PARSI LAW

PARSI LAW

CONTAINING

THE LAW APPLICABLE TO PARSIS AS REGARDS SUCCESSION AND INHERITANCE, MARRIAGE AND DIVORCE, &C

FRAMJEE A RÁNÁ

GYAN

Published by

GYAN

Gyan Publishing House
5, Ansari Road
Daryaganj, New Delhi-110002
Phone: 011-47034999, 9811692060
E-mail: books@gyanbooks.com

Distribution Network
gyanbooks.com
India, USA, Canada, UK, Australia

ISBN: 978-93-7133-082-4 (PB)
First Published, 1902

2nd Impression 2025

Printed at: Gyan Press, Delhi.

PARSI LAW
Author Framjee A Ráná

PARSI LAW.

PARSI LAW

CONTAINING

THE LAW APPLICABLE TO PARSIS AS REGARDS SUCCESSION AND INHERITANCE, MARRIAGE AND DIVORCE, &c.

BY

FRAMJEE A. RÁNÁ, B.A., LL.B.,

VAKIL, HIGH COURT.

JOINT AUTHOR OF "AN EPITOME OF HINDU LAW", "AN EPITOME OF MAHOMEDAN LAW" AND "AN EPITOME OF THE PRINCIPLES OF EQUITY."

Bombay:

PRINTED AT THE "EXAMINER PRESS."

1902.

TO

THE REVERED MEMORY

OF

SIR JAMSETJEE JIJIBHOY,

THE FIRST PARSI BARONET,

PATRON OF THE PARSI LAW ASSOCIATION,

This Little Book

IS RESPECTFULLY INSCRIBED,

WITH FEELINGS OF ESTEEM AND VENERATION

FOR

HIS MUNIFICENT AND WORLD-WIDE CHARITIES,

HIS GREAT ZEAL IN THE CAUSE OF EDUCATION,

AND

HIS UNCEASING EFFORTS TO PROMOTE THE WELFARE AND AMELIORATE THE CONDITION OF THE VARIOUS INDIAN COMMUNITIES IN GENERAL, AND HIS OWN CO-RELIGIONISTS IN PARTICULAR.

PREFACE.

Encouraged by the success of the works on Hindu Law, Mahomedan Law and Principles of Equity which have been successively published by the author jointly with Mr. C. K. Mulji during the last seven years, the author has attempted in the present work to place before the public a manual of the principles of Parsi Law, as embodied in the Acts relating to testamentary and intestate Succession, Marriage and Divorce which govern the personal relations of the Community at the present day and which have been developed and enunciated by authority from the Bench in the various decisions of the High Court.

This is the first attempt of its kind as there is no other book which comprises the whole field of Parsi Law as provided for by Statutes and formulated by High Court decisions.

All available sources of information have been carefully consulted and no pains have been spared by the author to make the book accurate and trustworthy.

It is hoped that the work will prove useful and serviceable both to practitioners and students as also to the Parsi Community in general.

July 1902.

EXPLANATION OF ABBREVIATIONS.

B. H. C.	Bombay High Court Reports.
Bom.	Indian Law Reports, Bombay Series.
Bom. L. R.	Bombay Law Reporter.
Cal.	Indian Law Reports, Calcutta Series.
Henderson.	Henderson's Testamentary Succession in India, 2nd edition.
I. S. Act.	Indian Succession Act X of 1865.
M. I. A.	Moore's Indian Appeals.
Mad.	Indian Law Reports, Madras Series.
P. J.	Printed Judgments of the Bombay High Court.
Stokes.	Indian Succession Act by Whitley Stokes, 1865.

EXPLANATION OF ABBREVIATIONS

CONTENTS.

The references throughout are to pages.

PART I.

INHERITANCE AND SUCCESSION.

	PAGE.
Introductory	1
Parsi Intestate Succession Act XXI of 1865 (with commentaries)...	5
Summary of Indian Succession Act X of 1865 ...	14

PART II.

MARRIAGE AND DIVORCE.

Introductory	43
Parsi Marriage and Divorce Act XV of 1865 (with commentaries)...	45
Rules and Orders under Parsi Marriage and Divorce Act	68
Law as to bridal presents amongst Parsis	70

APPENDICES.

Appendix **A**.

Parsi Chattels Real Act IX of 1837 ... ... I.

Appendix **B**.

Indian Succession Act X of 1865 ... ... II.

Appendix **C**.

Rules and Regulations for Parsi Chief Matrimonial Court in Bombay Presidency ... ... CI.

Tables of Fees ... ...

TABLE OF CASES.

Ardaseer Cursetji v. Pirozbai, 44,49,61,63.
Ardeseer v. Avabai, 62,64.
Avabai v. Jamasji, 51,58.
Avery v. Bowden, 60.

Bai Shirinbai v. Kharshedji, 49,62.
Burjorji v. Pestonji, 70.
Burnett v. Manu, 7.
Byramji v. Jamsetji, 70.

Cursetji v. Rustomji, 18.

De Souza v. Secretary of State, 35.
Dhanjibhai v. Hirabai, 62.
Dhanjibhai v. Navazbai, 10,17.
Dhanjishaw v. Sorabji, 40.
Dorabji v. Jerbai, 49,55,58,64.

Erasha v. Jerbai, 5,9,11.

Fardunji v. Navazbai, 38.
Fardunji N. Banaji v. Mithibai, 28.

Graham v. Londonderry, 17.

Harris v. Harries, 17.
Hill v. Administrator General, 20.
Hirabai v. Dhunjibhoy, 59,61.
Hirjibhai v. Burjorji, 9,11.
Homabaee v. Punjeabhaee, 6.
Hormusji v. Rustomji, 29.
Hulme v. Tenant, 15.

Jehangir v. Pirozbai 2,3,8.

Kawasji v. Sirinbai, 61,62.

Limji v. Bapuji, 29.

Mancherji v. Motibai, 60.
Mancherji Davar v. Mithibai, 8.
Manchershaw v. Kamarunisa Begam, 2.
Merbai v. Perozbai, 15.
Merwanji v. Avabai, 50,61.
Merwanji v. Rustomji, 70.
Miller v. Administrator General, 20.
Modee Kaikhoshru v. Cooverbai, 14.
Motabhai v. Dosibai, 6.
Motibai v. Motibai, 60.
Muncherji v. Nusserwanji, 70.

Naoroji v. Rogers, 2,50.
Natall v. Natall, 17.
Navroji v. Pirozbai, 3,23.

Peshotam Hormusji Dastoor v. Meherbai, 43,48, 49,50,63.

Rogers v. Naoroji, 2.

S. v. B., 56.
Sarkies v. Prosonomoyee Dossee, 16.
Sorabji v. Buchoobai, 50,57.

Taylor v. Meads, 15.
Tullet v. Armstrong, 15.

Wallis v. Hodgson, 7.

PARSI LAW.

PART I.

INHERITANCE AND SUCCESSION.

INTRODUCTORY.

From the clear and able report of the Parsi Law Commission (13th October 1862) it appears that before the year 1865 the law applicable to the Parsis in the Presidency Towns as regards their social relations widely differed from that which prevailed in the Mofussil; for, while they were governed in the Presidency Towns, as regards division of property, according to the English Statute of Distribution, in the Mofussil they were governed according to Regulation IV of 1827, and undefined and precarious usage constituted the only guide there.

In the year 1835 a Parsi died intestate and his eldest son preferred a claim in the Supreme Court of Bombay to be entitled to the whole immovable property of his deceased father by right of primogeniture to the exclusion of the next-of-kin. This circumstance caused great anxiety among the Parsis residing in Bombay. Becoming apprehensive that the English law of real property was for the first time about to be applied or might be applied in that case, they petitioned to the Legislature on the 20th November 1835 to be protected against such threatened application of the English law. Their appeal was not unheeded, for on the 15th May 1837 the Parsi Chattels Real Act (IX of 1837) was passed to emancipate the Parsis of the Presidency Towns from the English law of succession to real property.

This Act (repealed by Act VIII of 1868) applied to all the Presidency Towns and not to the Town of Bombay alone. (*Rogers* v. *Naoroji*, 4 B. H. C. at p. 114.)

This Act (IX of 1837) provided "that all immovable property situate within the jurisdiction of any of the Courts established by His Majesty's Charter shall, as far as regards the transmission of such property on the death and intestacy of any Parsi having a beneficial interest in the same, or by the last will of any such Parsi, be taken to be and to have been of the nature of chattels real and not of freehold."

The principle which the Mofussil Courts had adopted was that there was no *lex loci* in British India, and their practice had been to ascertain, in the best manner they could, what the law of the country of the parties before them was; and the Courts, there, acting under Regulation IV of 1827, sections 26 and 27, took evidence of, and enforced what were proved to be the usages of the Parsis in the locality. (*Jehangir v. Firozbai*, 11 Bom. at p. 4.)

Section 26 of Regulation IV of 1827 provided "that the law to be observed in the trial of suits shall be Acts of Parliament and Regulations of Government applicable to the case; in the absence of such Acts and Regulations, the usage of the country in which the suit arose; if none shall appear, the law of the defendant; and in the absence of specific law and usage, equity and good conscience alone."

In Manchershaw v. Kamarunisa Begam, 5 B. H. C. 109, Couch, C. J., held that according to section 26 of Regulation IV of 1827, the law of the defendant who was a Parsi governed the case. That there was no law generally applicable to Parsis in India, but the law applicable to them within the jurisdiction of the High Courts on its Original Side was that which was applicable to British-born subjects, and in the absence of any specific law for the Parsis in the Mofussil, the rule of justice, equity, and good conscience should be observed; and in such cases the practice of the Courts of Equity in England with certain necessary modifications should be followed.

The judgment in *Naoroji v. Rogers*, 4 B. H. C. 1., has set at rest any doubts, which ever existed as to the law by which the Parsis are governed. Since the decision in that case it cannot be disputed that until the legislation of 1865 (Acts X, XV, and XXI of 1865), "the law uniformly applied to Parsis and their property in the Island of Bombay by the Supreme Court and, since it was closed, by the High Court at its Original Jurisdiction Side has been the English law" subject to certain specified exceptions. (*Navroji v. Pirozbai*, 23 Bom. at pp. 98, 87.)

Before the passing of Act XXI of 1865 the Parsis in the town and island of Bombay were, as to succession, governed by the English law as modified by Act IX of 1837; and in the mofussil, the Courts acting under Regulation IV of 1827, sections 26 and 27, took evidence of and enforced what were proved to be the usages of the Parsis in the locality. (*Jehangir v. Pirozbai, 11 Bom. at p. 4.*)

Though the Parsis in the Presidency Towns were somewhat benefited by the passing of Act IX of 1837, the Mofussil Parsis derived no benefit from it. Even the Parsis in the Presidency Towns got only partial relief, for, though it relieved them from the operation of the English law of Primogeniture as regards immovable property, yet as regards *all* sorts of property in cases of intestacy they were left under the subjection of the English Statute of Distributions, which, being wholly unsuited to their requirements and quite at variance with their usages and customs, caused real and pressing inconvenience to the Parsis of the Presidency Towns.

In all cases of intestacy the Parsis of the Presidency Towns *as regards every description of property* were subjected to the English Statute of distribution by which a third went to the widow and the residue was distributed equally amongst the children and their representatives.

Having no recognized code among themselves, and neither ancient books of law, nor any authoritative account even of their unwritten law, no one of the Parsis knew the extent of his family rights, or the obligation of his family duties, and a better and more satisfactory and permanent settlement of their inheritance and succession laws being entirely necessary, the Parsis held a great meeting at Bombay, on the 20th August 1855, to consider and adopt measures for procuring the enactment of laws adapted to them. The Managing Committee of the Parsi Law Association, appointed for that purpose, drew up a draft code and presented it to the Legislative Council on the 31st March 1860. The Select Committee of the Legislative Council then submitted their report and a Commission was thereupon appointed *to enquire into the usages recognized as laws by the Parsi Community of India, and into the necessity of special legislation in connection with them* (26th December 1861). The Parsi Law Commission then made a report on the 13th October 1862, and at last a long standing grievance was removed by the passing of the Parsi Succession Act (XXI of 1865), which came into force on the 10th April 1865.

This Act, which contains special provisions as to succession amongst Parsis, in cases of intestacy, applies to Parsis in the whole of British India, except the scheduled districts: The Indian Succession Act (X of 1865) applies to Parsis in cases of succession under wills.

THE PARSI INTESTATE SUCCESSION ACT.

ACT NO. XXI OF 1865.

Passed on the 10th April 1865.

An Act to define and amend the Law relating to Intestate Succession among the Parsis.

By section 3 of the Laws Local Extent Act (XV of 1874) this Act has been declared to be in force in the whole of British India, except as regards the Scheduled Districts.

It has been declared, under the Scheduled Districts Act, 1874, to be in force in the following Scheduled Districts :—

Sindh ; West Jalpaiguri ; The Districts of Hazaribagh, Lohárdaga, and Mánbhum, and Pargana Dhálbhum, and the Kolhán in the District of Singbhum ; The Jhánsi Division ; Kumaon and Garhwál ; The Scheduled portion of the Mirzápur district ; Jaunsar Báwar ; The Districts of Hazara Peshawar, Kohát, Bannu, Dera Ismail Khan, and Dera Gházi Khan ; Ajmer and Merwára ; The District of Silhat.

It has been extended, under the same Act, to the Scheduled District of the *North Western Provinces Tarái.*

It has been declared, under same Act, *not* to be in force in the Scheduled *District of Lahaul.*

Preamble.

Whereas it is expedient to define and amend the law relating to intestate succession among the Parsis: It is enacted as follows :—

A man is considered to die *intestate* in respect of all property of which he has not made a testamentary disposition which is capable of taking effect. (S. 25. I. S. Act.)

A Parsi by his will expressly directed that neither his daughter nor his widow should take any share of his property, the whole of which he bequeathed to his brother, who, however, predeceased him. The bequest thus in his brother's favour lapsed and there was an *intestacy* and the daughter and his widow took the property. Use of mere negative words unaccompanied by any effective disposition of his property could not exclude them. (*Erasha* v. *Jerbai*, 4 Bom. 537.)

Division of property among widow and children of intestate.

1. Where a Parsi dies leaving a widow and children, the property of which he shall have died intestate shall be divided among the widow and children, so that the share of each son shall be double the share of the widow, and that her share shall be double the share of each daughter.

In accordance with this section, the widow gets twice as much as each daughter, and each son gets twice as much as the widow.

The children may be either by the widow or a predeceased wife. (Stokes. 203.)

The word property occurring in this Act includes both movables and immovables.

Previous to this Act, a Parsi widow had only a right to be provided by her husband's heir during her life time with a suitable abode and maintenance. She took no proprietary right in the house assigned to her, but the estate therein, as in the other property of her husband, vested in his heir. Such an estate would not be in the nature of a reversion, but would be an absolute estate burdened with a liability, and the death of the widow would make no change in the nature of the estate, but merely extinguish the liability. (*Motabhai* v. *Dosibai*, P. J. for 1877. at p. 106.)

The words "Son" and "Daughter" here do not include a step-son or step-daughter, nor an adopted son or adopted daughter, but they do include a posthumous son and posthumous daughter as is explained below.

Step-child.

One's step-child is only a child of one's husband or wife by a former marriage and consequently it does not inherit anything in the estate of the step-parent.

Adoption.

There is nothing like strict adoption amongst Parsis. A Parsi can adopt a son to perform his funeral ceremonies, but such adopted person will not inherit any portion of the deceased's estate, except under his will. Such adopted person is called "Paluk" or "Dharm-putr." It may be pointed out here that under the General Clauses Act X of 1897, the word "son" occurring in all Acts of the Governor General in Council made after the commencement of that Act and in all Acts of the Governor General in Council made after the 3rd day of January 1868, includes an adopted son, in the case of any one whose personal law permits adoption. As however this definition does not apply to the Parsi Succession Act which was passed in 1866, it is not necessary to discuss whether the personal law of Parsis permits adoption or not.

An adoption made by a Parsi immediately before his death would render extremely improbable the execution of a will by him a short time previous thereto, and therefore calls for a very clear proof to establish its existence. Although in the cases of adoption by "Dhurm-putr" (a partial adoption) it is not indispensably necessary that a declaration should be made on the third day after the decease, yet it is usual to make such a declaration and to take a writing from the "Dharm-putr." In the absence of any such writing, and upon the whole evidence the adoption (in the case) was pronounced to be as a "Paluk-putr" and not merely as a "Dhurm-putr." A "Paluk" is appointed by the adoptive father in his life-time; while a "Dhurm-putr" is appointed after his death, for the performing of his funeral ceremonies. (*Homabaee v. Punjeabhaee*, 1 utherland's P. C. Judgments, page 28.)

Posthumous children.

As regards posthumous children, they would inherit though no express mention is made of them. Before the Parsi Intestate Succession Act was passed, a Parsi posthumous child would have inherited to his father dying intestate, under the English Law. By the Common Law of England, a child *en ventre* (i. e., in the womb) is looked upon as a person in *rerum natura*, so that such child is to all intents and purposes a child as much as if born in the father's life-time. Such a child succeeds under the English Statutes of Distribution to an intestate, although those statutes contain no provision similar to what is found in section 23 of the Indian Succession Act X of 1865 as to the position of a child *en ventre*. (*Wallis V. Hodgson*, 2 Atk. p. 116; *Burnett V. Manu*, 1 Ves. 156.) From the fact that part third of the Indian Succession Act (which includes section 23) is excluded from application to Parsis, it might, at first sight, appear that a Parsi posthumous child would not inherit to a Parsi intestate. But section 23 is a mere declaratory section as to the position a child *en ventre* occupies and the omission of the part third containing it, affords no ground for the argument that it was intended that a Parsi child *en ventre* should occupy a different position after the Parsi Intestate Succession Act than it did defore in cases of succession. Section 86 of the Indian Succession Act, which applies to Parsis enacts that in a will, all words expressive of relationship apply to a child in the womb who is afterwards born alive. This also points to the conclusion that, the Legislature could not have intended a result in the case of an intestary different from that in the case of a will.

As the point was somewhat doubtful the author went to the cost of procuring the opinion of an eminent counsel, viz., Mr. Inverarity on it.

Division of property among widower and children of intestate.

2. Where a female Parsi dies leaving a widower and children, the property of which she shall have died intestate shall be divided among the widower and such children, so that his share shall be double the share of each of the children.

The children may be by the widower or the female's predeceased husband. Sons and daughters share equally. (Stokes. 204.)

Division of property amongst children of male intestate leaving no widow.

3. Where a Parsi dies leaving children, but no widow, the property of which he shall have died intestate shall be divided amongst the children, so that the share of each son shall be four times the share of each daughter.

Division amongst children of female intestate leaving no widower.

4. Where a female Parsi dies leaving children, but no widower, the property of which she shall have died intestate shall be divided amongst the children in equal shares.

The son gets four times as much as a daughter out of the father's property, while the son and the daughter share equally their mother's property.

5. **If any child of a Parsi intestate shall have died in his or her life time, the widow or widower and issue of such child shall take the share which such child would have taken if living at the intestate's death in such manner as if such deceased child had died immediately after the intestate's death.**

Division of predeceased child's share among widow or widower and issue of such child.

By "widower," in this section, is meant a widower, relatively to the deceased wife only, and without consideration of the fact or possibility of the widower re-marrying. If the framers of the Act had wished to provide against re-marriage in cases under section 5, they might have used adequate language as in the 2nd Schedule, articles 10 and 14 which refer to section 7. The omission to employ similar express words for cases falling under section 5 is significant. (*Jehangir v. Pirozbai*, 11 Bom. at p. 5.)

D, a Parsi, died intestate on the 19th September 1885, leaving a widow (the defendant), two daughters, and heirs of a predeceased daughter J, surviving him. J had been the wife of the plaintiff, and had died 34 years before the date of his suit, leaving as her heirs, her husband (the plaintiff), and one daughter, who was still living. After J's death the plaintiff married again, and his second wife was living at the date of this suit. Letters of administration to D's estate were granted to his widow, the defendant. The plaintiff claimed a share in D's estate, contending that he was the widower of J, one of the daughters of the intestate and entitled as such under section 5 of the Parsi Intestate Succession Act XXI of 1865. It was held that he was the widower of J within the meaning of the said section, and as such was entitled to a share in D's estate. (*Ibid. 1.*)

It is not necessary, in order for the widow or widower to take, and for the issue to take, that there should be in existence, at the death of the intestate, both *widow or widower and issue*. It is not a condition precedent to the application of this section that the predeceased son of an intestate Parsi shall have left both a widow *and* issue. Where a Parsi died intestate leaving him surviving a widow, sons, daughters, children of a predeceased son and the widow of another predeceased son who had died without issue, and a posthumous daughter was afterwards born to the intestate, it was held that the last mentioned widow was entitled to one moiety of the share in the intestate's estate, which her husband would have taken had he survived the intestate, and that the other moiety of such share devolved on the surviving issue of the intestate, including the posthumous daughter and the children of his other predeceased son. (*Mancherji Davar v. Mithibai*, 1 Bom. at pp. 506, 511.)

6. Where a Parsi dies leaving a widow or widower, but without leaving any lineal descendants, his or her father and mother, if both are living, or one of them if the other is dead, shall take one moiety of the property, as to which he or she shall have died intestate, and the widow or widower shall take the other moiety.

Division of property when intestate leaves widow or widower but no lineal descendants.

Where both the father and the mother of the intestate survive him or her, the father's share shall be double the share of the mother.

Where neither the father nor the mother of the intestate survives him or her, the intestate's relatives on the father's side, in the order specified in the first schedule hereto annexed shall take the moiety which the father and the mother would have taken if they had survived the intestate.

The next of kin standing first in the same schedule shall be preferred to those standing second, the second to the third, and so on in succession, provided that the property shall be so distributed as that each male shall take double the share of each female, standing in the same degree of propinquity.

If there be no relatives on the father's side, the intestate's widow or widower shall take the whole.

The first six sections of the Act are intended to embrace all cases of a Parsi leaving lineal descendants or a widow or widower. Section 7 applies to cases where the intestate leaves neither widow or widower, nor lineal descendants.

Division of property when intestate leaves neither widow nor widower nor lineal descendants.

7. Where a Parsi dies leaving neither lineal descendants nor a widow or widower, his or her next-of-kin, in the order set forth in the second schedule hereto annexed, shall be entitled to succeed to the whole of the property as to which he or she shall have died intestate.

The next of kin standing first in the same schedule shall always be preferred to those standing second, the second to the third, and so on in succession; provided that the property shall be so distributed as that each male shall take double the share of each female standing in same degree of propinquity.

Where there is no kin, the Crown would, of course, take as *ultimus hæres*. (Henderson. 240.)

Under the Act widows and children rank before brothers or sisters. Section 7, schedule II, art. 2 of the Act is applicable only where the deceased leaves neither lineal descendants, nor a widow or widower. (Erasha v. Jerbai, 4 Bom. 537.)

In both sections 6 and 7 of this Act, the words "next-of-kin" and "relatives" are synonymous, and are collective names for the persons mentioned in the first and second schedules respectively. (*Hirjibhai v. Burjorji*, 22 Bom. 909.)

One Jerbai, a Parsi widow, died intestate and without issue. Her father, mother, three brothers and two sisters had predeceased her. Two of the brothers and one of the sisters had left children. Some of these children had also predeceased her, leaving children (grand-nephews and nieces of Jerbai). Two of this last mentioned class had also predeceased

Jerbai, leaving children (great-grand-nephews and nieces of Jerbai). It was held that Jerbai's property should, in the first instance, be divided into three shares, i. e., one for each of the two predeceased brothers who left children, and one for the predeceased sister who left a child, each brother's share to be two-fifths and the sister's one-fifth ; such respective shares to be sub-divided among the descendants of the two brothers and the sister respectively, no descendant being entitled to share concurrently with his or her ancestor and, on each division and sub-division, each male taking double the share of each female standing in the same degree of propinquity. (*Ibid.*)

Exemption of Parsis from parts of Indian Succession Act, 1865.

8. The following portions of the Indian Succession Act, 1865, shall not apply to Parsis (that is to say),—the whole of Part III, the whole of Part IV, excepting section 25, the whole of Part V and section 43.

The scheme of the Parsi Succession Act being so different from the English system of distribution, the rule as to advancement does not affect the Parsis, though section 42 of the Succession Act does apply to them. In excluding, from application to Parsis, section 42 of the Indian Succession Act, which does away with the English rule that children's advancements are to be brought into hotchpot, it was not the intention of the Legislature to preserve the English provision for that community. (*Dhanjibhai* v. *Navazbai*, 2 Bom. 75.)

THE FIRST SCHEDULE.

(1.) Brothers and sisters, and the children or lineal descendants of such of them as shall have predeceased the intestate.

The words "brothers" and "sisters" in this article refer to "brothers" and "sisters" on the father's side without reference to who the mother is and consequently all brothers and sisters by the *same father* whether by the same mother or not come in under this article. The words "brothers" and "sisters" here refer both to brothers and sisters of the full-blood (i. e. those by the same father and same mother) as also to half-brothers and sisters by the *same father* but by different mothers.

(2.) Grandfather and Grandmother.

(3.) Grandfather's sons and daughters, and the lineal descendants of such of them as shall have predeceased the intestate.

(4.) Great-grandfather and great-grandmother.

(5.) Great-grandfather's sons and daughters, and the lineal descendants of such of them as shall have predeceased the intestate.

The words grandfather and grandmother, as also great-grandfather and great-grandmother occurring in articles 2 to 5 (first schedule) clearly refer only to the paternal grand-parents and great-grand-parents. Section 6 says that where neither the father nor the mother of the intestate survives him or her, the *intestate's relatives on the father's side*, in the order specified in the first schedule hereto annexed shall take the moiety, &c.

THE SECOND SCHEDULE.

(1.) Father and mother.

(2.) Brothers and sisters, and the lineal descendants of such of them as shall have predeceased the intestate.

The words "brothers" and "sisters" in this article are intended for "brothers" and "sisters" on the father's side including all by the same father no matter who the mother is. It will be noticed that this article and article 1 of the first schedule are exactly in the same words and therefore the same meaning must be given to them when brothers and sisters on the mother's side are specially mentioned in article 7 of this (second) schedule. The words "brothers" and "sisters" here refer both to full-blood brothers and sisters (i. e., those by the same father and the same mother) as also to half-brothers and sisters by the same father but by different mother.

Under this Act widows and children rank before brothers or sisters. Section 7, schedule II, article 2 of the Act is applicable only where the deceased leaves neither lineal descendants, nor a widow or widower. (Erasha v. Jerbai, 4 Bom. 537.)

In construing the (second) schedule, section 7 so far helps us as to show (1) that where it was intended that any class of relatives should, if living, absolutely exclude any other, they were placed within a separate article; (2) that, within the particular articles, differences in propinquity of blood are so far recognized that each degree constitutes a class, not for the purpose of excluding or being preferred to any other, but for the purpose of giving each male double the share of each female with it; (3) that all males within a particular article, or even within a particular degree of propinquity, do not necessarily take equal shares. Apart from section 7, there are no other legal provisions which appear to throw much light on the construction of article 2. It would not be safe to base any inferences regarding the article upon the provisions of the English law or those of the Indian Succession Act in reference to the distribution of an intestate's property. Act XXI of 1865 was enacted for the express purpose of withdrawing the Parsis from the English law of intestate succession, which until then had governed them. Section 8 was enacted for the express purpose of exempting them from parts III, IV, and V, of the Indian Succession Act, which was passed in the same year. There does not appear to be any usage, as district from law, existing among Parsis prior to 1865, upon which article 2 may have been based or which might throw light upon its construction. (*Hirjibhai* v. *Burjorji*, 22 Bom. at pp. 916, 917.)

In this article (art. 2, Sch. 2.), the gift to lineal descendants is substitutional in the sense that they take nothing if the head of their branch of the family is living, whereas if he is dead, they stand in his place and take the share which he would have taken. In distributing an estate, therefore, "among brothers and sisters and the lineal descendants of such of them as have predeceased the intestate," the primary division must be *per stirpes.* If there are surviving brothers and lineal descendants of a predeceased brother, then each surviving brother will take equal shares with the lineal descendants (of the predecased brother) collectively. If all the brothers are dead, then the share which each would have taken, had he survived, will be taken by his lineal descendants. If in either case the predeceased was a sister, her lineal descendants will take her share only (which would be half of her brother). (*Ibid.* 909.)

(3.) Paternal grandfather and paternal grandmother.

(4.) Children of the paternal grandfather, and the lineal descendants of such of them as shall have predeceased the intestate.

(5.) Paternal grandfather's father and mother.

(6.) Paternal grandfather's father's children, and the lineal descendants of such of them as shall have predeceased the intestate.

(7.) Brothers and sisters by the mother's side, and the lineal descendants of such of them as shall have predeceased the intestate.

The words "brothers and sisters by the mother's side" in this article mean only "brothers and sisters" by the *same mother* but by different fathers.

(8.) Maternal grandfather and maternal grandmother.

(9.) Children of the maternal grandfather, and the lineal descendants of such of them as shall have predeceased the intestate.

(10.) Son's widow, if she have not re-married at or before the death of the intestate.

Express words are used in this article as also in article 14 below providing against remarriage.

(11.) Brother's widow, if she have not re-married at or before the death of the intestate.

(12.) Paternal grandfather's son's widow, if she have not re-married at or before the death of the intestate.

(13.) Maternal grandfather's son's widow, if she have not re-married at or before the death of the intestate.

(14.) Widowers of the intestate's deceased daughters, if they have not re-married at or before the death of the intestate.

(15.) Maternal grandfather's father and mother.

(16.) Children of the maternal grandfather's father, and the lineal descendants of such of them as shall have predeceased the intestate.

(17.) Paternal grandmother's father and mother.

(18.) Children of the paternal grandmother's father, and the lineal descendants of such of them as shall have predeceased the intestate.

SUMMARY OF IMPORTANT PORTIONS OF THE INDIAN SUCCESSION ACT, X OF 1865.

[*Out of that part of the Indian Succession Act which is applicable to the Parsis, the most important portions have been culled out and given here in a summarized form with a view to making them easily intelligible even to a layman. The entire Act is given in full as an appendix.*]

The Indian Succession Act regulates testamentary succession to Parsis domiciled in British India. (*Modee Kaikhoshru* v. *Cooverbai*, 6 M. I. A. 449.)

The 4th section of the Indian Succession Act which applies to Parsis has introduced a very important change in the law in the case of persons to whom hitherto the English law was applicable. It gets rid of the principle, so far as property is concerned that husband and wife are *one person* in law, for it provides that after the 1st day of January 1866 no person shall, by marriage, acquire any interest in the property of the person whom he or she marries, nor become incapable of doing any act in respect of his or her own property, which he or she could have done if unmarried.

The Common Law of England, which hitherto applied to Parsis in the Presidency Towns, merged the wife in the husband and declared her absolutely incapable, during coverture, of contracting, holding and disposing of property.

By virtue of the English Common Law relating to husband and wife, the wife can exercise no independent disposing control, during her husband's life-time, over any property whatever, not even over that which comes to her, or is given to her, from or by her own family.

During coverture a married woman could acquire no legal right to *personal property*. Immediately upon her marriage, the contracts between the husband and the wife came to an end, and goods, chattels and effects in possession belonging to the wife at the time of her marriage became the absolute property of the husband by virtue of the marriage.

The wife's *personal chattels in possession*, belonging to her at the time of her marriage and not settled to her separate use, vested absolutely in the husband, except her *paraphernalia.*

The *paraphernalia* of the wife include such apparel and ornaments given to the wife as are suitable to her condition in life, and as are expressly given to be worn as ornaments of her person only, e. g , rings, watches and other jewels given to the wife by her husband to be worn merely as ornaments. The wife cannot dispose of her paraphernalia during her husband's life-time ; but the husband can dispose of it by sale or gift *inter vivos*, though not by will, and on his death subject to payment of his debts, the wife is absolutely entitled to it.

The fact of the husband's great control over, and interest in his wife's property at law, gave rise in Equity to the doctrine of "*separate estate*," that is ownership of property by a married woman apart from her husband for her exclusive use. Such property is free from the debts and control of her husband; and unless restrained by stipulation she may alone alienate it by deed or will, or charge it with her debts. (Indermaur, 347 ; *Tullet v. Armstrong*, 1 Beave. 1 ; *Hulme v. Tenant*, 1 W. &. T. 536 ; *Taylor v. Meads*, 34 *L.* J. Ch. 203).

Closely allied to separate property is *pin-money* which may be defined as a yearly allowance settled upon the wife before marriage for the purchase of clothes and ornaments, or otherwise for her separate expenditure, and in order to deck her person suitably to the rank and agreeably to the tastes of her husband. It is allowed to her in order to save the constant recurrence by the wife to the husband for trifling expenses.

As regards the wife's *choses-in-action* (i. e., things which are enforceable by her only by suit) e. g., debts, legacies, &c., they did not become the husband's until he reduced them into possession; consequently if he failed so to reduce them, they survived to the wife, and if she died before he had reduced them into possession they formed part of her estate and became his property subject to payment of her debts.

Resting on the doctrine of unity of persons between husband and wife, the husband, as to her *chattels real*, became possessed of them by marriage in her right. Not only was he entitled to their rents and profits, but he might also dispose of them as he pleased during coverture. They were liable for his debts ; and if he survived her, they were absolutely his. He could not, however, devise them by will and if he failed to dispose of them in his life-time, and in case he died before his wife, she became entitled to them absolutely.

By the 4th section of the Succession Act (which applies to Parsis) a woman married after the 1st day of January 1866 will hold all her property as a *feme coverte* in England holds property settled to her separate use.

Among Parsis a gift may be made to the separate use of a married woman, or of a woman about to be married. (*Merbai v. Perozbai*, 5 *Bom.* 268.)

The 4th section of the Indian Succession Act sweeps away the husband's right to his wife's personalty, his interest in her realty as tenant by the courtesy, and the wife's right to her husband's land as tenant by dower; and as to her property the section has the effect of a settlement of it to her own use without restraint on anticipation. This section abolishes the unity of persons between husband and wife; consequently when an estate is conveyed or devised during coverture to husband and wife, they will take as joint-tenants with equal undivided shares, and each can alienate his or her own moiety in his or her life-time. At Common Law in such a case they would take by entireties, and the husband may do what he likes with the rents and profits during coverture. Further, the husband is no longer able, by his endorsement alone, to pass his wife's negotiable instruments, nor can he release or assign her *choses-in-action.* (Stokes Anglo Indian Codes. Vol. I. page 296.)

This section (S. 4. I. S. Act.) has altogether done away with the Common Law rule that where a man marries his creditor the debt is thereby released.

The 4th section does not affect the right to make a settlement nor the usual effect thereof. It does not apply to marriages contracted before the 1st day of January 1866. It is prospective, and does not affect rights which had already been acquired before the passing of the Act. (*Sarkies* v. *Prosono-moyee Dossee*, 6 Cal. 794.)

Since the 4th section of the Succession Act (which applies to Parsis) is prospective and does not affect rights which had already been acquired before the 1st day of January 1866, it is evident that if a female Parsi who was married before 1st January 1866, dies leaving property, that property would not go to her heirs as on an intestacy, or to the persons named in her will, but will be governed by the English law. At Common Law a wife's will was void as to lands, and as to chattels she had no testamentary power, unless the husband was banished or transported, or unless the will was restricted to property of which she was executrix or administratrix, or unless it was made with her husband's special permission. But equity holds a wife's will valid as an execution of a power, or in pursuance of an agreement, or as disposition of her separate estate. In fact the will of such a Parsi female would be valid only so far as it relates to the disposition of her separate estate, or if her husband gave his consent to the will, or if she survived him.

In the absence of any rule applicable to Parsis other than the English law, following *Graham* v. *Londonderry* (3 Alk. 393), a Parsi husband has no right to demand from the widow of his deceased father, in whose hands they are, delivery to himself of ornaments purchased for his wife by his deceased father, as they are the separate property of his wife. (*Dhanjibhai* v. *Navazbai*, 2 Bom. 75.)

In England the position as to wife's property at Common Law was to some extent altered by the Married Woman's Property Act 1870. (33 & 34, Vict. C. 93.)

In India the Married Woman's Property Act III of 1874 declares provisions similar to those declared by Statute 33 & 34, Vict. C. 93.

The 4th section of the Indian Succession Act did not remove the disability of married women to contract; this was removed by the Married Woman's Property Act III of 1874. (*Natall* v. *Natall*, 9 Mad. 12.)

Section 4 of Act III of 1874 enacts that the wages and earnings of a married woman after the passing of the Act shall be deemed to be her separate property, and her receipts alone shall be good discharges.

Section 5 provides that she may effect a policy of insurance on her own behalf and independently of her husband.

Section 7 empowers her to sue in her own name for recovery of any property which by force of the Indian Succession Act or the Act itself was her separate property.

Section 8 makes the wife (whether married before or after the 1st January 1866) liable to be sued to the extent of her separate property by any one contracting with her as to such property.

Sections 7 and 8 provide for the remedies of a married woman, who is within the 4th section, for injuries to her property. (*Harris* v. *Harries*, 1 Cal. 285.)

The object of the Legislature in passing Act X of 1865 and Act III of 1874 was to assimilate the position of a married woman to that of an unmarried one, so far as regards her dealings with her own property. Section 4 of the former Act combined with section 7 of the latter Act enables women, married since 1st of January 1866, to possess and sue and be sued in respect of such property as though they were unmarried. These sections do not, however, deal with their capacity to contract. Section 8 of the latter Act deals with that capacity, and applies to women married as well before as after the 1st of January 1866, and provides that such women can contract as though they were unmarried at the date of the contract, but that on such contracts they will be liable only to the extent of their separate estate. (Cursetji *v.* Rustomji, 11 Bom. 352, 353.)

Under section 8 (Act III of 1874) a married woman has power to charge property settled upon herself, for her separate use without power of anticipation, with the payment of debts incurred by her subsequently to her marriage, and such a charge is valid and binding. (*Ibid.* 348.)

The husband, however, stands responsible for debts contracted by his wife's agency.

Lastly, section 9 (Act III of 1874) relieves the husband married after 31st December 1865 from his wife's *ante-nuptial* debts. At Common Law the husband stood liable jointly with his wife for her debts contracted before marriage. The wife's separate property is now held liable for her own contracts.

Domicile.

Part II of the Indian Succession Act which applies to Parsis treats of domicile.

Succession to a deceased person's immovable property in British India is regulated by the law of British India wherever he may have had his domicile at the time of his death; and succession to his movable property is regulated by the law of the country in which he had his domicile at the time of his death. (S. 5. I. S. Act.)

"Immovable property" includes land, incorporeal tenements, and things attached to the earth, or permanently fastened to anything which is attached to the earth. "Movable property" means property of every description except immovable property. (S. 3. I. S. Act.)

A person can only have one domicile for the purpose of succession of his movable property. (S. 6. I. S. Act.)

The domicile of origin of every person of legitimate birth is in the country in which, at the time of his birth, his father was domiciled : or if he is a posthumous child, in the country in which his father was domiciled at the time of the father's death. The domicile of origin of an illegitimate child is in the country in which, at the time of his birth, his mother was domiciled. (Ss. 7, 8. I. S. Act.)

Domicile is the legal conception of residence of which there are three kinds :—(1). *Domicile by birth*, or *of origin*. As no man can be without a domicile the law attributes to every individual as soon as he is born, the domicile of his father, if the child is legitimate; and the domicile of his mother, if the child is illegitimate. This is called the *domicile of origin* and is involuntary. (2) *Domicile by operation of law.* This sort of domicile attaches to those (*a*) who are under the control of another, e. g., wife, minor and servant, and (*b*) on whom the state affixes domicile, e. g., officer, prisoner. (3) *Domicile of choice.* This is where one is abandoned and another is acquired.

The domicile of origin prevails until a new domicile has been acquired. A man acquires a new domicile by taking up his fixed habitation in a country which is not that of his domicile of origin. (Ss. 9, 10. I. S. Act.)

No man acquires a domicile in British India merely by residing in H. M.'s Civil or Military service, or in the exercise of any profession or calling, or in the discharge of the duties of any public office. (Ss. 10, 12. I. S. Act.)

The special mode of acquiring a domicile in British India is treated of in section 11 of the Succession Act, which provides that any person may acquire a domicile in British India by making and depositing in some office in British India (to be fixed by the Local Government) a declaration in writing under his hand of his desire to acquire such domicile, provided that he shall have been resident in British India for one year immediately preceding the time of his making such declaration.

A new domicile continues until the former domicile has been resumed, or another has been acquired. (S. 13. I. S. Act.)

The domicile of a minor follows the domicile of the parent from whom he derived his domicile of origin. During minority he cannot acquire a new domicile. His domicile however does not change with that of his parent, if the minor is married, or holds any office or employment in the service of Her Majesty, or has set up, with the consent of the parent, in any distinct business. (Ss. 14, 17. I. S. Act.)

"Minor" means any person who shall not have completed the age of eighteen years, and "Minority" means the status of such person. (S. 3. I. S. Act.)

The age of majority of persons domiciled in British India is provided for as follows by the 3rd section of the Indian Majority Act, IX of 1875: —Every minor of whose person or property, or both, a guardian, other than a guardian for a suit within the meaning of Chapter XXXI of the Code of Civil Procedure, has been or shall be appointed or declared by any Court of Justice before the minor has attained the age of eighteen years, and every minor of whose property the superintendence has been or shall be assumed by any Court of Wards before the minor has attained that age, shall, notwithstanding anything contained in the Indian Succession Act, X of 1865, or in any other enactment, be deemed to have attained his majority when he shall have completed his age of twenty-one years, and not before; and every other person domiciled in British India shall be deemed to have attained his majority when he shall have completed his age of eighteen years, and not before.

By marriage a woman acquires the domicile of her husband, if she had not the same domicile before. The wife's domicile during marriage follows her husband's, except when they are separated by sentence of a competent Court, or when the husband is undergoing a sentence of transportation. (Ss. 15, 16. I. S. Act.)

An insane person cannot acquire a new domicile in any other way than by his domicile following that of another person. (S. 18. I. S. Act.)

If a man dies leaving movable property in British India, in the absence of proof of any domicile elsewhere, succession to the property is regulated by the law of British India. (S. 19. I. S. Act.)

Section 44 of the Indian Succession Act provides that in the case of the marriage of a person not having a British Indian domicile to a person having such domicile, neither party acquires by the marriage any rights in respect of the other's property not comprised in an ante-nuptial settlement which he or she would not acquire thereby if both were domiciled in British India at the time of the marriage.

The meaning is this: where either of the parties has an Indian domicile, all his or her rights, as regards the other's property, whether movable or immovable, are regulated by the territorial law of India. (*Miller* v. *Administrator General*, 1 Cal. 420.)

In the above case (at. p. 412) it was held that section 4 of the Indian Succession Act does not apply in respect of the movable property of persons not having an Indian domicile and that while the 4th section lays down a general rule as to the effect of marriage in respect of movable property where both the married persons have an Indian domicile, the 44th section of the Indian Succession Act lays down a special rule to govern a particular case.

In the case of *Hill* v. *Administrator General of Bengal*, 23 Cal. at pp. 511, 512, however, Sale J. held that, since in the case of *Miller v. Administrator General* the applicability of the sections 4 and 44 was considered in connection with the question of domicile, but the particular question whether these sections in any way affect the rights of succession was not dealt with as necessarily arising in the case, these sections read together should be understood as laying down a general rule as to the immediate effect of marriage in respect of movable property belonging to each or either of the married persons not comprised in an ante-nuptial settlement, and not as laying down a rule intended to affect the law of succession.

Wills and Codicils.

"Will" means the legal declaration of the intentions of the testator with respect to his property, which he desires to be carried into effect after his death.

"Codicil" means an instrument made in relation to a will, and explaining, altering, or adding to its dispositions. It is considered as forming an additional part of the will. (S. 3. I. S. Act.)

The chief requisites for a valid will are :—

1. Soundness of mind and age of majority.

Every person of sound mind and not a minor may dispose of his property by will.

A married woman may dispose of by will any property which she could alienate by her own act during her life.

Persons who are deaf, or dumb, or blind, are not thereby incapacitated for making a will if they are able to know what they do by it.

One who is ordinarily insane may make a will during an interval in which he is of sound mind.

No person can make a will while he is in such a state of mind, whether arising from drunkenness, or from illness, or from any other cause, that he does not know what he is doing. (S. 46. I. S. Act.)

All persons, whether married or single, male or female, of sound mind who have completed the age of 18 years are capable of making wills.

Though a person who is a minor cannot dispose of his property by will, yet section 47 of the Succession Act empowers a father of whatever age to appoint testamentary guardians for his child during minority.

2. Freedom from fraud, coercion or importunity.

A will or any part of a will, the making of which has been caused by fraud or coercion, or by such importunity as takes away the free agency of the testator, is void. (S. 48. I. S. Act).

3. Proper execution.

Section 50 of the Succession Act deals with the execution of *unprivileged* (ordinary) wills, that is wills executed by persons, not being soldiers employed in expedition, or engaged in actual warfare, or mariners at sea. And three rules are to be observed in the execution of such wills.

First.—The testator shall sign or shall affix his mark to the will, or it shall be signed (not marked) by some other person in his presence and by his direction.

Secend.—The signature or mark of the testator, or the signature (not the mark) of the person signing for him, shall be so placed that it shall appear that it was intended thereby to give effect to the writing as a will.

The form of a paper does not affect its title to probate as a will, provided that it is the intention of the deceased that it should operate after his death. Thus, documents in the form of deeds, agreements, letters, bills of exchange, powers-of-attorney, or other instruments, may take effect as wills, if duly executed, where a testamentary intention can be collected, and the dispositions are not to take effect until after the death of the persons making them. (Henderson. 3.)

It is immaterial in what language a will may be written. A will or codicil, or any part thereof, may be written on paper, parchment or any other substance, in any character, at large, or abbreviations, or in cypher, and may be made or altered in pencil as well as in ink. (Stokes. 27.)

Third.—The will shall be attested by two or more witnesses, each of whom must have seen the testator sign or affix the mark to the will, or have seen some other person (not an attesting witness) sign the will in the presence and by the direction of the testator, or have received from the testator a personal acknowledgment of his signature or mark, or of the signature of such other person; and each of the witnesses must sign the will in the presence of the testator, but it shall not be necessary that more than one witness be present at the same time, and no particular form of attestation shall be necessary.

As regards *attestation* a will shall not be considered as insufficiently attested by reason of any benefit thereby given, either by way of bequest or by way of appointment, to any person attesting it, or to his or her wife or husband; but the bequest or appointment shall be void so far as concerns the person so attesting, or the wife or husband of such person, or any person claiming under either of them.

A legatee under a will does not lose his legacy by attesting a codicil which confirms the will. (S. 54. I. S. Act.)

The rules governing the execution of privileged wills which are less formal than ordinary wills are dealt with in section 53 of the Succession Act.

The formalities to be observed in the case of a bequest to religious or charitable uses by a testator having a nephew or niece or any nearer relative are that the will must be executed not less than 12 months before his death and within 6 months from its execution the same must be deposited in some place provided by law for safe custody of the wills of living persons. (S. 105. I. S. Act.)

Revocation of Wills.

A will is said to be *ambulatory* until the testator's death because he may revoke or alter it at any time when he is competent to dispose of his property by will.

An unprivileged will or codicil shall be revoked (*a*) by marriage of the maker, except when made in exercise of a power of appointment, or (*b*) by another will or codicil, or (*c*) by some writing declaring an intention to revoke the same and executed as an unprivileged will, or (*d*) by burning, tearing, or otherwise destroying the same by the testator, or by some person in his presence and by his direction, with the intention of revoking the same. (Ss. 55, 57. I. S. Act.)

As regards *revival of a will* section 60 of the Succession Act provides that where an unprivileged will or codicil, or any part thereof shall be revoked, the same shall be revived only by its re-execution, or by a codicil executed as required, and showing an intention to revive the same ; and when any will or codicil which shall be partly revoked, and afterwards wholly revoked, shall be revived, such revival shall not extend to so much thereof as shall have been revoked before the revocation of the whole thereof, unless an intention to the contrary shall be shown by the will or codicil.

Construction of Wills.

Rules as to interpretation of Wills are contained in sections 61—91 of the Succession Act.

The fundamental principle in the construction of wills is to effectuate the testator's intention so far as it is consistent with the rules of law.

It is sufficient if the wording of a will is such that the intentions of the testator can be known therefrom ; no technical words or terms of art need necessarily be used. (S. 61. I. S. Act.)

A will not expressive of any definite intention is void for uncertainty. (S. 76. I. S. Act.)

The meaning of any clause in a will is to be collected from the entire instrument, and all its parts are to be construed with reference to each other ; and for this purpose a codicil is to be considered as part of the will. (S. 69. I. S. Act.)

If in a Parsi will written in Gujarati the words used are such as to create a joint interest, it is impossible to escape the consequence that the beneficiaries take as joint tenants with the benefit of survivorship. (*Navroji v. Pirozbai,* 23 Bom. at p. 99.)

No part of a will is to be rejected as destitute of meaning if it is possible to put a reasonable construction upon it and testator's intention is not to be set aside because it cannot take full effect, but is to be effectuated as far as possible. (Ss. 72, 74. I. S. Act.)

Where any word material to the full expression of the meaning has been omitted, it may be supplied by the context. (S. 64. I. S. Act.)

Erroneous particulars in the description of the subject-matter of a bequest shall be rejected. A part of the description, however, shall not be rejected as erroneous, if any object answers the whole description. (Ss. 65, 66. I. S. Act.)

Section 65 is a paraphrase of the rule *Falsa demonstratio non nocet cumde corpore constat.* "The characteristic of cases within the rules is that the description so far as it is false, applies to no subject at all, and so far as it is true, applies to one only." (Stokes. 48.)

Extrinsic evidence of the testator's intention is admissible in cases of latent ambiguity only. It is inadmissible in cases of patent ambiguity or deficiency. (Ss. 67, 68. I. S. Act.)

Where a clause is susceptible of two meanings, according to one of which it has some effect, and according to the other it can have none, the former is to be preferred. And where two clauses in a will are inconsistent and not reconcilable, the last shall prevail. (Ss. 71, 75. I. S. Act.)

A will speaks from the testator's death.

Where property is bequeathed to any person, he is entitled to the whole interest of the testator therein, unless a restricted interest appears to have been intended for him. In the case of a bequest in the alternative, the legatee first named shall be entitled to the legacy, if he be alive at the time when it takes effect; but if he be then dead, the person or class of persons named in the second branch of the alternative shall take the legacy. (Ss. 82, 83. I. S. Act.)

Section 88 of the Succession Act lays down four rules of construction where a will purports to make two bequests to the same person, and nothing appears in the will to show the testator's intention whether the latter bequest was to be cumulative or to be substitutional only.

First.—If the same specific thing is bequeathed twice to the same legatee in the same will, or in the will and again in a codicil, he is entitled to receive that specific thing only.

Second.—Where one and the same will or one and the same codicil purports to make, in two places, a bequest to the same person of the same quantity or amount of anything, he shall be entitled to one such legacy only.

Third.—Where two legacies of unequal amount are given to the same person in the same will, or in the same codicil, the legatee is entitled to both.

Fourth.—Where two legacies, whether equal or unequal in amount, are given to the same legatee, one by a will and the other by a codicil, or each by a different codicil, the legatee is entitled to both legacies.

N. B.—In the four last rules, the word "will" does not include a codicil.

In sections 80, 81, 84, 86 and 87 are laid down certain rules for construction of gifts to objects under particular designations descriptive of relationship or membership of a class.

Legacies.

Legacies are either *general*, *specific* or *demonstrative*.

A *general* legacy is one which does not relate to any individual thing, or sum of money, as distinguished from other things of the same kind, or other moneys.

Where a general legacy is given to be paid at a future time the executor must invest a sum sufficient to meet it in authorized securities. The intermediate interest in such a case forms part of the residue of the testator's estate. (S. 302. I. S. Act.)

Where *no time is fixed* for the payment of a general legacy, interest begins to run from the expiration of one year from the testator's death, except where the legacy is bequeathed in satisfaction of a debt, or where the testator was a parent or a more remote ancestor of the legatee, or has put himself in *loco parentis* to the legatee, or where a sum is bequeathed to a minor with a direction to pay for his maintenance out of it; in all these cases interest on the legacy runs from the testator's death. Where a *time has been fixed* for the payment of a general legacy interest begins to run from the *time fixed* (the interest up to such time forming part of the residue of the testator's estate), except where the testator was a parent or a more remote ancestor of the legatee or has put himself in *loco parentis* to the legatee or the legatee is a minor, in which cases the interest begins to run from the testator's death unless a specific sum for maintenance is given by the will. (Ss. 311, 312. I. S. Act.)

Where a testator bequeaths to any person a specified part of his property, which is distinguished from all other parts of his property, the legacy is said to be *specific*. (S. 129. I. S.Act.)

A specific legacy has two advantages over a general one. (1) It does not abate with the latter on a deficiency of assets. (2) When given to a person in being and producing interest, it carries with it that interest from the date of the testator's death. But if it should get adeemed or be inadequate to its object, the legatee is not entitled to recompense or satisfaction out of the testator's estate. When other assets are insufficient to pay debts it will have to abate in proportion. (Griffith p. 85.)

A bequest of a sum certain, merely because the stocks, funds, or securities in which it is invested are described in the will, or a bequest of any stock in general terms, merely because the testator had, at the date of his will, an equal or greater amount of the specified kind, or a bequest of money, merely because it is not payable until some part of the testator's property is disposed of in a certain way, is not specific. So where a will contains a bequest of the residue of the testator's property along with an enumeration of some items of property not previously bequeathed, the articles enumerated shall not be deemed to be specifically bequeathed. (Ss. 130—133. I. S. Act.)

Where a specific legacy is subject at the testator's death to any charge, the legatee, if he accepts the legacy, takes it subject to such charge, and is liable to make good the amount of the charge. The testator's estate is liable, however, (*a*) for anything to be done to complete the testator's title to the thing bequeathed ; or (*b*) for payment of rent or land-revenue (of immovable property any interest in which is given in a bequest) payable periodically, up to the testator's death ; or (*c*) for call and other payment due from the testator at his death in respect of stock in a joint stock company, which is specifically bequeathed ; the specific legatee bears the call or other payment becoming due in respect of such stock after the testator's death. (Ss. 155—157. I. S. Act.)

The legatee of a specific legacy is entitled to the produce thereof from the testator's death.

Demonstrative legacy means a legacy directed to be paid out of specified property. (S. 137. I. S. Act.)

It is in its nature a general legacy but there is a particular fund pointed out to satisfy it.

A demonstrative legacy is so far general that if the fund be called in or fail the legatee will not be deprived of his legacy, but be permitted to receive it out of the general assets : but it is so far specific that it will not be liable to abate with general legacies upon a deficiency of assets. It is however, liable to abate when it becomes a general legacy by reason of the failure of the fund out of which it is payable. And a demonstrative legacy of stock does not carry interest from the testator's death. (Stokes. III.)

Sections 164, 165 of the Succession Act treat about legacies to creditors and portioners.

Where a debtor bequeaths a legacy to his creditor, and it does not appear from the will that the legacy is meant as a satisfaction of the debt, the creditor is *primâ facie* entitled to the legacy as well as to the amount of the debt. So where a parent who is under obligation by contract to provide a portion for a child fails to do so, and afterwards bequeaths a legacy to the child, and does not intimate by his will that the legacy is meant as a satisfaction of the portion, the child is entitled to receive the legacy as well as the portion. (Ss. 164, 165. I. S. Act.)

The executor's assent is necessary to complete a legatee's title to his legacy and when given, it gives effect to a legacy from the testator's death. The executor, however, is not bound to pay or deliver any legacy until after one year from the testator's death. (Ss. 292, 296, 297. I. S. Act.)

Annuities.

An annuity created by will is payable to the legatee for his life only, whether it is directed to be paid out of the property generally, or a sum of money is bequeathed to be invested in the purchase of it. (S. 160. I. S. Act.)

Where no time is fixed for the commencement of an annuity given by a will it commences from the testator's death; but the first payment is made at the end of a year next after that event. Where, however, there is a direction that the annuity be paid quarterly or monthly, the first payment becomes due and may be paid out at the end of the first quarter or first month, as the case be, after the testator's death; but the executor is not bound to pay it till the end of the year. And where there is a direction that the first payment is to be made within a given time from the testator's death, or on a day certain, the successive payments are to be made on the anniversary of the earliest day on which the will authorizes the first payment to be made; and in the interval between the times of payment if the annuitant were to die, an apportioned share of the annuity is to be paid to his representative.

Doctrine of Lapse.

If the legatee does not survive the testator, the legacy cannot take effect, but shall lapse and form part of the residue of the testator's property. In order to entitle the representatives of the legatee to receive the legacy, it must be proved that he survived the testator. (S. 92. I. S. Act.)

A bequest, however, does not lapse when the dying legatee is the testator's child or other lineal descendant and leaves a lineal descendant living at the testator's death, nor when the legatee is a trustee for another. So also a legacy does not lapse if one of two joint legatees die before the testator, but the survivor takes the whole. Where, however, there are words showing the testator's intention to give to legatees distinct shares, and if any legatee die before the testator, the legacy intended for him shall fall into residue of the testator's property. (Ss. 96, 97, 93, 94. I. S. Act.)

Residue means all of which no effectual disposition is made by the will *other than the residuary clause;* but when the disposition of the residue itself fails, to the extent to which it fails, the will is inoperative, and the testator will be taken to have died intestate in respect to it.

A residuary legatee may be constituted by any words that show an intention on the testator's part that the person designated shall take the surplus or residue of his property. Under a residuary bequest, the legatee is entitled to all property belonging to the testator at the time of his death, of which he has not made any other testamentary disposition which is capable of taking effect. (Ss. 89, 90. I. S. Act.)

The residue after usual payments is to be paid to the residuary legatee (if any) appointed by the will. (S. 326. I. S. Act.)

Void Bequests.

A bequest not expressive of any definite intention is void for uncertainty. (S. 76. I. S. Act.)

A bequest to a person by a particular description, there being no one answering such description at the testator's death, is void. (S. 99. I. S. Act.)

Sections 100 and 101 of the Indian Succession Act lay down restrictions upon the power conferred by section 99. By section 100 a bequest to a person not in existence at the testator's death subject to a prior bequest is void, unless it comprises the whole of the testator's remaining interest in the thing bequeathed.

In other words the section provides, in effect, that the deferred bequest must comprise the whole of the testator's remaining interest.

Section 101 puts a serious restriction upon the testator's power of creating successive interests in property by will. It treats of the rule against perpetuity, and provides that any bequest the vesting whereof is delayed beyond a life or lives in being at the testator's death, and the minority of the donee who must be living (born) at the close of the last life, is void.

The bequest is thus good if delayed from being vested beyond the life-time of persons in being for the period only of the minority of some person born in their life-time.

The members of a Parsi family, the heirs of F. deceased, entered into an agreement dated the 24th May 1851, by which they agreed that the remaining income (after paying the deceased's debts) of a certain estate, situated in the island of Salsette which had belonged to the deceased should be appropriated in certain shares among themselves as heirs of the deceased and "*after their death their shares are to be enjoyed and received by their heirs and children from generation to generation for ever*." In a previous suit (I. L. R. 6 Bom. 151) it was decided that under this agreement the signatories thereto took only a life interest in their respective shares. In the present suit it was contended and was held by the Division Court that the subsequent gift to the "heirs and children (of the signatories) from generation to generation for ever" was void as infringing the rule against perpetuities. On appeal it was held that the settlement in favour of the heirs and children of each signatory was in law a valid settlement and not void as creating a perpetuity. In the absence of words in the context showing that they were intended to take less, the respective heirs and children of the signatories took an absolute estate.

A gift to the heirs of A from generation to generation confers on them when ascertained the same estate as if the gift were to X and Y, the heirs of A *nominatum*.

(*Fardunji N. Banaji* v. *Mithibai*, 22 Bom. 355.)

Section 104 of the Succession Act provides that a direction to accumulate the income arising from any property shall be void; and that the property shall be disposed of as if no accumulation had been directed. Where, however, the property is immovable, or where accumulation is directed to be made from the testator's death, the directon shall be valid in respect only of the income arising from the property within one year next following the testator's death; and at the end of the year such property and income shall be disposed of respectively, as if the period during which the accumulation has been directed to be made had elapsed. (S. 104. I. S. Act.)

This section allows accumulation in two cases: (1) When the property is immovable and (2) when the accumulation is directed to be made "from the death of the testator." In each case the accumulable income must arise "within one year next following the testator's death" which period is to be calculated exclusively of the day of his death. (Stokes. 84.)

Mortmain gifts, *i e.*, bequests to religious or charitable uses have been declared void by section 105 of the Act. The section provides against death-bed bequests to charitable uses by person having nephews or nieces or any nearer relatives. In such cases the will must be executed at least twelve months before the testator's death, and deposited within six months after execution in some place provided by law for the deposit of wills of living persons.

Bequests to be valid as charitable bequests, must be of a *public* character. Bequest for objects which are merely for the benefit of individuals are therefore void. The performance of the *baj rozgar* ceremonies, the consecration of the *nirangdin*, the recitation of the *yezashne*, and the annual *gahambár* and *doslá* ceremonies are ceremonies performed among Parsis rather with a view to the private advantage of individuals than for public benefit and consequently trusts for such objects are set aside by the Court. (*Limji* v. *Bapuji*, 11 Bom. 441.)

"Charitable purpose" includes relief of the poor, education, medical relief, and the advancement of any other object of general public utility, but does not include a purpose which relates exclusively to religious teaching or worship. (S. 2 Charitable Endowments Act VI of 1890.)

The fact that certain bequests to religious uses in will were void, because the will had not been deposited as required by section 105 of Act X of 1865, does not render all the bequests in the will null and void. The exclusion of certain of a testator's heirs by a will does not exclude them from sharing in that portion of the property which has to be treated as intestate owing to certain bequests to religious uses being void. (*Hormusji* v. *Rustamji*, P. J. for 1893, at p. 333.)

It appears from the motion made by the Hon'ble Mr. Anderson in the Council held on the 7 April 1865 at Calcutta to consider the Succession and Inheritance (Parsis') Bill that the President of the Parsi Law Association had urged upon the Hon'ble member that section 105 of the Indian Succession Act—(the Mortmain section) was inapplicable to Parsis, as they were in no degree priest-ridden and it was consequently suggested that the Parsis should be exempted from the operation of that section.

The Hon'ble Mr. Anderson, however, appears not to have thought it at all advisable to allow this exemption. He said "I would remark that the section alluded to imports into India the 9th Geo. II. Cap. 36, commonly called the Statute of Mortmain. Now opinions may differ as to the propriety of that law ; but it will be generally conceded that if such a law is made applicable to any portion of the community subject to the Succession Act, it must be made applicable to all who are so subject. I freely admit that the Parsis are not priest-ridden ; but there is a principal which underlies all laws of Mortmain, and which address itself to a sentiment of deeper growth than priestly influence. That sentiment is the desire which many men of all creeds and races feel on their death-beds to make terms, as it were, with the mysterious future by a liberality exercised at the expense of their heirs. It is one of the subtlest of those mixed questions of laws and morals, to what extent a man is justified in influencing by testation the distribution of his property. The wisdom of successive generations has determined with reference to this kind of testation, that there ought to be the most ample security not merely that the testator is in possession of his faculties, but that his mind is in an entirely healthy state capable of looking before and looking after, and in no way thrown off its balance by the fear of approaching dissolution. On considerations of this kind the laws of Mortmain have been founded, and to such considerations the Parsis are as subject as their fellow-men. I was unable therefore to recommend the amendment proposed by my friend to the select committee for adoption. And I may add that Parsis make such munificent use of their wealth during their lives, that the legislature is bound to guard, in some measure, their heirs from any testamentary profusion in favour of public objects, which the fear of death may possibly suggest."

The other bequests which are treated as void under the Succession Act are bequests upon impossible, or illegal or immoral conditions. (Ss. 113, 114. I. S. Act.)

Vesting of Legacies.

If a legacy be given in general terms, without specifying the time when it is to be paid, the legatee has a vested interest in it from the day of the death of the testator, and if he dies without having received it, it shall pass to his representatives. (S. 91. I. S. Act.)

Whenever the enjoyment of the property is postponed to some date subsequent to the testator's decease, if the vesting of the property is not postponed, the representatives of the donee, surviving the testator but dying before the date of the will, take it.

Where, by the terms of a bequest, the legatee is not entitled to immediate possession of the thing bequeathed, a right to receive it at the proper time shall become vested in the legatee on the testator's death, and shall pass to the legatee's representatives if he dies before that time and without having received the legacy. And in such cases the legacy is, from the testator's death, said to be *vested in interest.* (S. 106. I. S. Act.)

An intention that a legacy to any person shall not become vested in interest in him is not to be inferred merely from a provision whereby the payment or possession of the thing bequeathed is postponed, or whereby a prior interest therein is bequeathed to some other person, or whereby the income arising from the fund bequeathed is directed to be accumulated until the time of payment arrives, or from a provision that if a particular event shall happen the legacy shall go over to another person. (*Ibid.*)

A legacy bequeathed in case a specified uncertain event shall happen does not vest until that event happens. A legacy bequeathed in case a specified uncertain event shall not happen does not vest until the happening of that event becomes impossible. In either case, until the condition has been fulfilled, the interest of the legatee is called *contingent.* (S. 107. I. S. Act.)

Where a fund is bequeathed to any person upon his attaining a particular age, and the will also gives to him absolutely the income to arise from the fund before he reaches that age, or directs the income, or so much of it as may be necessary, to be applied for his benefit, the bequest of the fund is not contingent. (*Ibid.*)

Section 108 deals with gifts to a contingent class and provides that where a bequest is made only to such members of a class as shall have attained a particular age, a person who has not attained that age cannot have a vested interest in the legacy.

Contingent bequests are treated of in Sections 111 and 112 of the Succession Act.

Sections 109 and 110 of the Succession Act which deal with *onerous* bequests, provide that where a bequest imposes an obligation on the legatee, he can take nothing by it unless he accepts it fully ; but that where a will contains two separate and independent bequests to the same person, the legatee is at liberty to accept one of them, and refuse the other, although the former may be beneficial, and the latter onerous.

Sections 115 to 124 of the Succession Act treat about *conditional* bequests.

Where a will imposes a *condition precedent* to the vesting of a legacy, the condition shall be considered to have been fulfilled if it has been *substantially* complied with. Where, however, there is a bequest with a *condition subsequent*, as distinguished from a condition precedent, the bequest takes effect only when the condition is *strictly* fulfilled.

In case of a condition *precedent* the legatee has no vested interest until the condition is performed and the condition is taken as performed if it has been substantially complied with ; in case of a condition *subsequent*, the interest vests in the legatee in the first instance, subject to be divested by the non-performance of the condition.

The original bequest is not affected by the invalidity of the second (ulterior) bequest.

Where there is a bequest to one person, and on its failure to another, of the same thing, the second bequest takes effect on the failure of the first, though the failure may not have occurred in the way contemplated by the testator, unless the will shows an intention on the testator's part that the first bequest shall fail in a particular way before the second can take effect, and then in such a case the second bequest takes effect only on failure of the first bequest in that particular way.

Sections 125 to 127 of the Succession Act treat about bequests with *directions as to application or enjoyment.*

It has been said that "equity like nature will do nothing in vain." Following this principle section 125 lays down that where a fund is bequeathed absolutely to or for the benefit of any person, but the will contains a direction that it shall be applied or enjoyed in a particular manner, the legatee shall be entitled to receive the fund as if the will had contained no such direction.

Where a testator *absolutely* bequeaths a fund, so as to sever it from his own estate, but directs that the mode of enjoyment of it by the legatee shall be restricted so as to secure a specified benefit for the legatee, if that benefit cannot be obtained for the legatee, the fund belongs to him as if the will had contained no such direction. Where a testator does *not absolutely* bequeath a fund, so as to sever it from his own estate but gives it for certain purposes, and part of those purposes cannot be fulfilled, the fund, or so much of it as has not been exhausted upon the objects contemplated by the will, remains a part of the estate of the testator. (Ss. 126, 127. I. S. Act.)

Ademption of Legacies.

If anything which has been specifically bequeathed does not belong to the testator at the time of his death, or has been converted into property of a different kind, the legacy is adeemed; that is, it cannot take effect by reason of the subject-matter having been withdrawn from the operation of the will. (S. 139. I. S Act.)

Where, however, the change between the date of the will and the testator's death, takes place by operation of law, or in execution of the provisions of any legal instrument in which the thing bequeathed was held, or without the testator's knowledge or sanction, the specific legacy is not adeemed. (Ss. 150, 151. I. S. Act.)

A demonstrative legacy is not adeemed by reason that the property on which it is charged by the will does not exist at the testator's death or has been converted into property of a different kind; but is payable in such case from the general assets of the testator. (S. 140. I. S. Act.)

A specific bequest of goods under a description connecting them with a certain place is not adeemed by reason that they have been removed from such place (*a*) from any temporary cause, or (*b*) by fraud, or (*c*) without the testator's knowledge or sanction. Nor does the removal of the thing bequeathed from the place in which it is stated in the will to be situated constitute an ademption, where the place is only referred to in order to complete the description of what the testator meant to bequeath. (Ss. 147, 148. I. S. Act.)

So also stock specifically bequeathed does not adeem (*a*) if it is lent to a third party on condition that it be replaced, and it is replaced accordingly, or (*b*) if it is sold and an equal quantity of the same stock is afterwards purchased and belongs to the testator at his death. (Ss. 152, 153. I. S. Act.)

A specific bequest of a right to receive something of value from a third party, gets adeemed by the testator himself receiving it; but where the bequest is of a valuable to be received by the testator from a third person, it does not get adeemed by the testator or his representative receiving the same, unless he mixes it up with his general property in which case the legacy gets adeemed. (Ss. 141, 149. I. S. Act.)

The receipt by the testator of a part of an entire thing specifically bequeathed operates as an ademption of the legacy to the extent of the sum so received. So the receipt by him of a portion of an entire fund or stock specifically bequeathed operates as an ademption only to the extent of the amount so received. (Ss. 142, 143, I. S. Act.)

Where stock specifically bequeathed does not exist in whole or in part at the testator's death the legacy is adeemed so far as regards the whole or the part as the case be. (Ss. 145, 146. I. S. Act.)

No bequest is wholly or partially adeemed by a subsequent provision made by settlement or otherwise for the legatee. (S. 166. I. S. Act.)

Abatement of Legacies.

If the assets, after payment of debts, necessary expenses, and specific legacies, are not sufficient to pay all the general legacies in full, the latter shall abate or be diminished in equal proportions. (S. 287. I. S. Act.)

On a deficiency of assets to pay legacies, a specific legacy is not liable to abate with the general legacies. (S. 136. I. S. Act.)

When the assets are not sufficient to pay debts and specific legacies, then only the specific legacies abate rateably. Where the assets are sufficient to pay debts and necessary expenses specific legacies do not abate.

Demonstrative legacies under similar circumstances where the assets are sufficient to pay debts and necessary expenses do not also abate, if the funds from which they are directed to be paid exist. These, however, are liable to abate when they become general legacies by reason of the primary funds out of which they are payable ceasing to exist. (Ss. 287.—290. I. S. Act.)

Where there is a deficiency of assets general legacies first abate, then demonstrative and then specific. If the fund out of which the demonstrative legacy is payable fails, the demonestrative legacy is payable out of the general assets, and then it abates with the general legacies. Where specific legacy fails it is not payable out of the general assets. Where the assets are not sufficient to pay all the legacies an annuity abates in the same proportion as the other pecuniary legacies given by the will.

Refunding of Legacies.

In the event of the *assets proving insufficient* to pay all the legacies, an executor may call upon a legatee to refund, if he has paid the legacy under Judge's order, but not if he has paid it voluntarily, and in this case (when he has paid a legacy voluntarily) the executor if solvent must be first proceeded against by the unsatisfied legatee; but if the executor be insolvent, then such a legatee can oblige each satisfied legatee to refund in proportion. So each satisfied legatee is compellable to refund in proportion when the executor has paid away the assets in legacies and he is afterwards obliged to discharge a debt of which he had no previous notice. If *assets were sufficient* to satisfy all the legacies at the time of the testator's death, an unpaid legatee or one who has been compelled to refund by creditor, cannot call upon the legatee who has received payment in full to refund. An unpaid creditor, however, may call upon a satisfied legatee to refund, whether the assets were, or were not sufficient at the time of the testator's death, to pay both debts and legacies, and whether the payment of the legacy by the executor was voluntary or not. (Ss. 316, 317, 323, 319, 322, 321. I. S. Act.)

A creditor may call upon a legatee to refund within 2 years.

The refunding shall in *all* cases be without interest. (S. 325. I. S. Act.)

Election.

Where a testator by his will, either believing or not believing that which he professes to dispose of to be his own, professes to dispose of something, which he has no right to dispose of, the person to whom the thing belongs has to elect either to conform to such disposition or to dissent from it; and in the latter case, he forfeits all interest (benefit) under the will. The interest so relinquished devolves as if it had not been disposed of in the legatee's favour, subject, nevertheless, to the charge of making good to the disappointed legatee the amount or value of the gift attempted to be given to him by the will.

A person taking no benefit directly under the will, but deriving a benefit under it indirectly, is not put to his election. (S. 171. I. S. Act.)

Acceptance of a benefit given by the will constitutes an election by the legatee to take under the will, (*a*) if he has knowledge of his right to elect, and of those circumstances which would influence the judgment of a reasonable man in making an election, or (*b*) if he waives inquiry into the circumstances. And such knowledge or waiver of inquiry *shall* be presumed by enjoyment by the legatee for two years of the benefits provided for him by the will without doing any act to express dissent, or it *may* be inferred from any act of the legatee which renders it impossible to place the persons interested in the subject-matter of the bequest in their original positions. (Ss. 173—175. I. S. Act.)

If the legatee does not elect within one year after the testator's death, he may be called upon after that time to make an election; and if he does not comply with such requisition within a reasonable time he shall be deemed to have elected to conform the will. S. 176. I. S. Act.)

Gifts in Contemplation of Death.

Donatio Mortis Causâ.

A gift is said to be made in contemplation of death where a man who is ill, and expects to die shortly of his illness, delivers to another the possession of any movable property to keep as a gift in case the donor shall die of that illness. Any movable property which the donor could dispose of by will, may be the subject of such a gift. It may be resumed by the giver and it does not take effect if he recovers from the illness during which it was made; nor if he survives the person to whom it was made. (S. 178. I. S. Act.)

Probate and Letters of Administration.

The executor or administrator, as the case may be, of a deceased person, is his legal representative for all purposes, and all the property of the deceased person vests in him as such. (S. 179. I. S. Act.)

"Executor" means a person to whom the execution of the last will of a deceased person is, by the testator's appointment, confided. (S. 3. I. S. Act.)

"Administrator" means a person appointed by competent authority to administer the estate of a deceased person when there is no executor. (Ibid.)

It is only the actual property of the deceased that vests in the executor or administrator and consequently property vested in a testator as executor of another does not vest in his executor. (*De Souza* v. *Secretary of State*, 12 B. L. R. 422.)

Probate can be granted only to an executor appointed by the will. (S. 181. I. S. Act.)

"Probate" means the copy of a will certified under the seal of a Court of competent jurisdiction with a grant of administration to the estate of the testator. (S. 3. I. S. Act.)

The appointment of an executor may be express or implied; and it may be for any limited purpose, specified in the will, when probate shall be limited to that purpose. (Ss. 182, 219. I. S. Act.)

Probate and letters of administration cannot be granted to any person who (1) is a minor, or (2) is of unsound mind, nor (3) to a married woman without her husband's previous consent. (Ss. 183, 189. I. S. Act.)

There is no objection to an infant being appointed executor; but probate will not be granted during his minority. Where, however, a minor is *sole* executor, letters of administration with the will annexed may be granted to his legal guardian, or to such other person as the Court thinks fit, until the minor completes the age of 18 years, when and not till then, probate of the will is to be granted to him. And where there are two or more minor executors, and no executor has attained majority, administration is granted limited until one of them completes the age of 18 years. (Ss. 215, 216. I. S. Act.)

In case of a sole executor or a person entitled to letters of administration being a lunatic, letters of administration, with or without the will annexed, as the case be, may be granted to his committee or to such other person as the Court thinks fit, for the use and benefit of the lunatic until he becomes of sound mind. (S. 217. I. S. Act.)

When probate or letters of administration have been granted to a married woman, she has all the powers of an ordinary executor or administion. (S. 275. I. S. Act.)

When several executors are appointed, probate may be granted to them all simultaneously or at different times. (S. 184. I. S. Act.)

A separate probate of a codicil discovered after the grant of probate, may be granted to the executor if the codicil in no way repeals the appointment of executors made by the will. But if different executors are appointed by the codicil, the probate of the will must be revoked, and a new probate granted of the will and the codicil together. (S. 185. I. S. Act.)

If after the grant of letters of administration with the will annexed, a codicil be discovered, it may be added to the grant on due proof and identification, and the grant altered and amended accordingly. (S. 233. I. S. Act.)

Upon the death of one or more of several executors or administrators all the powers of the office become vested in the survivors or survivor. This means that even where probate has not been granted, the office becomes vested in the survivor or survivors. (S. 272. I. S. Act; Henderson. 165.)

No right as executor (or legatee) can be established in any Court of Justice unless probate, or letters of administration to the estate of the deceased shall have been granted by a competent Court within the province. So also no right to any

part of an intestate's property can be established in any Court of Justice, unless letters of administration have been granted by a competent Court. (Ss. 187, 190. I. S. Act.)

S. 180 of the Indian Succession Act provides that when a will has been proved in a competent Court, situated beyond the limits of the province, whether in the British dominions or in a foreign country, and a properly authenticated copy of the will is produced in British India, letters of administration may be granted here with a copy of such copy annexed.

Probate of a will when granted, (1) establishes the will from the testator's death, and (2) renders valid all intermediate acts of the executor as such. Letters of administration entitle the administrator to all rights belonging to the intestate as effectually as if the administration had been granted at the moment after his death, but do not render valid any of his intermediate acts tending to the diminution or damage of the intestate's estate. (Ss. 188, 191, 192. I. S. Act.)

Renunciation by Executor.

The renunciation of executorship may be made (1) orally in presence of the judge, or (2) by a writing signed by the person renouncing, and when made shall preclude him from ever thereafter applying for probate of the will appointing him executor. (S. 193. I. S. Act.)

If the executor renounce, or fail to accept the executorship within the time limited, the will may be proved and letters of administration with a copy of the will annexed may be granted to the person, who would be entitled to administration in case of intestacy.

Where the appointed executor has not renounced the executorship, letters of administration are granted to another person after issue of a citation calling upon the executor to accept or renounce his executorship. Where, however, one or more of several executors have proved a will, on the death of the survivors of those who have proved, administration may be granted without citing those who have not proved. (S. 193. I. S. Act.)

Letters of administration with the will annexed when and to whom given.

When the testator has failed to appoint an executor in his will, or when the appointed executor is legally incapable or refuses to act, or has died before the testator or before he has proved the will, or before he has administered all the estate after having proved the will, the following persons successively may be admitted to prove the will, and letters of administration with the will annexed may be granted to them of the whole or so much of the estate, as may be unadministered: (1) Universal or residuary legatee. (2) The representative of a residuary legatee having a beneficial interest dying before the estate has been fully administered. (3) Administrators on intestacy. (4) Legatee having a beneficial interest. (5) creditor. (Ss. 196, 198. I. S. Act.)

Administrators on Intestacy.—When the deceased has died intestate (1) persons connected with him either by marriage or by consanguinity are entitled to obtain letters of administration of his estate and effects in the following order:—(*a*) widow of the intestate, unless the Court sees cause to exclude her either on the ground of personal disqualification, or because she has no interest in his estate. The Court may associate with her in the administration any person or persons who would be solely entitled to the administration in the default of a widow; (*b*) in default or on exclusion of a widow, person or persons beneficially entitled to the estate according to the rules of distribution of an intestate's estate; provided that when the mother of the deceased shall be one of the class of persons so entitled she shall be solely entitled to administration; (2) in default of persons connected by marriage or consanguinity, administration may be granted to a creditor, (Ss. 200, 203, 206. I. S. Act.)

Those who stand in equal degree of kindred to the deceased, are equally entitled to administrations. The widower has the same right of administration of his wife's estate as the widow has in respect of her husband's estate. (Ss. 204, 205. I. S. Act.)

A district Judge cannot, under section 210, of the Succession Act, grant letters of administration to a Parsi if the deceased had not at the time of his death a fixed place of abode or any property within his district. (*Fardunji v. Navazbai*, 17 Bom. 689.)

Where the deceased has left property in British India, letters of administration must be granted according to these rules although he may have been a domiciled inhabitant of a country in which the law relating to testate and intestate succession differs from the law of British India. (S. 207. I. S. Act.)

Executors and Administrators.

Their Powers.

1. An executor or administrator has the same power (*a*) to sue in respect of all causes of action that survive the deceased and (*b*) to destrain for all rents due to him at the time of his death, as the deceased had when living. (S. 267. I. S. Act.)

2. All demands whatsoever, and all rights to prosecute or defend any action or special proceeding existing in favour or against the deceased survive to and against his executors or administrators, except (*a*) causes of action for defamation, (*b*) assault as defined in the I. P. Code, (*c*) other personal injuries not causing the death of the party, and (*d*) cases where after

the party's death the relief sought could not be enjoyed or the granting it would be nugatory. (S. 268. I. S. Act.)

3. He may dispose of the property of the deceased in any manner he likes. (S. 269. I. S. Act.)

Their Duties.

1. On application for probate an executor must state the amount of assets which are likely to come to his hands. (S. 244. I. S. A.)

2. An executor or administrator must exhibit within six months from the grant of probate or letters of administration, or within such further time as the Court, which granted the probate or letters, may from time to time appoint, an inventory containing a full and true estimate of all the property in possession and all the credits, and also all the debts owing by any person to which the executor or administrator is entitled in that character, and must exhibit within a year from the same date an account of the estate, shewing the assets which may have come to his hands and the manner in which they have been applied or disposed of. (S. 277. I. S. Act.)

In all cases where a grant has been made of probate or letters of administration intended to have effect throughout the whole of British India, the executor or administrator to the effects of any person dying in British India and leaving property in more than one province shall include in the inventory of the effects of the deceased his movables and immovables situate in such of the provinces, and the value of such property situate in the said provinces respectively, shall be separately stated in such inventory. (*Ibid*)

3. The executor or administrator must collect the property of, and the debts owing to, the deceased. (S. 278. I. S. Act.)

4. After paying in order (*a*) funeral expenses, deathbed charges including fees for medical attendance, board and lodging for one month previous to the death of the deceased; (*b*) expenses of obtaining probate or letters of administration; and (*c*) wages of labourers, artizans, or domestic servants for three months before death of the deceased, the executor or administrator must pay all such debts as he knows of, including his own, equally and rateably, as far as the assets of the deceased will extend. (Ss. 279—282. I. S. Act.)

The executor or administrator must observe the rules of priority laid down in sections 279, 280, 281. Thus funeral expenses, &c., are to be paid by him before all debts. (S. 279.) The expenses of probate, &c., are to be paid by him next after the funeral expenses and death-bed charges. (S. 280.) Wages of labourers, &c., are next to be paid (S. 281.) and then the other debts of the deceased.

5. Debts of every description must be paid before any legacy. (S. 285. I. S. Act.)

Their Liabilities.

1. When an executor or administrator misapplies the estate of the deceased, or subjects it to loss or damage, he is liable to make good the loss or damage so occasioned. (S. 327. I. S. Act.)

2. When he occasions a loss to the estate by neglecting to get in any part of the deceased's property, he is liable to make good the amount. (S. 328. I. S. Act.)

Sections 327, 328 of the Succession Act make the executors liable for negligence in the discharge of their duties, if it results in loss to the estate, even if they may be not guilty of fraud or collusion or corruption. (*Dhanjishaw* v. *Sorabji*, *P. J. for* 1896, at p. 512.)

Note.—An executor cannot in part refuse. He must refuse entirely, or not at all. Nor can he renounce after probate.

When a person improperly intermeddles with the estate of the deceased, while there is no rightful executor or administrator in existence he is called an "executor of his own wrong" (executor *de son tort*), and is answerable to the rightful executor or administrator, or to any creditor or legatee of the deceased to the extent of the assets which may have come to his hands, after deducting payments made to the rightful executor or administrator, and payments made in due course of administration. (Ss. 265, 266. I. S. Act.)

Limited Grants of Administration.

Grants Limited in Duration.

Probate may be granted, of a copy or the draft of a lost or destroyed will and so may the probate of the *contents of a lost or destroyed* will be granted in case there is no copy nor its draft as also of a *copy* of a will *where the original exists*, but is in possession of a person outside of the Court's jurisdiction, limited until the original or an authenticated copy of it be produced. (Ss. 208, 210, 209. I. S. Act.)

Where a will is known to exist but is not forthcoming, administration letters may be granted until the will or an authenticated copy of it be produced. (S. 211. I. S. Act.)

Grants for the Use and Benefit of others having Right.

Letters of administration with the will annexed may be granted, to the attorney of an absent executor for the use and benefit of his principal, as also to the attorney of an absent person, who if present would be entitled to administration, and *letters of administration* may be grant to the attorney of an absent person, who would be entitled to administration in case of intestacy, limited until he shall obtain probate or letters of administration granted to him. (Ss. 212, 214. I. S. Act.)

Letters of administration with the will annexed in case of a minor and a lunatic being a sole executor or a sole residuary legatee, may be granted to the legal guardian of the minor and to the committee of the lunatic or to such other person as the Court thinks fit to appoint, until the minor attains the age of 18 years and the lunatic becomes sane. (Ss. 215, 217. I. S. Act.)

And under section 218 I. S. Act administrator *pendente lite* may be appointed by the Court with all the rights and powers of a general administrator other than the right of distributing the estate.

For Special Purpose.

Probate shall be limited to the purpose specified in the will and letters of administration with the will annexed limited to a particular purpose may be given to an attorney of an executor appointed generally under sections 219 and 220 I. S. Act.

When it is necessary that a deceased person's representative be made a party to a pending suit, and the executor or person entitled to administration is unable or unwilling to act, letters of administration may be granted to the nominee of a party in such suit, limited for the purpose of representing the deceased in the said suit. (S. 222. I. S. Act.)

If, at the expiration of 12 months from the date of probate or letters of administration, the executor or administrator is absent, letters of administration may be granted, to any person the Court thinks fit, limited to the purpose of becoming a party to a suit to be brought against the executor or administrator and carrying the decree which may be made therein into effect. (S. 223. I. S. Act.)

Wherever necessary letters of administration may be granted, to any person the Court thinks fit, limited to the collection and preservation of the deceased's property. (S. 224. I. S. Act.)

Grants with Exception and of the Rest.

Wherever the nature of the case requires that an exception be made, probate of a will or letters of administration with or without the will annexed shall be granted subject to such exception, and whenever such a grant with an exception has been made and there is another estate of the deceased, then the person entitled to probate or administration of the remainder of the deceased's estate may take a grant of probate or letters of administration, as the case may be, of the rest (*cœterorum*) of the estate. (Ss. 226—228. I. S. Act.)

Grants of Effects Unadministered—de bonis non.

Where the executor to whom probate is granted dies, leaving the estate partly unadministered, a new representative may be appointed for the purpose of administering such part of the estate, and the grant is called *de bonis non*; and when a limited grant has expired, and there is still some part of the deceased's estate unadministered, supplemental (*cessate*) grants are made and letters of administration shall be granted to those to whom original grants might have been made. (Ss. 229, 231. I. S. Act.)

These supplemental or *cessate* grants are a re-grant of the whole of the deceased's estate as in the original grant.

Revocation of, and alteration in, grants.

The grant of probate or letters of administration may be revoked or annulled for just cause. (S. 234. I. S. Act.)

Just cause is, (1) that the proceedings to obtain the grant were defective in substance; (2) that the grant was obtained fraudulently by making a false suggestion, or by concealing from Court something material to the case; (3) that the grant was obtained by means of an untrue allegation of a fact essential in point of law to justify the grant, though such allegation was made in ignorance or inadvertently; (4) that the grant has become useless and inoperative through circumstances.

Errors in names and descriptions, or in setting forth the time and place of the deceased's death, or the purpose in a limited grant, may be rectified by the Court, and probate or letters of administration may be altered and amended accordingly. (S. 232. I. S. Act.)

PART II.

MARRIAGE AND DIVORCE.

INTRODUCTORY.

From their arrival in India in A. D. 717 up to 1865 the Parsis had no recognized laws to govern their social relations. When they settled in Western India they probably brought with them a system, both of law and custom, from Persia. But it was all unwritten and fell into desuetude, and this mere handful of Persian strangers gradually and naturally adopted much of the law and usage that obtained in the Hindu community, *inter alia*, as to marriage. (*Peshotam v. Meherbai*, 13 Bom. at p. 307.)

Before the year 1865, the English law of marriage was made applicable to the Parsis who had scarcely the idea of illegitimacy, and the law of divorce was applied to them to whom the indissolubility of marriage and the pecuniary penalty for dishonour were equally abhorrent.

Previous to the establishment of the High Court of Judicature the Parsis of the town of Bombay, a body constituting the preponderating majority of the entire Parsi population of India, far in advance of any other portion of the Parsi race in wealth, intelligence and civilization, had, since the Privy Council decision in 1856, been living in a state of lawlessness as to all that regards the marriage tie. They had no law at all on the subject. Each man did as seemed good in his own eyes. (Report of the Commission appointed by Bombay Government, dated 13th October, 1862.)

The urgency of taking some action was demonstrated in the year 1856 when the Privy Council decided in the case of *Ardaseer Cursetji v. Pirozbai*, that the Supreme Court on its ecclesiastical side had no jurisdiction to entertain a suit brought by a Parsi wife against her husband for restitution of conjugal rights, or for maintenance. This decision practically left the Parsis without any tribunal to enforce the duties and obligations arising out of the marriage union with the exception of those connected with mere property. The Parsis thereupon made repeated representations to the Government, as a consequence whereof a commission was appointed by the Bombay Government to enquire into the usages recognized by Parsis in India, and into the necessity of special legislation in connection with them. A large body of the leading Parsis formed themselves into the Parsi Law Association, and on the 15th February 1862 a numerously attended deputation from the managing committee of that association presented the Draft of a "Supplemental Code of Betrothment, Marriage and Divorce," to the said commission appointed by the Government of Bombay. *(Ibid.)*

The Parsis did not ask in vain from the great British Government the vindication by enactment of their moral law, for, on the 7th day of April, 1865, "The Parsi Marriage and Divorce Act" was passed.

THE PARSI MARRIAGE AND DIVORCE ACT.

ACT NO. XV of 1865.

Passed on the 7th April 1865.

An Act to define and amend the Law relating to Marriage and Divorce among the Parsis.

By section 3 of the Laws Local Extent Act (XV of 1874) this Act has been declared to be in force in the whole of British India, except the Scheduled Districts.

It has been declared under the Scheduled District Act, XIV of 1874, to be in force in the following Scheduled Districts:—

Sindh; West Jalpaiguri; The Districts of Hazaribagh, Lohárdaga, and Mánbhum, and Pargana of Dhálbhum, and the Kolhán in the District of Singbhum; The Scheduled portion of the Mirzapur District; Jaunsar Báwar; The Districts of Hazara, Peshawar, Kohát, Bannu, Dera Ismail Khan, and Dera Gházi Khan; The District of Silhat; The rest of Assam (except the North Lushai Hills).

It has been extended, under the same Act to the following Scheduled Districts:—

Kumáon and Garhwál; The North Western Provinces Tarái; British Baluchistan.

It has been declared, under the same Act, *not* to be in force in the *Scheduled District of Lahaul.*

Preamble.

Whereas the Parsi Community has represented the necessity of defining and amending the law relating to marriage and divorce among Parsis; And whereas it is expedient that such law should be made conformable to the customs of the said community: It is enacted as follows:—

I.—Preliminary.

Short title.

1. This Act may be cited as "The Parsi Marriage and Divorce Act 1865.

Interpretation clause.

2. In this Act, unless there be something repugnant in the subject or context.—

Words in the singular number include the plural, and words in the plural number include the singular :

"Priest" means a Parsi Priest and includes Dastúr and Mobed :

"Marriage" means a marriage between Parsis whether contracted before or after the commencement of this Act ; and "husband" and "wife" respectively mean a Parsi husband and a Parsi wife :

"Section" means a section of this Act :

"Chief Justice" includes Senior Judge :

"Court" means a court constituted under this Act :

"British India" means the territories which are or shall be vested in her Majesty or her successors by the Statute 21 & 22 Vic., cap. 106, entitled "An Act for the better Government of India ;"

And, in any part of British India in which this Act operates, "Local Government" means the persons authorized to administer executive Government in such part of India, or the chief executive officer of such part when it is under the immediate administration of the Governor-General of India in Council, and when such officer shall be authorized to exercise the powers vested by this Act in a Local Government; and "High Court" means the highest Civil Court of appeal in such part.

II.—Of Marriages between Parsis.

Requisites to validity of Parsi marriages.

3. No marriage contracted after the commencement of this Act shall be valid, if the contracting parties are related to each other in any of the degrees of consanguinity or affinity prohibited among Parsis and set forth in a table which the Governor-General of India in Council shall, after due inquiry, publish in the *Gazette of India*, and unless such marriage shall be solemnized according to the Parsi form or ceremony called "Asírvád" by a Parsi priest in the presence of two witnesses independently of such officiating priest; and unless, in the case of any Parsi who shall not have completed the age of twenty-one years, the consent of his or her father or guardian shall have been previously given to such marriage.

Table.

A man shall not marry his—

1 Paternal grand-father's mother.
2 Paternal grand mother's mother.
3 Maternal grand-father's mother.
4 Maternal grand-mother's mother.
5 Paternal grand-mother.
6 Paternal grand-father's wife.
7 Maternal grand-mother.
8 Maternal grand-father's wife.
9 Mother or step-mother.
10 Father's sister or step-sister.
11 Mother's sister or step-sister.
12 Sister or step-sister.
13 Brother's daughter or step-brother's daughter, or any direct lineal descendant of a brother or step-brother.
14 Sister's daughter or step-sister's daughter, or any direct lineal descendant of a sister or step-sister.
15 Daughter or step-daughter, or any direct lineal descendant of either.
16 Son's daughter or step-son's daughter, or any direct lineal descendant of a son or step-son.
17 Wife of son or of step-son, or of any direct lineal descendant of a son or step-son.
18 Wife of daughter's son or of step-daughter's son, or of any direct lineal descendant of a daughter or step-daughter.
19 Mother of daughter's husband.
20 Mother of son's wife.
21 Mother of wife's paternal grand-father.
22 Mother of wife's paternal grand-mother.
23 Mother of wife's maternal grand-father.
24 Mother of wife's maternal grand-mother.
25 Wife's paternal grand-mother.
26 Wife's maternal grand-mother.
27 Wife's mother or step-mother.
28 Wife's father's sister.
29 Wife's mother's sister.
30 Father's brother's wife.
31 Mother's brother's wife.
32 Brother's son's wife.
33 Sister's son's wife.

A woman shall not marry her—

1 Paternal grand-father's father.
2 Paternal grand-mother's father.
3 Maternal grand-father's father.
4 Maternal grand-mother's father.
5 Paternal grand-father.
6 Paternal grand-mother's husband.
7 Maternal grand-father.
8 Maternal grand-mother's husband.
9 Father or step-father.
10 Father's brother or step-brother.
11 Mother's brother or step-brother.
12 Brother or step-brother.
13 Brother's son or step-brother's son, or any direct lineal descendant of a brother or step-brother.
14 Sister's son or step-sister's son, or any direct lineal descendant of a sister or step-sister.
15 Son or step-son, or any direct lineal descendant of either.
16 Daughter's son or step-daughter's son or any direct lineal descendant of a daughter or step-daughter.
17 Husband of daughter or of step-daughter, or of any direct lineal descendant of a daughter or step-daughter.
18 Husband of son's daughter or of step-son's daughter, or of any direct lineal descendant of a son or step-son.
19 Father of daughter's husband.
20 Father of son's wife.
21 Father of husband's paternal grand-father.
22 Father of husband's paternal grand-mother.
23 Father of husband's maternal grand-father.
24 Father of husband's maternal grand-mother.
25 Husband's paternal grand-father.
26 Husband's maternal grand-father.
27 Husband's father or step-father.
28 Brother of husband's father.
29 Brother of husband's mother.
30 Husband's brother's son, or his direct lineal descendant.
31 Husband's sister's son, or his direct lineal descendant.
32 Brother's daughter's husband.
33 Sister's daughter's husband.

Note.—In the above table the words "Brother" and "Sister" denote brother and sister of the whole as well as half-blood. Relationship by step means relationship by marriage.

(Gazette of India, 9th September, 1865, pp. 9-81, 982.)

The requisites to the validity of a Parsi marriage are :—(1) The marriage should not be contracted within the prohibited degrees of consanguinity and affinity ; (2) it must be celebrated according to the ceremony called "Asirvad ;" (3) the ceremony must be performed by a "Parsi priest ;" (4) the ceremony must be performed in the presence of two "Parsi witnesses ;" and (5) in case of either party being under twenty-one, the consent of his or her father or guardian must be previously obtained.

In 1868 the plaintiff and defendant, then of the ages of seven and six years respectively, went through the ceremony of marriage in the presence of their respective parents and according to the rites of their religion. The formal consent on behalf of the plaintiff was not given by his father, but by his uncle, with whom he was living and by whom he had been adopted. Nineteen years afterwards the plaintiff filed a suit praying for a declaration that the pretended marriage was null and void and did not create the *status* of husband and wife between him, the plaintiff, and the defendant. The defendant resisted the suit and claimed to be the lawful wife of the plaintiff. The plaintiff and defendant never lived together as man and wife, nor was the marriage ever consummated. It was *held* that under the circumstances the formal consent of the uncle and the tacit consent of the father were enough to satisfy the requirements of section 3 of Act XV of 1865, which requires the previous consent of the father or guardian to the marriage ; that such a suit not being in the category of suits relegated to a special court by Act XV of 1865, the jurisdiction to try it remained in the High Court, to which it had been given by section 12 of the Letters Patent ; that the law to be applied was the English law, subject, however, to any well-established usage ; that by the English law such a marriage would be inchoate and imperfect marriage capable of repudiation by either party after arriving at years of discretion, but capable also of being made a valid and binding marriage by the consent of the parties thereto after they had arrived at such age; that the circumstances of the case showed that there had been such acquiescence in, and acceptance of, the marriage by the plaintiff after arriving at years of discretion as to render the marriage valid and binding on him, and incapable of subsequent repudiation. Consummation is the best proof of consent to a marriage, but is not the only proof. (*Peshotam Hormusji Dastoor v. Meherbai*, 13 Bom. 302.)

The plaintiff and defendant were Parsis. The husband filed this suit in April, 1891, stating that in March, 1885, he and the defendant went through the ceremony of *Ashirvád* at Akola in the Berár Assigned Districts. He alleged that he was at the time only nineteen years of age and that his mother and guardian had not given her previous consent to the ceremony, nor was she present at it. He and the defendant, subsequently, cohabited at Bhusáwal until the 8th April, 1885, but since then he had not lived with the defendant. He further alleged that the defendant had been guilty of adultery, and he prayed that, if necessary, it might be delcared that the Ashirvád ceremony did not constitute a valid marriage, but that if the marriage should be declared valid, it might be dissolved. The delegates having found that at the marriage the requirements of section 3 were complied with, *held*, assuming that there was no special law or usage in the Berars on the subject as to the requisites of a valid marriage between Parsis in that district, or that, if there was no such law or usage, it was in accordance with section 3 of the Act, the marriage between the plaintiff and the defendant was valid and capable of being dessolved. (*Dorabji v. Jerbai*, 16 Bom. 136.)

Within three years after attaining the age of 21 years, a Parsi female can sue to have her marriage ceremony performed while she was only 3 years of age declared null and void. She attains her majority on reaching the age of 21 years.

A Parsi female, within three years after she had attained the age of twenty-one, brought a suit in the Court of the Subordinate Judge at Broach for a declaration that a marriage ceremony performed in 1869, when she was not three years old, did not create the *status* of husband and wife between her and the defendant. She had never lived with the defendant as his wife. The Subordinate Judge held that the marriage was valid and binding, being of opinion that the custom of infant marriage among the Parsis was well established and recognized. On appeal the Judge confirmed the decree, holding that at all events in 1869, when the marriage took place, the custom was common and recognized as binding. On second appeal the High Court concurred with the opinion expressed in *Peshotam v. Meherbai*, 13 Bom. 302, that the Zoroastrian system did not contemplate marriage in infancy, but the lower Courts having found that a custom had grown up among Parsis in India validating such marriages, and that the custom was in force in 1869, did not consider it open on second appeal to arrive at an independent finding as to whether the evidence established the existence of such a custom. It was *held* that the plaintiff having for the purpose of bringing the suit attained her majority at twenty-one, the suit was not barred. (*Bai Shirinbai v. Kharshedji*, 22 Bom. 430.)

Section 3 of the Indian Majority Act IX of 1875 provides that "every person domiciled in British India shall be deemed to have attained his majority when he shall have completed his age of eighteen years and not before," but by section 2, clause *(a)* it is enacted that nothing in the Act "shall affect the capacity of any person to act in the following matters (namely), Marriage, Dower, Divorce, and Adoption." A Parsi suing to have a marriage declared void is "acting in the mattor of marriage," and, therefore, the Majority Act IX of 1875, which makes the age of eighteen the age of majority, does not apply to a question of limitation with regard to such suit. The age of majority in such a case is that prescribed by the Parsi Marriage and Divorce Act XV of 1865, viz: twenty-one years. (*Ibid.*)

Act XV of 1865 contains no provision as to the age at which a Parsi can contract marriage. Though the legislative in section 37 impliedly recognizes the validity of the marriage of a Parsi woman under the age of fourteen and of a Parsi male under the age of sixteen years, it does not deal with the age at which a Parsi marriage can be validly contracted. That matter is left to the general law which governs Parsis in that particular just as the English Marriage Act (4 Geo. IV. c. 76.) leaves the same matter to be dealt with by the Common Law of England. Now in *Ardaseer v. Pirozbai*, 6 M. I. A. 348, it is assumed by the Privy Council that the validity of a Parsi marriage must be determined by Parsi law and not by English law. That opinion was expressed in a case which was brought in the late Supreme Court on its ecclesiatical side, but the *dictum* is of general application and applies with even more force outside the limits of the Presidency Town where under Regulation IV of 1827 the law to be observed is, in the absence of Acts and Regulations, the usage of the country in which the suit arose; if none such appears, the law of the defendant, and in the absence of specific law and usage, justice, equity and good conscience alone. (*Ibid.* at p. 436.)

"When the Parsi Marriage and Divorce Act XV of 1865 was passed, twenty-one was the age of majority for Parsis in the Presidency Towns, as the English law in that respect applied to them—*Peshotam v. Meherbai*, 13 Bom. 309; *Naroji v. Rogers*, 4 B. H. C. 1. There is no evidence to show that a different law as to the age of majority amongst Parsis prevailed in the Mofussil. The Legislature in Act XV of 1865 adopted twenty-one years as the age of majority for Parsis, enacting by section 3 that no marriage contracted after the commencement of the Act should be valid, unless in the case of any Parsi who should not have completed the age of twenty-one years the consent of his or her father or guardian should have been previously given to such marriage. The schedule to the Act shows that the age of twenty-one was inserted in section 3 as denoting the limit of the age of infancy. For the purpose of the Act it must, therefore, be taken that minority does not cease amongst Parsis until the age of twenty-one, and it was so held by Candy, J. in *Sorabji v. Buchoobai*, 18 Bom. 366. The present suit is not, however, brought under the provisions of that Act (P. M. & D. Act), as (probably by an oversight) no provision is contained in it dealing with a case like the present where it is alleged that a marriage though in form a marriage is invalid in law, the element of consent being absent.—*Peshotam v. Meherbai*. It is, we think, to be regretted that a case like this cannot be tried before the special Parsi tribunal constituted by the Legislature for the trial of cognate cases." (*Ibid.* at pp. 434, 435.)

Re-marriage save after divorce unlawful during life-time of first wife or husband.

4. No Parsi shall, after the commencement of this Act, contract any marriage in the life-time of his or her wife or husband, except after his or her lawful divorce from such wife or husband by sentence of a Court as hereinafter provided; and every marriage contracted contrary to the provisions of this section shall be void.

Before the year 1865, when this Act came into force there was no restriction as regards marrying by a person in his or her life-time.

Formerly second marriages among Parsis (the first wife being alive) were not strictly allowed without sufficient cause; but such second marriages had been very numerous among members of the Parsi community, without any former precedent of the rigid enforcement of the penalties of the law, if any such existed, and such second marriages had been frequent down to the date on which Act XV of 1865 came into operation. (*Merwanji v. Avabai*, 2 Bom. 231.)

Unless a decree of nullity of marriage under sections 27 or 28 of thi Act, or a decree for dissolution of marriage under section 29 of thi Act, or a decree for divorce under section 32 of this Act is obtained, n Parsi can now, (*i. e.* after the commencement of this Act.), legally re marry in the life-time of his or her wife or husband. Then again the provisions of section 43 of this Act must be complied with. That section allows the respective parties to marry again (as if the prior marriage had been dissolved by death) only when the time limited for appealing (*viz* ;—three calendar months) against any decree dissolving a marriage shall have expired without any such appeal being presented, or when, any such appeal shall have been dismissed, or when, in the result of any appeal, any marriage shall be declared to be dissolved.

Punishment of bigamy.

5. Every Parsi who shall, after the commencement of this Act and during the life-time of his or her wife or husband, contract any marriage without having been lawfully divorced from such wife or husband, shall be subject to the penalties provided in sections 494 and 495 of the Indian Penal Code for the offence of marrying again during the life-time of a husband or wife.

Before this Act came into operation a Parsi contracting a second marriage in the life-time of his or her wife or husband could not be punished under the Indian Penal Code. (*Avabai v. Jamasji*, 3 B. H. C. at p. 115.)

Whoever, having a husband or wife living, marries in any case in which such marriage is void by reason of its taking place during the life of such husband or wife, shall be punished with imprisonment of either description for a term which may extend to seven years, and shall also be liable to fine.

Exception.—The section does not extend to any person, whose marriage with such husband or wife has been declared void by a Court of competent jurisdiction, nor to any person who contracts a marriage during the life of a former husband or wife, if such husband or wife, at the time of the subsequent marriage, shall have been continually absent from such person for the space of seven years, and shall not have been heard of by such person as being alive within that time, provided the person contracting such subsequent marriage shall, before such marriage takes place, inform the person with whom such marriage is contracted, of the real state of facts, so far as the same are within his or her knowledge. (S. 494. I. P. Code.)

Whoever commits the offence defined in the last preceding section, having concealed from the person with whom the subsequent marriage is contracted the fact of the former marriage, shall be punished with imprisonment of either description for a term which may extend to ten years, and shall also be liable to fine. (S. 495. I. P. Code.)

Certificate and registry of marriages.

6. Every marriage contracted after the commencement of this Act shall, immediately on the solemnization thereof, be certified by the officiating priest in the form contained in the schedule to this Act.

The certificate shall be signed by the said priest, the contracting parties, or their fathers or guardians when they shall not have completed the age of twenty-one years, and two witnesses present at the marriage; and the said priest shall thereupon send such certificate, together with a fee of two rupees to be paid by the husband, to the registrar of the place at which such marriage is solemnized.

The registrar on receipt of the certificate and fee shall enter the certificate in a register to be kept by him for that purpose, and shall be entitled to retain the fee.

Appointment of Registrar.

7. For the purposes of this Act a registrar shall be appointed.

Within the local limits of the ordinary original civil jurisdiction of a High Court, the registrar shall be appointed by the Chief Justice of such Court, and, without such limits, by the Local Government.

Every registrar so appointed may be removed by the Chief Justice or Local Government appointing him.

Marriage-register to be open for public inspection.

8. The register of marriages mentioned in section 6 shall, at all reasonable times, be open for inspection; and certified extracts therefrom shall, on application, be given by the registrar on payment to him by the applicant of two rupees for each such extract.

Every such register shall be evidence of the truth of the statements therein contained.

Transmission of certified copies of certificates in marriage-register to Registrar-General of Births, Deaths, and Marriages.

8A. Every registrar, except the registrar appointed by the Chief Justice of the High Court of Judicature at Bombay, shall, at such intervals as the Governor-General in Council from time to time directs, send to the Registrar-General of Births, Deaths, and Marriages for the territories administered by the Local Government by which he was appointed, a true copy certified by him, in such form as the Governor-General, from time to time, prescribes, of all certificates entered by him in the said register of marriages since the last of such intervals.

Penalty for solemnizing marriage contrary to section 4.

9. Any priest knowingly and wilfully solemnizing any marriage contrary to and in violation of section 4 shall, on conviction thereof, be punished with simple imprisonment for a term which may extend to six months, or with fine which may extend to two hundred rupees, or with both.

Penalty for priest's neglect of requirements of section 6.

10. Any priest neglecting to comply with any of the requisitions affecting him contained in section 6 shall, on conviction thereof, be punished for every such offence with simple imprisonment for a term which may extend to three months, or with fine which may extend to one hundred rupees, or with both.

Penalty for omitting to subscribe and attest the certificate.

11. Every other person required by section 6 to subscribe or attest the said certificate, who shall wilfully omit or neglect so to do, shall, on conviction thereof, be punished for every such offence with a fine not exceeding one hundred rupees.

12. Every person making or signing or attesting any such certificate containing a statement which is false, and which he either knows or believes to be false, or does not know to be true, shall be deemed to be guilty of the offence of forgery as defined in the Indian Penal Code, and shall be liable, on conviction thereof, to the penalties provided in section 466 of the said Code.

Penalty for making, &c., false certificate.

Whoever forges a document, purporting to be a record or proceeding of or in a Court of Justice, or a register of birth, baptism, marriage, or burial, or a register kept by a public servant as such, or a certificate or document purporting to be made by a public servant in his official capacity, or an authority to institute or defend a suit, or to take any proceedings therein, or to confess judgment, or a power of attorney, shall be punished with imprisonment of either description for a term which may extend to seven years, and shall also be liable to fine. (S. 466. I. P. Code.)

13. Any registrar failing to enter the said certificate pursuant to section 6 shall be punished with simple imprisonment for a term which may extend to one year, or with fine which may extend to one thousand rupees, or with both.

Penalty for not registering certificate.

14. Any person secreting, destroying or dishonestly or fraudulently altering the said register in any part thereof, shall be punished with imprisonment of either description as defined in the Indian Penal Code for a term which may extend to two years, or, if he be a registrar, for a term which may extend to five years, and shall also be liable to fine which may extend to five hundred rupees.

Penalty for secreting, destroying, or altering the register.

III.—Of Parsi Matrimonial Courts.

15. For the purposes of hearing suits under this Act, a special Court shall be constituted in each of the presidency-towns of Calcutta, Madras, and Bombay, and in such other places in the territories of the several Local Governments as such Governments respectively shall think fit.

Constitution of special Courts under Act.

16. The Court so constituted in each of the presidency-towns shall be entitled the Parsi Chief Matrimonial Court of Calcutta, Madras, or Bombay, as the case may be.

Parsi Chief Matrimonial Courts.

The local limits of the jurisdiction of a Parsi Chief Matrimonial Court shall be conterminous with the local limits of the ordinary original civil jurisdiction of the High Court.

The Chief Justice of the High Court, or such other Judge of the same Court as the Chief Justice shall, from time to time, appoint, shall be the Judge of such Matrimonial Court, and, in the trial of cases under this Act, he shall be aided by eleven delegates.

Parsi District Matrimonial Courts.

17. Every Court so constituted at a place other than a presidency-town shall be entitled the Parsi District Matrimonial Court of such place.

Subject to the provisions contained in the next following section, the local limits of the jurisdiction of such Court shall be conterminous with the limits of the district in which it is held. The Judge of the principal Court of original civil jurisdiction at such place shall be the Judge of such Matrimonial Court; and in the trial of cases under this Act, he shall be aided by seven delegates.

Power to alter territorial jurisdiction of District Courts.

18. The Local Government may, from time to time, alter the local limits of the jurisdiction of any Parsi District Matrimonial Court, and may include within such limits any number of districts under its government.

Certain districts to be within jurisdiction of Chief Matrimonial Court.

19. Any district, which the Local Government, on account of the fewness of the Parsi inhabitants, shall deem it inexpedient to include within the jurisdiction of any District Matrimonial Court, shall be included within the jurisdiction of the Parsi Chief Matrimonial Court for the territories under such Local Government where there is such Court.

Court-seal.

20. A seal shall be made for every Court constituted under this Act, and all decrees and orders, and copies of decrees and orders of such Court, shall be sealed with such seal, which shall be kept in the custody of the presiding Judge.

Appointment of delegates.

21. The Local Government shall, in the presidency-towns and districts subject to their respective Governments, respectively appoint persons to be delegates to aid in the adjudication of cases arising under this Act.

The persons so appointed shall be Parsis: their names shall be published in the official Gazette; and their number shall, within the local limits of the ordinary original civil jurisdiction of a High Court, be not more than thirty, and in districts beyond such limits, not more than twenty.

Power to appoint new delegate.

22. The appointment of a delegate shall be for life.

But whenever a delegate shall die, or be desirous of relinquishing his office, or refuse or become incapable or unfit to act, or be convicted of an offence under the Indian Penal Code or other law for the time being in force, then and so often the Local Government may appoint any other person being a Parsi to be a delegate in his stead; and the name of the person so appointed shall be published in the official Gazette.

Delegates to be deemed public servants.

23. All delegates appointed under this Act shall be considered to be public servants within the meaning of the Indian Penal Code.

Selection of delegates under sections 16 and 17 from those appointed under section 21.

24. The delegates selected under sections 16 and 17 to aid in the adjudication of suits under this Act shall be taken under the orders of the presiding Judge of the Court in due rotation from the delegates appointed by the Local Government under section 21.

Practitioners in Matrimonial Courts.

25. All advocates, vakils, and attornies-at-law entitled to practise in a High Court shall be entitled to practise in any of the Courts constituted under this Act; and all vakils entitled to practise in a District Court shall be entitled to practise in any District Matrimonial Court constituted under this Act.

Court in which suits to be brought.

26. All suits instituted under this Act shall be brought in the Court within the limits of whose jurisdiction the defendant resides at the time of the institution of the suit.

When defendant has left British India.

When the defendant shall, at such time, have left British India, such suit shall be brought in the Court at the place where the plaintiff and defendant last resided together.

At the time of the filing of the suit the plaintiff and defendant (both Parsis) were living in Bombay. It was held that the Court's Jurisdiction was not barred merely by the circumstance that the parties were married at Akola in the Berars. The Parsi marriage and Divorce Act is not in force at Akola; but section 26 of the Act permits a Parsi husband or wife to bring a suit in the Court established under the Act within the limits of whose Jurisdiction the defendant resides at the time of the institution of the suit. (*Dorabji v Jerbai*, 16 Bom. at p. 139.)

IV.—*Of Matrimonial Suits.*

(*a*) *For a Decree of Nullity.*

27. If a Parsi, at the time of his or her marriage, was a lunatic or of habitually unsound mind, such marriage may, at the instance of his or her wife or husband, be declared null and void upon proof that the lunacy or habitual unsoundness of mind existed at the time of the marriage and still continues.

In case of lunacy or mental unsoundness.

Provided that no suit shall be brought under this section if the plaintiff shall at the time of the marriage have known that the respondent was a lunatic or of habitually unsound mind.

28. In any case in which consummation of the marriage is from natural causes impossible, such marriage may, at the instance of either party thereto, be declared to be null and void.

In case of impotency.

In March, 1882, the plaintiff and defendant, Parsis, were married according to the rites and ceremonies of their religion. In October, 1882, the plaintiff attained puberty, and for seventeen months from that time she lived with the defendant in his parents' house; but there was no consummation of the marriage. There was no physical defect in either plaintiff or defendant, nor any unwillingness in the plaintiff to consummate the marriage; but the defendant had always entertained such hatred and disgust for the plaintiff as to result, in the opinion of the medical experts, in an incurable impotency in the defendant *as regards the plaintiff*. The delegates unanimously found, on the evidence, that the consummation of this marriage had from its commencement been impossible; because the defendant was from a physical cause, namely, impotency, as regards the plaintiff, unable to effect consummation. They also found that there was no collision or connivance between the parties. *Held*, on this finding, that such impotency *quoad* the plaintiff must be regarded as one of the causes going to make consummation of a marriage impossible under section 28 of Act 15 of 1865, there being nothing in the Act to suggest a contrary opinion. (*S. v. B.*, 16 Bom. 639.)

(*b*) *For a Decree of Dissolution in Case of Absence.*

29. If a husband or wife shall have been continually absent from his or her wife or husband for the space of seven years, and shall not have been heard of as being alive within that time by those persons who would naturally have heard of him or her had he or she been alive, the marriage of such husband or wife may, at the instance of either party thereto, be dissolved.

In case of absence for seven years.

(See S. 108 Indian Evidence Act. I of 1872.)

(c) *For Divorce or Judicial Separation.*

On ground of wife's adultery.

30. Any husband may sue that his marriage may be dissolved, and a divorce granted, on the ground that his wife has, since celebration thereof, been guilty of adultery;

On ground of husband's adultery, &c.

and any wife may sue that her marriage may be dissolved, and a divorce granted, on the ground that, since the celebration thereof, her husband has been guilty of adultery with a married or fornication with an unmarried woman not being a prostitute, or of bigamy coupled with adultery, or of adultery coupled with cruelty, or of adultery coupled with wilful desertion for two years or upwards, or of rape, or of an unnatural offence.

In every such suit for divorce on the ground of adultery the plaintiff shall, unless the Court shall otherwise order, make the person with whom the adultery is alleged to have been committed a co-defendant, and in any such suit by the husband the Court may order the adulterer to pay the whole or any part of the costs of the proceedings.

Dissolution of marriage is allowed in the following cases :—

1. Lunacy or habitual unsoundness of mind at the time of marriage of any one of the parties.
2. Consummation being rendered impossible from natural causes.
3. Continual absence of any one of the parties for seven years.
4. Adultery of the wife.
5. Adultery, or bigamy with adultery, or adultery with cruelty, or adultery with wilful desertion for 2 years or upwards, or rape or unnatural offence, of the husband.

Cruelty or personal violence on the part of the husband entitles the wife to judicial separation.

In a suit by a husband for divorce under this section (section 30), the defendant, if under the age of 21 years, although more than 18, must be deemed to be a minor, and a guardian for the suit of the defendant must be appointed. (*Sorabjee v. Buchoobai*, 18 Bom. 366.)

"Section 30 provides for suits for the dissolution of a marriage and the word "marriage" is defined in section 2 as meaning "a marriage between Parsis whether contracted before or after the commencement" of the Act. The provisions of section 33 do not, therefore, apply only to marriages celebrated in accordance with the requirements of section 3. That section applies to marriages whensoever celebrated. It applies also to valid marriages wheresoever celebrated. If it had been the intention of the Legislature to give relief to Parsi husbands and wives, in proper cases, only if they had been married in British India, that intention would have been clearly expressed. In the Indian Divorce Act IV of 1869 the Courts established thereunder have their jurisdiction in respect of marriages expressly limited. Those Courts can make no decree of dissolution of marriage unless the marriage has been solemnized in India, or unless the husband, has, since the solemnization of the marriage, exchanged his profession of Christianity for the profession of some other form of religion. No such limitation of the jurisdiction of this Court is to be found in Act XV of 1865." As in this case, both the parties were domiciled within the territorial jurisdiction of the Court at the time of the marriage, and were so domiciled at the time of the filing of the suit, and the adultery was also committed within the jurisdiction, it was held that the Court had jurisdiction and its jurisdiction was not barred merely by the circumstance that the parties were married at Akola. (*Dorabji v. Jerbai*, 16 Bom. at p. 139.)

A Parsi residing in Bombay, after this Act was passed, but before it came into operation, contracted a second marriage during the life-time of his first wife, from whom he had not been divorced, and whom he had wilfully deserted for two years. On appeal from an order by the Judge of the Parsi Matrimonial Court rejecting a plaint for divorce by the first wife, on the ground that the subject-matter of the plaint did not constitute a cause of action, it was *held* that the facts alleged in the plaint did not amount to "bigamy coupled with adultery," nor to "adultery coupled with wilful desertion," within the meaning of section 30 of Act XV of 1865, as a second marriage contracted by a Parsi during the life-time of his first wife was not unlawful before the Act came into operation, and the Act itself did not in any way affect the validity or the consequences of such a marriage. (*Avabai v. Jamasji*, 3 B. H. C. 113.)

Grounds of Judicial separation.

31. If a husband treat his wife with such cruelty or personal violence as to render it in the judgment of the Court improper to compel her to live with him, or if his conduct afford her reasonable grounds for apprehending danger to life or serious personal injury, or if a prostitute be openly brought into or allowed to remain in the place of abode of a wife by her own husband, she shall be entitled to demand a judicial separation.

Suits for divorce or judicial separation.

32. In a suit for divorce or judicial separation under this Act, if the Court be satisfied of the truth of the allegations contained in the plaint, and

that the offence therein set forth has not been condoned, and

that the husband and wife are not colluding together, and

that the plaintiff has not connived at, or been accessory to the said offence, and

that there has been no unnecessary or improper delay in instituting the suit, and

that there is no other legal ground why relief should not be granted, then and in such case, but not otherwise, the Court shall decree a divorce or judicial separation accordingly.

On either of three following grounds a wife can get judicial separation from her husband :—

1. Cruelty or personal violence by the husband rendering it improper to compel the wife to live with her husband.

2. His conduct affording her reasonable grounds for apprehending danger to life or serious personal injury.

3. The husband's openly bringing a prostitute into or allowing to remain in the wife's abode.

Judicial separation does not dissolve the marriage union as in divorce and neither the wife nor the husband can re-marry in his or her life-time.

The word "cruelty" in this section means "legal cruelty," *i. e.* "injury causing danger to life or limb or health, or reasonable apprehension of injury to life or limb or health.

Alimony *pendente lite.*

33. In any suit under this Act for divorce or judicial separation, if the wife shall not have an independent income sufficient for her support and all the necessary expenses of the suit, the Court, on the application of the wife, may order the husband to pay her monthly or weekly during the suit, such sum not exceeding one-fifth of her husband's net income, as the Court, considering the circumstances of the parties, shall think reasonable.

The Parsi Matrimonial Court, constituted under this Act, has no power to award alimony "*pendente lite,*" after decree and pending appeal. An unsuccessful wife cannot claim alimony after final decree and pending appeal, nor for the period during which she is seeking review of judgment. (*Hirabai V. Dhunjibhoy*, 17 Bom. 146.)

In no section of this Act does the word "suit" or "sue" necessarily take the meaning which includes appeal: such a meaning would conflict with sections 15 and 16 about jurisdiction and section 44 about custody of children. It may be supposed that if the Legislature had meant to empower this Court to award alimony after appeal made, it would have used as plain language as in section 36 of the Indian Divorce Act IV of 1869. Section 33 of Act XV of 1865 empowers the Court to order the husband to pay alimony "during the suit." (*Ibid*, at p. 150.)

Permanent alimony.

34. The Court may, if it shall think fit, on any decree for divorce or judicial separation, order that the husband shall, to the satisfaction of the Court, secure to the wife such gross-sum, or such monthly or periodical payments of money for a term not exceeding her life, as, having regard to her own property (if any), her husband's ability, and the conduct of the parties, shall be deemed just, and for that purpose may require a proper instrument to be executed by all necessary parties, and suspend the pronouncing of its decree until such instrument shall have been duly executed.

In case any such order shall not be obeyed by her husband, he shall be liable to damages at her suit, and further to be sued by any person supplying her with necessaries during the time of such disobedience, for the price or value of such necessaries.

In leaving the question of cruelty to the delegates in trials under this Act, the Court should adopt the rule expressed by the Court of Exchequer Chamber in the case of *Avery v. Bowden*, 6 E. and B. 973 "that if the evidence was such that the jury could conjecture only and not judge, it ought not to go to the jury. Where the amount of alimony awarded to the wife by the Parsi Chief Matrimonial Court did not exceed one-third of the husband's income, the High Court refused to interfere in appeal, following the practice of the Court of Divorce in England. (*Mancherji v. Motibai*, P. J. for 1894 at p. 109.)

By an order of the Parsi Matrimonial Court the deceased was directed to execute a proper instrument charging his immovable property with the payment of Rs. 70. per mensem by way of permanent alimony to his wife during her life. The instrument was executed accordingly. On his death his widow was held entitled, in addition to the Rs. 70 per mensem charged on her deceased husband's immovable property, to a distributive share in his estate. (*Motibai v. Motibai*, 24 Bom. 465.)

This section which deals with permanent alimony, does not contain the proviso for varying, &c., the orders for permanent alimony contained in section 37 of the Indian Divorce Act, IV of 1869. Section 34 of the Parsi Marriage and Divorce Act corresponds with section 32 of 20 & 21 Vict. Ch. 85, under which it has been held that the order for permanent alimony is permanent and incapable of being varied. (*Ibid.* at p. 469.)

Payment of alimony to wife or to her trustee.

35. In all cases in which the Court shall make any decree or order for alimony, it may direct the same to be paid either to the wife herself, or to any trustee on her behalf to be approved by the Court, and may impose any terms or restrictions which to the Court may seem expedient, and may, from time to time, appoint a new trustee, if for any reason it shall appear to the Court expedient so to do.

(*d*) *For Restitution of Conjugal Rights.*

Suit for restitution of conjugal rights.

36. Where a husband shall have deserted, or without lawful cause ceased to cohabit with his wife, or where a wife shall have deserted, or without lawful cause ceased to cohabit with her husband, the party so deserted, or with whom cohabitation shall have so ceased, may sue for the restitution of his or her conjugal rights, and the Court, if satisfied of the truth of the allegations contained in the plaint, and that there is no just ground why relief should not be granted, may proceed to decree such restitution of conjugal rights accordingly.

If such decree shall not be obeyed by the party against whom it is passed, he or she shall be liable to be punished with simple imprisonment for a term which may extend to one month, or with fine which may extend hundred rupees, or with both.

The Privy Council in the year 1856 before the enactment of this Act in the case of *Ardaseer v. Pirozbai* (6 M. I. A. 348), declared that the Supreme Court of Bombay, on its ecclesiastical side, was incompetent to entertain a suit for restitution of conjugal rights at the instance of a Parsi wife against her husband, as there existed such a difference between the duties and obligations of a matrimonial union among Parsis from that of Christians, that the Court, if it made a decree, had no means of enforcing it, except according to the principles governing the matrimonial law in Doctor's Commons, which were in such a case incompatible with the laws and customs of Parsis.

Their Lordships in the above case at pages 390 and 392 say: "For the reasons we have stated, we think that a suit for the restitution of conjugal rights strictly an ecclesiastical proceeding, could not, consistently with the principles and rules of ecclesiastical law, be applied to parties who profess the Parsi religion; but we should much regret if there were no court and no law whereby a remedy could be administered to the evils which must be incidental to married life amongst them. We do not pretend to know what may be the duties and obligations attending upon the matrimonial union between Parsis, nor what remedies may exist, for the violation of them, but we conceive that there must be some laws, or some custom having the effect of laws, which apply to the married state of persons of this description. It may be that such laws and customs do not afford what we should deem, as between Christians, an adequate relief; but it must be recollected that the parties themselves could have contracted for the discharge of no other duties and obligations than such as, for time out of mind, were incident to their own caste; nor could they reasonably have expected more extensive remedies, if aggrieved, than were customarily afforded by their own usages. Such remedies we conceive that the Supreme Court on the civil side might administer, or at least remedies as nearly approaching to them as circumstances would allow. In suits commenced on the civil side, the peculiar difficulties which belong to the exercise of ecclesiastical jurisdiction in some matrimonial cases would not arise. Proceedings might be conducted on the civil side with such adaptation to the circumstances of the case as justice might require, though on the ecclesiastical side such modification would be wholly irreconcilable with ecclesiastical law."

"We have been led to make these observations, not merely by general considerations, but more particularly by the case of *Merwanji v. Avabai*, 2 Borr. Bom. S. D. Rep. 209. That case shows that the *Sudder Adawlut* at *Bombay* will take cognizance of matrimonial suits between Parsis, and will afford them such relief as a due regard to their own laws and customs will allow; it also proves, as indeed must be expected, that those laws and customs are wholly at variance with the principles which govern the matrimonial law of the Diocese of *London*, and incompatible with the ecclesiastical law, as in such cases is administered. One instance, will suffice. It appears that, under many circumstances, the husband is permitted to take a second wife, the first being alive."

"We have not neglected to observe that in two or three cases, the ecclesiastical side of the Supreme Court has not refused to entertain suits of this description, but we have no reason to think that the difficulties which occur to us were brought prominently before that Court, or that, after duly considering them, the judges came to the conclusion that they were unimportant. There is no such course of decision as should make us hesitate in giving effect to our own opinion."

The word "lawful" in this section must refer not to English ecclesiastical law to which Parsis were never subject, but to the law to which they are subject—*Kawasji v. Sirinbai*, 23 Bm. at p. 281. (*Hirabai v. Dhunjibhoy*, 2 Bom. L. R. at p. 847.)

The word "just" in this section is not intended to have any different signification from the word "lawful" in the same section. (*Ibid.* 845.)

Some grounds which suggest themselves as clearly lawful grounds justifying refusal to cohabit are, adultery, which entitles a husband under the Parsi marriage and Divorce Act to obtain a divorce from his wife, and an agreement to separatl, consticuting a binding contract between the parties. Cruelty or personal violence of the kind mentioned in section 31 (of the Act) constitutes another lawful ground why a wife may refuse to cohabit with her husband. All these grounds are clearly sanctioned by some express law binding on Parsis and they are therefore lawful. But they do not seem to be exhaustive. It seems reasonable to treat the word "lawful" in this section as having a wider meaning and as indicating the law, whether statutory or customary governing the marriage relations of Parsis. The statutory law must doubtless be pointed out by the Court, but the customary law is a matter, like other matters of fact, within the cognizance of the delegates. That the customs binding on the conscience of Parsis, and as such forming the law subject to which the status of marriage is entered into is to be ascertained as a question of fact, like any other customary law peculiar to a particular community, needs little support from authority as it is a principle which is universally recognized by the Courts. But if authority is desired, reference may be made to *Bai Sirinbai v. Kharshedji*, 22 Bom. 430, in which this Court treated as a question of fact, not open to second appeal, the finding as to the existence of a custom binding amongst Parsis sanctioning infant marriages. The fact that in regard to Mahomedans and Hindus governed by Mahomedan and Hindu laws the Courts have determined as questions of law the grounds on which they refuse to direct wives to return to their husbands, affords no argument for taking out of the cognizance of the delegates the determination of the question what constitutes a lawful ground amongst a special community such as the Parsis for the refusal of a husband to live with his wife. (*Ibid.* at pp. 847, 848.)

To justify a refusal for the restitution of conjugal rights, the causes must be grave and weighty and such as to show a moral impossibility that the duties of married life can be discharged. (*Ibid.* 845.)

Discretion when applied to a Court of Justice means sound discretion guided by law. It must be governed by rule, not by humour ; it must not be arbitrary, vague, and fanciful, but legal and regular. (*Ibid.*)

Under this section (section 36) a contract by which a husband has agreed to allow his wife to live separate is a good defence to a subsequent suit by him for restitution of conjugal rights. (*Kawasji v. Sirinbai*, 23 Bom. 279.)

A decree for restitution of conjugal rights under this Act is enforceable only in the manner provided by this section (section 36) ; such provision is in substitution of, and not in addition to, the ordinary remedies provided by section 200 of the Civil Procedure Code, and the penalty therein provided operates not only as a purging of the contempt in not obeying the decree, but in full satisfaction of the decree. (*Ardeseer v. Avabai*, 9 B. H. C. 290.)

Having regard to section 23 of the Indian Limitation Act, 1877 and article 35 in the second schedule to that Act, a suit under the Parsi Marriage and Divorce Act by a wife for restitution of her conjugal rights is barred by lapse of time when restitution has been demanded by her and refused by the husband being of full mind, more than two years prior to the commencement of the suit.

Per Jenkins, C. J.—The words of article 35, Sch. II, Limit. Act read by themselves do impose on the special remedy of restitution of conjugal rights a time bar when there has been a demand and refusal though that may not be a necessary part of the cause of action. (*Dhunjibhai v. Hirabai*, 3 Bom. L. R. 371.)

37. *No suit to enforce marriage or contract arising out of marriage when husband under 16, or wife under 14 years.*

Notwithstanding anything herein before contained, no suit shall be brought in any Court to enforce any marriage between Parsis, or any contract connected with or arising out of any such marriage, if, at the date of the institution of the suit, the husband shall not have completed the age of sixteen years, or the wife shall not have completed the age of fourteen years.

This is the only section in which reference to infant marriages is made. The section says that no suit can be brought to enforce a marriage if at the date of the suit, the husband is not over sixteen, or the wife is not over fourteen.

Although the practice of infant marriages is one which finds no warrant in their own religious system, the Parsis in Western India have in the course of centuries so generally adopted them from their Hindu neighbours as to give such marriages amongst themselves all the validity they possess amongst Hindus, making them independent of any question of subsequent consent or non-consent by the parties thereto. (*Peshotam v. Meherbai*, 13 Bom. 303.)

When the Parsis settled in Western India in 717 A. D. they probably brought with them a system, both of law and custom, from Persia. But it was all unwritten, and fell into disuetude, and this mere handful of Persian strangers gradually and naturally adopted much of the law and usage that obtained in the Hindu community in whose midst they were forced to dwell. There is no doubt they adopted, amongst other things, the injurious practice of infant marriage. From the high level of education and civilization which the Parsi community of the present day has reached, these marriages are now discountenanced, but such marriages still are practised and recognized. The Parsi Law Association in 1862 sent to the Parsi Law Commission, which produced the Parsi Marriage Act, eighty-five delegates, all of them leading Parsis, to ask that the *Panchayet* should have power to dissolve marriages contracted before puberty "in consequence of the custom of marriages taking place during infancy amongst the Parsi community." This was refused; the Commission declined to insert either this provision or any explicit legislative sanction or prohibition of infant marriages being a matter of custom which though it appeared to be injurious, was yet admitted by the Parsi community. It is difficult to conceive a stronger proof of the prevalence of the usage than this petition which emanated from the great majority of the Parsi community. (*Ibid.* at pp. 311, 312.)

There is no doubt but that the Parsis in India are, as a general rule, subject to English law. They brought no written code of laws from Persia, and all ordinary disputes between Parsis are now regulated in conformity with the laws of England. But in Parsi Matrimonial matters a special Court has been created. The special Court has only power to grant a decree of nullity of marriage; it has no power to deal with a case where there never was a marriage at all. In *Ardeseer Cursetji v. Pirozbai*, 6 M. I. A. 348, it was held by the Privy Council that the Parsis were not subject to the ecclesiastical jurisdiction of the Court on disputes arising out of the marriage contract but that the ecclesiastical jurisdiction extended only to Christians in questions of the restitution of conjugal rights. It was, however, at the same time intimated by their Lordships that the Supreme Court on its civil side might possibly administer some kind of remedy for the violation of the duties and obligations arising out of the matrimonial union between Parsis. The High Court inherited all the powers of the Supreme Court, and was also specially empowered in the exercise of its ordinary original civil jurisdiction to "try suits of every description." This wide jurisdiction would cover such cases as are not within the jurisdiction of the special Parsi Court. The object of the charter which granted the Letters Patent was to invest the High Court with power to determine cases of every description and to apply a remedy to every wrong. Therefore the words "to try suits of every description" comprise matrimonial suits, subject of course to the provisions of Parsi Marriage Act, which assigns to a special tribunal most of the questions incidental to the matrimonial contract. (*Ibid.* at pp. 309, 310.)

Suits with closed doors.

38. In every suit prefered under this Act, the case shall be tried with closed doors should such be the wish of either of the parties.

39. [*Repealed by Court Fees Act VII of 1870.*]

Civil Procedure Code applied.

40. The provisions of the Code of Civil Procedure shall, so far as the same may be applicable, apply to suits instituted under this Act.

Vide, case of *Ardeseer v. Avabai*, 9. B. H. C. 290 given under notes to section 36 *ante.*

Determination of questions of law, and procedure, and fact.

41. In suits under this Act, all questions of law and procedure shall be determined by the presiding judge; but the decision on the facts shall be the decision of the majority of the delegates before whom the case is tried.

The decision of the majority of the delegates is conclusive under this section. In this case six of the delegates found that since the celebration of the marriage, the defendant was guilty of the alleged adultery. (*Dorabji v. Jerbai*, 16 Bom. at p. 138.)

Appeal to High Court.

42. An appeal shall lie to the High Court from the decision of any Court established under this Act, whether a Chief Matrimonial Court or District Matrimonial Court, on the ground of the decision being contrary to some law, or usage having the force of law, or of a substantial error or defect in the procedure or investigation of the case which may have produced error or defect in the decision of the case upon the merits and on no other ground:

Provided that such appeal be instituted within three calendar months after the decision appealed from shall have been pronounced.

Liberty to parties to marry again.

43. When the time hereby limited for appealing against any decree dissolving a marriage shall have expired and no appeal shall have been presented against such decree, or

when any such appeal shall have been dismissed, or

when in the result of any appeal any marriage shall be declared to be dissolved, but not sooner,

it shall be lawful for the respective parties thereto to marry again, as if the prior marriage had been dissolved by death.

V.—*Of the Children of the Parties.*

Custody of children *pendente lite.*

44. In any suit under this Act for obtaining a judicial separation or decree of nullity of marriage, or for dissolving a marriage, the Court may from time to time pass such interim orders and make such provision in the final decree as it may deem just and proper, with respect to the custody, maintenance and education of the children under the age of sixteen years, the marriage of whose parents is the subject of such suit,

Orders as to custody of children after final decree.

and may, after the final decree, upon application by petition for the purpose, make from time to time all such orders and provisions with respect to the custody, maintenance, and education of such children as might have been made by such final decree, or by interim orders in case the suit for obtaining such decree were still pending.

Settlement of wife's property for benefit of children.

45. In any case in which the Court shall pronounce a decree of divorce or judicial separation for adultery of the wife, if it shall be made to appear to the Court that the wife is entitled to any property either in possession or reversion, the Court may order such settlement as it shall think reasonable to be made of such property or any part thereof, for the benefit of the children of the marriage or any of them.

VI.—*Of the Mode of enforcing Penalties under this Act.*

Cognizance of offences under Act.

46. All offences under this Act may be tried by any officer exercising the powers of a Magistrate, unless the period of imprisonment to which the offender is liable shall exceed that which such officer is competent to award under the law for the time being in force in the place in which he is employed.

When the period of imprisonment provided by this Act exceeds the period that may be awarded by such officer, the offender shall be committed for trial before the Court of Session.

47. If any offence which by this Act is declared to be punishable with fine, or with fine and imprisonment not exceeding six months, shall be committed by any person within the local limits of the ordinary original civil jurisdiction of the High Court, such offence shall be punishable upon summary conviction by any Presidency Magistrate of the place at which such Court is held.

Punishment of offences under Act committed within local limits of High Court.

48. All fines imposed under the authority of this Act may, in case of non-payment thereof, be levied by distress and sale of the offender's movable property by warrant under the hand of the officer imposing the fine.

Levy of fines by distress.

49. In case any such fine shall not be forthwith paid, such officer may order the offender to be arrested and kept in safe custody until the return can be conveniently made to such warrant of distress, unless the offender shall give security to the satisfaction of such officer for his appearance at such place and time as shall be appointed for the return of the warrant of distress.

Procedure until return made to distress-warrant.

50. If upon the return of the warrant it shall appear that no sufficient distress can be had whereon to levy such fine, and the same shall not be forthwith paid, or

Imprisonment if no sufficient distress.

in case it shall appear to the satisfaction of such officer, by the confession of the offender or otherwise, that he has not sufficient movable property whereupon such fine could be levied if a warrant of distress were issued,

any such officer may, by warrant under his hand, commit the offender to prison for any term not exceeding two calendar months when the amount of fine shall not exceed fifty rupees, and for any term not exceeding four calendar months when the amount shall not exceed one hundred rupees, and for any term not exceeding six calender months in any other case, the commitment to be determinable in each of the cases aforesaid on payment of the amount of fine.

VII.—*Miscellaneous.*

51. Subject to the provisions contained or referred to in this Act, the High Court shall make such rules and regulations concerning the practice and procedure of the Parsi Chief and District Matrimonial Courts in the

Rules of procedure of Parsi Matrimonial Courts to be made by High Court.

Presidency or Government in which such High Court shall be established, as it may from time to time consider expedient, and shall have full power from time to time to revoke or alter the same.

All such rules, revocations and alterations shall be published in the official Gazette.

(*Vide* Appendix C.)

Power to invest chief executive officer with powers of Local Government.

52. The Governor-General of India in Council may invest the chief executive officer of any part of British India under the immediate administration of the Government of India with the powers vested by this Act in a Local Government.

53. [*Repealed by the Repealing Act XII of 1876.*]

SCHEDULE.

(*See section 6.*)

Date and place of marriage.	Names of the husband and wife.	Condition at the time of marriage.	Rank or profession.	Age.	Residence.	Names of the fathers or guardians.	Rank or profession.	Signature of the officiating priest.	Signature of the witnesses.	Signature of father or guardian when husband or wife is an infant.

RULES AND ORDERS UNDER PARSI MARRIAGE AND DIVORCE ACT, XV OF 1865.

(From Local Rules and Orders made under Enactments applying to Bombay. Volume I, edition of 1896, pages 27 and 28.)

Order constituting Parsi Chief Matrimonial Court in **Bombay** *and District Courts in* **Surat** *and* **Poona** *and their limits.*

" The Honourable the Governor in Council of Bombay is pleased to notify under the provisions of *Act XV of 1865, sections 15 and 18*, that the Parsi Chief Matrimonial Court of Bombay has been constituted in the Presidency Town of Bombay and that Parsi District Matrimonial Courts have been constituted in the towns of Surat and Poona respectively. "

" The local limits of the jurisdisction of the Parsi District Matrimonial Court of Surat include the District of Surat and Ahmedabad."

" The local limits of the jurisdiction of the Parsi District Matrimonial Court of Poona include the Districts of Poona, Ahmednagar, Satara, and Kaladgi (now Sholapur-Bijapur)."

" The District Registrars at Surat and Poona, appointed under Act XVI of 1864 (now Act III of 1877), have been appointed also Registrars for the purposes of *Act XV of 1865* under provisions of *section 7*."

(*Notification dated 30th August 1865, B. G. G., 1865, Vol. II p. 486.*)

Order constituting Parsi District Matrimonial Court for **Sind.**

" Under the provisions of *section 17 of Act XV of 1865*, the Honourable the Governor in Council is pleased to constitute the District Court of Karachi as the Parsi District Matrimonial Court for the Province of Sind, and to notify that the local limits of the jurisdiction of that Court will be conterminous with those of the Province of Sind."

" The Deputy Registrar appointed under Act XVI of 1864 (now Act III of 1877), is appointed Registrar of Parsi Marriages in Sind, under *section 7 of the Parsi Marriage and Divorce Act, 1865.*"

(*Notification dated 19th July 1865, B. G. G., 1865, Vol. II. p. 151.*)

Settlement of **Aden** *and* **its dependencies** *to be included within the jurisdiction of the Parsi Chief Matrimonial Court of Bombay.*

"The Governor in Council is pleased to direct under *section 19 of Act XV of 1865* (an Act to define and amend the law relating to Marriage and Divorce among the Parsis), that the Settlement of Aden and its dependencies shall be included within the jurisdiction of the Parsi Chief Matrimonial Court of Bombay."

(*Notification No. 2046A, dated 11th April 1891 as amended by Notification No. 3378 dated 24th June 1891. B. G. G., 1891, Part I. p. 337.*)

LAW AS TO BRIDAL PRESENTS AMONGST PARSIS.

Custom prevailing amongst Parsis as to ownership in presents made to bride at and after betrothal, and at and after marriage.

In the case of *Burjorji v. Pestonji*, decided on the 20th September 1877, *Bayley*, J., held that a custom was proved that "ornaments, moneys, &c., given on marriage by a husband, or his parents and relations, to his wife, are subject to the joint control of husband and wife during marriage, and on the death of either belong to the survivor."

In the case of *Merwanji v. Rustomji*, decided on the 4th September 1884, *Birdwood*, J· referred to the above case of *Burjorji v. Pestonji* and held, "that the above custom embraced gifts from the bride's side as well as from the husband's and was unaffected by the birth of children."

In *Byramji v. Jamsetji*, 16 Bom. 630, *Parsons*, J., finding the above two cases decided by the Bombay High Court upon the customs, as to ownership of presents made to a bride, held that by the custom prevailing amongst Parsis presents of money and ornaments made to a bride at betrothal and between betrothal and marriage, and at marriage, and the increment thereof, belong to the husband and wife jointly during their lives, and on the death of either pass absolutely to the survivor. Further that with regard to special and costly clothes (i. e., those intended to be worn only on special occasions and ceremonies) presented during the same period, the same custom prevails.

In *Muncherji v. Nusserwanji*, 20 Bom. 11. *Farran*, C. J., said : "It is customary amongst Parsis for the father of the bridegroom, on the occasion of the marriage of his sons, to give ornaments or money for the purchase of ornaments, to the bride. Such ornaments are considered to be the joint property of the husband and wife."

APPENDIX A.

THE PARSI CHATTELS REAL ACT.

ACT No. IX. of 1837.

I. It is hereby enacted, that from the 1st day of June 1837, all immovable property, situate within the Jurisdiction of any of the Courts established by His Majesty's Charter shall, as far as regards the transmission, of such property on the death and intestacy of any Parsi having a beneficial interest in the same, or by the last will of any such Parsi, be taken to be and to have been of the nature of chattels reals and not of freehold.

II. Provided always, that in any suit at Law or in Equity which shall be brought for the recovery of such immovable property as is aforesaid, no advantage shall be taken of any defect of title arising out of the transmission of such property upon the death and intestacy of any Parsi having a beneficial interest in the same or by the last last will of any such Parsi if such transmission took place before the said 1st day of June 1837, and if such transmission were either according to the Rules which regulate the transmission of freehold property, or else took place with the acquiescence of all persons to whom any interest in that property, would according to the Rules which regulate the transmission of chattels real, have accrued upon the death of such Parsi.

APPENDIX B.

THE INDIAN SUCCESSION ACT.

ACT X. OF 1865.

RECEIVED THE G.-G.'S ASSENT ON THE 16TH MARCH 1865.

An Act to amend and define the Law of Intestate and Testamentary Succession in British India.

Preamble.

Whereas it is expedient to amend and define the rules of law applicable to Intestate and Testamentary Succession in British India; It is enacted as follows:—

PART I.

PRELIMINARY.

Short title.

1. This Act may be cited as "The Indian Succession Act, 1865."

Act to constitute law of British India in cases of intestate or testamentary succession.

2. Except as provided by this Act, or by any other law for the time being in force, the rules herein contained shall constitute the law of British India applicable to all cases of intestate or testamentary succession.

Interpretation-clause.

3. In this Act, unless there be something repugnant in the subject or context,—

Number.
Gender.

Words importing the singular number include the plural; words importing the plural number include the singular; and words importing the male sex include females:

"Person."

"Person" includes any company or association, or body of persons, whether incorporated or not:

"Year."
"Month."

"Year" and "month" respectively mean a year and month reckoned according to the British calendar:

"Immovable property."

"Immovable property" includes land, incorporeal tenements, and things attached to the earth, or permanently fastened to anything which is attached to the earth:

"Movable property."

"Movable property" means property of every description except immovable property:

"Province." "Province" includes any division of British India having a Court of the last resort:

"British India." "British India" means the territories which are or may become vested in Her Majesty or Her Successors by the Statute 21 & 22 Vic., cap. 106 (*An Act for the better government of India.*)

"District Judge." "District Judge" means the Judge of a principal Civil Court of original jurisdiction:

"Minor." "Minority." "Minor" means any person who shall not have completed the age of eighteen years, and "minority" means the status of such person:

"Will." "Will" means the legal declaration of the intentions of the testator with respect to his property, which he desires to be carried into effect after his death.

"Codicil." "Codicil" means an instrument made in relation to a will and explaining, altering, or adding to its dispositions. It is considered as forming an additional part of the will:

"Probate." "Probate" means the copy of a will certified under the seal of a Court of competent jurisdiction, with a grant of administration to the estate of the testator:

"Executor." "Executor" means a person to whom the execution of the last will of a deceased person is, by the testator's appointment, confided:

"Administrator." "Administrator" means a person appointed by competent authority to administer the estate of a deceased person when there is no executor:

"Local Government." And in every part of British India to which this Act shall extend, "Local Government" shall mean the person authorized by law to administer executive goverment in such part; and

"High Court." "High Court" shall mean the highest Civil Court of Appeal therein, *and for the purposes of section 242, 242A, 246A, and 277A, shall include the Court of the Recorder of Rangoon.*

Interests and powers not acquired nor lost by marriage.

4. No person shall, by marriage, acquire any interest in the property of the person whom he or she marries, nor become incapable of doing any act in respect of his or her own property which he or she could have done if unmarried.

PART II.

OF DOMICILE.

Law regulating succession to deceased person's immovable and movable property respectively.

5. Succession to the immovable property in British India of a person deceased is regulated by the law of British India, wherever he may have had his domicile at the time of his death.

Succession to the moveable property of a person deceased is regulated by the law of the country in which he had his domicile at the time of his death.

Illustrations.

(*a.*) A, having his domicile in British India, dies in France, leaving movable property in France, movable property in England, and property, both movable and immovable, in British India. The succession to the whole is regulated by the law of British India.

(*b*) A, an Englishman, having his domicile in France, dies in British India, and leaves property, both movable and immovable, in British India. The succession to the movable property is regulated by the rules which govern, in France, the succession to the movable property of an Englishman dying domiciled in France, and the succession to the immovable property is regulated by the law of British India.

One domicile only affects succession to movables.

6. A person can only have one domicile for the purpose of succession to his movable property.

Domicile of origin of person of legitimate birth.

7. The domicile of origin of every person of legitimate birth is in the country in which, at the time of his birth, his father was domiciled: or, if he is a posthumous child, in the country in which his father was domiciled at the time of the father's death.

Illustration.

At the time of the birth of A, his father was domiciled in England. A's domicile of origin is in England, whatever may be the country in which he was born.

Domicile of origin of illegitimate child.

8. The domicile of origin of an illegitimate child is in the country in which, at the time of his birth, his mother was domiciled.

Continuance of domicile of origin.

9. The domicile of origin prevails until a new domicile has been acquired.

Acquisition of new domicile.

10. A man acquires a new domicile by taking up his fixed habitation in a country which is not that of his domicile of origin.

Explanation.—A man is not to be considered as having taken up his fixed habitation in British India merely by reason of his residing there in Her Majesty's civil or military service, or in the exercise of any profession or calling.

Illustrations.

(*a*) A, whose domicile of origin is in England, proceeds to British India, where he settles as a barrister or a merchant, intending to reside there during the remainder of his life. His domicile is now in British India.

(*b*) A, whose domicile is in England, goes to Austria, and enters the Austrian service, intending to remain in that service. A has acquired a domicile in Austria.

(*c*) A, whose domicile of origin is in France, comes to reside in British India under an engagement with the British Indian Government for a certain number of years. It is his intention to return to France at the end of that period. He does not acquire a domicile in British India.

(*d*) A, whose domicile is in England, goes to reside in British India for the purpose of winding up the affairs of a partnership which has been dissolved, and with the intention of returning to England as soon as that purpose is accomplished. He does not by such residence acquire a domicile in British India, however long the residence may last.

(*e*) A, having gone to reside in British India under the circumstances mentioned in the last preceding illustration, afterwards alters his intention and takes up his fixed habitation in British India. A has acquired a domicile in British India.

(*f*) A, whose domicile is in the French Settlement of Chandernagore, is compelled by political events to take refuge in Calcutta, and resides in Calcutta for many years in the hope of such political changes as may enable him to return with safety to Chandernagore. He does not, by such residence, acquire a domicile in British India.

(*g*) A, having come to Calcutta under the circumstances stated in the last preceding illustration, continues to reside there after such political changes have occurred as would enable him to return with safety to Chandernagore, and he intends that his residence in Calcutta shall be permanent. A has acquired a domicile in British India.

Special mode of acquiring domicile in British India.

11. Any person may acquire a domicile in British India by making and depositing in some office in British India (to be fixed by the Local Government) a declaration in writing under his hand of his desire to acquire such domicile, provided that he shall have been resident in British India for one year immediately preceding the time of his making such declaration.

Domicile not acquired by residence as representative of foreign Government, or as part of his family.

12. A person who is appointed by the Government of one country to be its ambassador, consul, or other representative in another country, does not acquire a domicile in the latter country by reason only of residing there in pursuance of his appointment; nor does any other person acquire such domicile by reason only of residing with him as part of his family or as a servant.

13. A new domicile continues until the former domicile has been resumed, or another has been acquired.

Continuance of new domicile.

14. The domicile of a minor follows the domicile of the parent from whom he derived his domicile of origin.

Minor's domicile.

Exception.—The domicile of a minor does not change with that of his parent if the minor is married, or holds any office or employment in the service of Her Majesty, or has set up, with the consent of the parent, in any distinct business.

Domicile acquired by woman on marriage.

15. By marriage a woman acquires the domicile of her husband, if she had not the same domicile before.

Wife's domicile during marriage.

16. The wife's domicile during the marriage follows the domicile of her husband.

Exception.—The wife's domicile no longer follows that of her husband if they be separated by the sentence of a competent Court, or if the husband is undergoing a sentence of transportation.

17. Except in the cases above provided for, a person cannot, during minority, acquire a new domicile.

Minor's acquisition of new domicile

18. An insane person cannot acquire a new domicile in any other way than by his domicile following the domicile of another person.

Lunatic's acquisition of new domicile.

Succession to movable property in British India in absence of proof of domicile elsewhere.

19. If a man dies leaving movable property in British India, in the absence of proof of any domicile elsewhere, succession to the property is regulated by the law of British India.

PART III.

This part does not apply to Parsis.

Of Consanguinity.

20. Kindred or consanguinity is the connexion or relation of persons descended from the same stock or common ancestor.

Kindred of consanguinity.

21. Lineal consanguinity is that which subsists between two persons, one of whom is descended in a direct line from the other, as between a man and his father, grandfather, and great-grand-father, and so upwards in the direct ascending line; or between a man, his son, grandson, great-grandson, and so downwards in the direct descending line.

Lineal consanguinity.

Every generation constitutes a degree, either ascending or descending.

A man's father is related to him in the first degree, and so likewise is his son; his grandfather and grandson in the second degree; his great-grandfather and great-grandson in the third.

Collateral consanguinity.

22. Collateral consanguinity is that which subsists between two persons who are descended from the same stock or ancestor, but neither of whom is descended in a direct line from the other.

For the purpose of ascertaining in what degree of kindred any collateral relative stands to a person deceased, it is proper to reckon upwards from the person deceased to the common stock, and then downwards to the collateral relative, allowing a degree for each person, both ascending and descending.

Persons held for purpose of succession to be similarly related to deceased.

23. For the purpose of succession, there is no distinction between those who are related to a person deceased through his father, and those who are related to him through his mother;

nor between those who are related to him by the full blood, and those who are related to him by the half-blood;

nor between those who were actually born in his life-time, and those who, at the date of his death, were only conceived in the womb, but who have been subsequently born alive.

Mode of computing degrees of kindred.

24. In the annexed table of kindred the degrees are computed as far as the sixth, and are marked by numeral figures.

The person whose relatives are to be reckoned, and his cousin-german or first cousin, are, as shown in the table, related in the fourth degree; there being one degree of ascent to the father, and another to the common ancestor, the grandfather; and from him one of descent to the uncle, and another to the cousin-german; making in all four degrees.

A grandson of the brother and a son of the uncle, *i. e.*, a great-nephew and a cousin-german, are in equal degree, being each four degrees removed.

A grandson of a cousin-german is in the same degree as the grandson of a great uncle, for they are both in the sixth degree of kindred.

VIII

TABLE OF CONSANGUINITY.

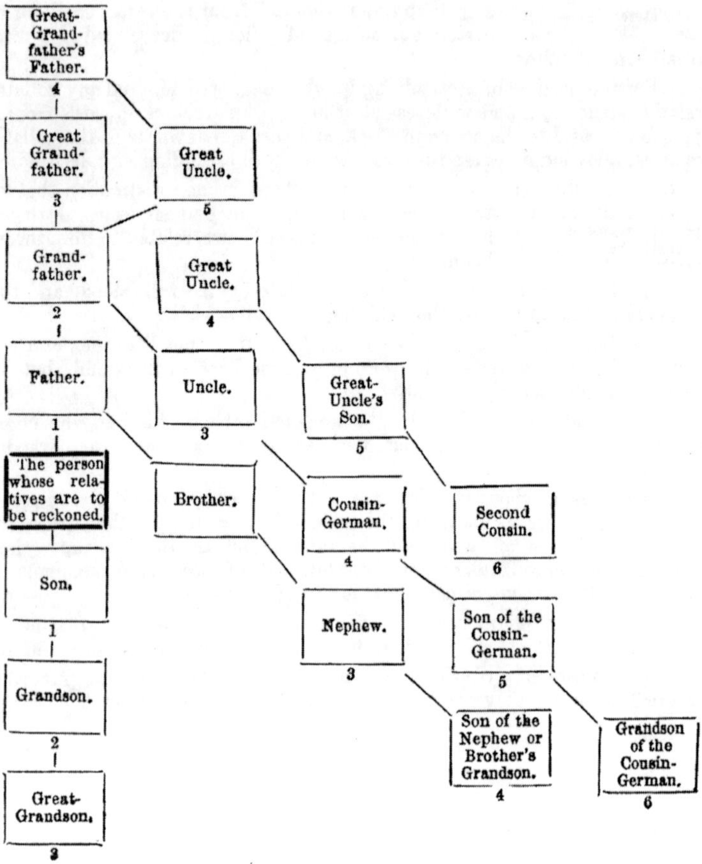

PART IV.

With the exception of section 25 this part does not apply to Parsis.

Of Intestacy.

As to what property deceased considered to have died intestate.

25. A man is considered to die intestate in respect of all property of which he has not made a testamentary disposition which is capable of taking effect.

Illustrations.

(*a.*) A has left no will. He has died intestate in respect of the whole of his property.

(*b.*) A has left a will, whereby he has appointed B his executor; but the will contains no other provisions. A has died intestate in respect of the distribution of his property.

(*c.*) A has bequeathed his whole property for an illegal purpose. A has died intestate in respect of the distribution of his property.

(*d.*) A has bequeathed 1,000*l.* to B and 1,000*l.* to the eldest son of C, and has made no other bequest; and has died leaving the sum of 2,000*l.* and no other property. C died before A without having ever had a son. A has died intestate in respect of the distribution of 1,000*l.*

Devolution of such property.

26. Such property devolves upon the wife or husband, or upon those who are of the kindred of the deceased, in the order and according to the rules herein prescribed.

Explanation.—The widow is not entitled to the provision hereby made for her, if, by a valid contract made before her marriage, she has been excluded from the distributive share of her husband's estate.

Where intestate has left widow and lineal descendants, or widow and kindred only, or widow and no kindred.

27. Where the intestate has left a widow, if he has also left any lineal descendants, one-third of his property shall belong to his widow, and the remaining two-thirds shall go to his lineal descendants, according to the rules herein contained.

If he has left no lineal descendant, but has left persons who are of kindred to him, one-half of his property shall belong to his widow, and the other half shall go to those who are of kindred to him, in the order and according to the rules herein contained.

If he has left none who are of kindred to him, the whole of his property shall belong to his widow.

Where intestate has left no widow, and where he has left no kindred.

28. Where the intestate has left no widow, his property shall go to his lineal descendants or to those who are of kindred to him, not being lineal descendants, according to the rules herein contained; and if he has left none who are of kindred to him, it shall go to the Crown.

PART V.

This part does not apply to Parsis.

OF THE DISTRIBUTION OF AN INTESTATE'S PROPERTY—

(*a.*)—*Where he has left Lineal Descendants.*

Rules of distribution.

29. The rules for the distribution of the intestate's property (after deducting the widow's share, if he has left a widow) amongst his lineal descendants are as follow :—

Where intestate has left child or children only.

30. Where the intestate has left surviving him a child or children, but no more remote lineal descendant through a deceased child, the property shall belong to his surviving child, if there be only one, or shall be equally divided among all his surviving children.

Where intestate has left no child, but grandchild or grandchildren.

31. Where the intestate has not left surviving him any child, but has left a grandchild or grandchildren, and no more remote descendant through a deceased grandchild, the property shall belong to his surviving grandchild, if there be only one, or shall be equally divided among all his surviving grandchildren.

Illustrations.

(*a*) A has three children, and no more: John, Mary, and Henry. They all die before the father. John leaving two children, Mary three, and Henry four. Afterwards A dies intestate, leaving those nine grandchildren and no descendant of any deceased grandchild. Each of his grandchildren shall have one-ninth.

(*b*) But, if Henry has died leaving no child, then the whole is equally divided between the intestate's five grandchildren, the children of John and Mary.

(*c*) A has two children, and no more: John and Mary. John dies before his father, leaving his wife pregnant. Then A dies, leaving Mary surviving him, and in due time a child of John is born. A's property is to be equally divided between Mary and such posthumous child.

Where intestate has left only great-grandchildren or remoter lineal descendants.

32. In like manner the property shall go to the surviving lineal descendants who are nearest in degree to the intestate, where they are all in the degree of great grandchildren to him, or are all in a more remote degree.

Where intestate leaves lineal descendants not all in same degree of kindred to him, and those through whom the more remote descended are dead.

33. If the intestate has left lineal descendants who do not all stand in the same degree of kindred to him, and the persons through whom the more remote are descended from him are dead, the property shall be divided into such a number of equal shares as may correspond with the number of the lineal descendants of the intestate who either stood in the nearest degree of kindred to him at his decease, or, having been of the like degree of kindred to him, died before him, leaving lineal descendants who survived him ; and

one of such shares shall be allotted to each of the lineal descendants who stood in the nearest degree of kindred to the intestate at his decease ; and

one of such shares shall be allotted in respect of each of such deceased lineal descendants ; and

The share allotted in respect of each of such deceased lineal descendants shall belong to his surviving child or children or more remote lineal descendants, as the case may be ; such surviving child or children or more remote lineal descendants always taking the share which his or their parent or parents would have been entitled to respectively, if such parent or parents had survived the intestate.

Illustrations.

(*a*) A had three children, John, Mary and Henry ; John died leaving four children, and Mary died leaving one, and Henry alone survived the father. On the death of A intestate, one-third is allotted to Henry, one-third to John's four children, and the remaining third to Mary's one child.

(*b*) A left no child, but left eight grandchildren, and two children of a deceased grandchild. The property is divided into nine parts, one of which is allotted to each grandchild ; and the remaining one-ninth is equally divided between the two great-grand-children.

(*c*) A has three children, John, Mary, and Henry. John dies leaving four children, and one of John's children dies leaving two children. Mary dies leaving one child. A afterwards dies intestate. One-third of his property is allotted to Henry ; one-third to Mary's child ; and one-third is divided into four parts, one of which is allotted to each of John's three surviving children, and the remaining part is equally divided between John's two grandchildren.

(*b*)—*Where the Intestate has left no Lineal Descendants.*

Rules of distribution where intestate has left no lineal descendants.

34. Where an intestate has left no lineal descendants, the rules for the distribution of his property (after deducting the widow's share, if he has left a widow) are as follow :—

Where intestate's father living.

35. If the intestate's father be living, he shall succeed to the property.

Where intestate's father dead, but his mother, brothers, and sisters living.

36. If the intestate's father is dead, but the intestate's mother is living and there are also brothers or sisters of the intestate living, and there is no child living of any deceased brother or sister, the mother and each living brother or sister shall succeed to the property in equal shares.

Illustration.

A dies intestate survived by the mother and two brothers of the full blood, John and Henry, and a sister Mary, who is the daughter of his mother, but not of his father. The mother takes one-fourth, each brother takes one-fourth, and Mary, the sister of half-blood, takes one-fourth.

Where intestate's father dead, and his mother, a brother or sister, and children of any deceased brother or sister, living.

37. If the intestate's father is dead, but the intestate's mother is living, and if any brother or sister, and the child or children of any brother or sister who may have died in the intestate's lifetime, are also living, then the mother and each living brother or sister, and the living child or children of each deceased brother or sister, shall be entitled to the property in equal shares, such children (if more than one) taking in equal shares only the shares which their respective parents would have taken if living at the intestate's death.

Illustration.

A, the intestate, leaves his mother, his brothers, John and Henry, and also one child of a deceased sister Mary, and two children of George, a deceased brother of the half-blood, who was the son of his father, but not of his mother. The mother takes one-fifth, John and Henry each take one-fifth, the child of Mary takes one-fifth, and the two children of George divide the remaining one-fifth equally between them.

Where intestate's father dead, and his mother and children of any deceased brother or sister living.

38. If the intestate's father is dead, but the intestate's mother is living and the brothers and sisters are all dead, but all or any of them have left children who survived the intestate's mother and the child or children of each deceased brother or sister shall be entitled to the property in equal shares, such children (if more than one) taking in equal shares only the shares which their respective parents would have taken if living at the intestate's death.

Illustration.

A, the intestate, leaves no brother or sister, but leaves his mother and one child of a deceased sister Mary, and two children of a deceased brother George. The mother takes one-third, the child of Mary takes one-third, and the children of George divide the remaining one-third equally between them.

Where intestate's father dead, but his mother living, and no brother, sister, nephew, or niece.

39. If the intestate's father is dead, but the intestate's mother is living, and there is neither brother nor sister nor child of any brother or sister of the intestate, the property shall belong to the mother.

Where intestate has left neither lineal descendant, nor father, nor mother.

40. Where the intestate has left neither lineal descendant, nor father, nor mother, the property is divided equally between his brothers and sisters and the child or children of such of them as may have died before him, such children (if more than one) taking in equal shares only the shares which their respective parents would have taken if living at the intestate's death.

Where intestate has left neither lineal descendants, nor parent, nor brother, nor sister.

41. If the intestate left neither lineal descendant, nor parent, nor brother, nor sister, his property shall be divided equally among those of his relatives who are in the nearest degree of kindred to him.

Illustrations.

(*a*) A, the intestate, has left a grandfather and a grandmother, and no other relative standing in the same or a nearer degree of kindred to him. They, being in the second degree, will be entitled to the property in equal shares, exclusive of any uncle or aunt of the intestate, uncles and aunts being only in the third degree.

(*b*) A, the intestate, has left a great grandfather or great grandmother and uncles and aunts, and no other relatives standing in the same or a nearer degree of kindred to him. All of these, being in the third degree, shall take equal shares.

(*c*.) A, the intestate, left a great-grandfather, and uncle, and a nephew, but no relative standing in a nearer degree of kindred to him. All of these, being in the third degree, shall take equal shares.

(*d.*) Ten children of one brother or sister of the intestate, and one child of another brother or sister of the intestate, constitute the class of relatives of the nearest degree of kindred to him. They shall each take one-eleventh of the property.

Children's advancements not brought into hotchpot.

42. Where a distributive share in the property of a person who has died intestate shall be claimed by a child, or any descendant of a child, of such person, no money or other property which the intestate may, during his life, have paid, given, or settled to, or for the advancement of, the child by whom or by whose descendant the claim is made, shall be taken into account in estimating such distributive share.

PART VI.

Section 43 of this part does not apply to Parsis.

OF THE EFFECT OF MARRIAGE AND MARRIAGE-SETTLEMENTS ON PROPERTY.

Rights of widower and widow respectively.

43. The husband surviving his wife has the same rights in respect of her property, if she die intestate, as the widow has in respect of her husband's property, if he die intestate.

Effect of marriage between person domiciled, and one not domiciled, in British India.

44. If a person whose domicile is not in British India marries in British India a person whose domicile is in British India, neither party acquires by the marriage any rights in respect of any property of the other party not comprised in a settlement made previous to the marriage, which he or she would not acquire thereby if both were domiciled in British India at the time of the marriage.

Settlement of minor's property in contemplation of marriage.

45. The property of a minor may be settled in contemplation of marriage, provided the settlement be made by the minor with the approbation of the minor's father or if he be dead or absent from British India, with the approbation of the High Court.

PART VII.

OF WILLS AND CODICILS.

Persons capable of making wills.

46. Every person of sound mind and not a minor may dispose of his property by will.

Explanation 1.—A married woman may dispose by will of any property which she could alienate by her own act during her life.

Explanation 2.—Persons who are deaf, or dumb, or blind, are not thereby incapacitated for making a will if they are able to know what they do by it.

Explanation 3.—One who is ordinarily insane may make a will during an interval in which he is of sound mind.

Explanation 4.—No person can make a will while he is in such a state of mind, whether arising from drunkenness, or from illness, or from any other cause, that he does not know what he is doing.

Illustrations.

(*a.*) A can perceive what is going on in his immediate neighbourhood, and can answer familiar questions, but has not a competent understanding as to the nature of his property or the persons who are of kindred to him, or in whose favour it would be proper that he should make his will. A cannot make a valid will.

(*b*) A executes an instrument purporting to be his will, but he does not understand the nature of the instrument, nor the effect of its provisions. This instrument is not a valid will.

(*c*) A being very feeble and debilitated but capable of exercising a judgment as to the proper mode of disposing of his property, makes a will. This is a valid will.

Testamentary guardian.

47. A father, whatever his age may be, may, by will appoint a guardian or guardians for his child during minority.

Will obtained by fraud, coercion, or importunity.

48. A will or any part of a will, the making of which has been caused by fraud or coercion, or by such importunity as takes away the free agency of the testator, is void.

Illustrations.

(*a*) A falsely and knowingly represents to the testator that the testator's only child is dead, or that he has done some undutiful act, and thereby induces the testator to make a will in his (A's) favour; such will has been obtained by fraud, and is invalid.

(*b*) A, by fraud and deception, prevails upon the testator to bequeath a legacy to him. The bequest is void.

(*c*) A, being a prisoner by lawful authority, makes his will. The will is not invalid by reason of the imprisonment.

(*d*) A threatens to shoot B, or to burn his house, or to cause him to be arrested on a criminal charge, unless he makes a bequest in favour of C. B in consequence makes a bequest in favour of C. The bequest is void, the making of it having been caused by coercion.

(*e*) A, being of sufficient intellect, if undisturbed by the influence of others, to make a will, yet being so much under the control of B that he is not a free agent, makes a will dictated by B. It appears that he would not have executed the will but for fear of B. The will is invalid.

(*f*) A, being in so feeble a state of health as to be unable to resist importunity, is pressed by B to make a will of a certain purport, and does so merely to purchase peace, and in submission to B. The will is invalid.

(*g*) A being in such a state of health as to be capable of exercising his own judgment and volition. B uses urgent intercession and persuasion with him to induce him to make a will of a certain purport. A, in consequence of the intercession and persuasion, but in the free exercise of his judgment and volition, makes his will in the manner recommended by B. The will is not rendered invalid by the intercession and persuasion of B.

(*h*) A, with a view to obtaining a legacy from B, pays him attention and flatters him, and thereby produces in him a capricious partiality to A. B. in consequence of such attention and flattery, makes his will, by which he leaves a legacy to A. The bequest is not rendered invalid by the attention and flattery of A.

Will may be revoked or altered.

49. A will is liable to be revoked or altered by the maker of it at any time when he is competent to dispose of his property by will.

PART VIII.

OF THE EXECUTION OF UNPRIVILEGED WILLS.

Execution of unprivileged wills.

50. Every testator, not being a soldier employed in an expedition or engaged in actual warfare or a mariner at sea, must execute his will according to the following rules:—

First.—The testator shall sign or shall affix his mark to the will, or it shall be signed by some other person in his presence and by his direction.

Second.—The signature or mark of the testator, or the signature of the person signing for him, shall be so placed that it shall appear that it was intended thereby to give effect to the writing as a will.

Third.—The will shall be attested by two or more witnesses, each of whom must have seen the testator sign or affix his mark to the will, or have seen some other person sign the will in the presence and by the direction of the testator, or have received from the testator a personal acknowledgment of his signature or mark, or of the signature of such other person; and each of the witnesses must sign the will in the presence of the testator, but it shall not be necessary that more than one witness be present at the same time, and no particular form of attestation shall be necessary.

Incorporation of papers by reference.

51. If a testator, in a will or codicil duly attested, refers to any other document then actually written, as expressing any part of his intentions, such document shall be considered as forming a part of the will or codicil in which it is referred to.

PART IX.

Of Privileged Wills.

Privileged will.

52. Any soldier being employed in an expedition, or engaged in actual warfare, or any mariner being at sea, may, if he has completed the age of eighteen years, dispose of his property by a will made as is mentioned in section 53.

Such wills are called privileged wills.

Illustrations.

(*a.*) A, the surgeon of a regiment, is actually employed in an expedition. He is a soldier actually employed in an expedition, and can make a privileged will.

(*b.*) A is at sea in a merchant-ship, of which he is the purser. He is a mariner, and, being at sea, can make a privileged will.

(*c*) A, a soldier serving in the field against insurgents, is a soldier engaged in actual warfare, and as such can make a privileged will.

(*d.*) A, a mariner of a ship in the course of a voyage, is temporarily on shore while she is lying in harbour. He is, in the sense of the words used in this clause, a mariner at sea, and can make a privileged will.

(*e.*) A, an admiral who commands a naval force, but who lives on shore, and only occasionally goes on board his ship, is not considered as at sea, and cannot make a privileged will.

(*f.*) A, a mariner serving on a military expedition, but not being at sea, is considered as a soldier, and can make a privileged will.

Mode of making, and rules for executing, privileged wills.

53. Privileged wills may be in writing, or may be made by word of mouth.

The execution of them shall be governed by the following rules :—

First.—The will may be written wholly by the testator with his own hand. In such case it need not be signed nor attested.

Second.—It may be written wholly or in part by another person, and signed by the testator. In such case it need not be attested.

Third.—If the instrument purporting to be a will is written wholly or in part by another person, and is not signed by the testator, it shall be considered to be his will if it be shown that it was written by the testator's directions, or that he recognized it as his will.

If it appear on the face of the instrument that the execution of it in the manner intended by him was not completed, the instrument shall not, by reason of that circumstance, be invalid, provided that his non-execution of it can be reasonably ascribed to some cause other than the abandonment of the testamentary intentions expressed in the instrument.

Fourth.—If the soldier or mariner shall have written instructions for the preparation of his will, but shall have died before it could be prepared and executed, such instructions shall be considered to constitute his will.

Fifth.—If the soldier or mariner shall, in the presence of two witnesses, have given verbal instructions for the preparation of his will, and they shall have been reduced into writing in his lifetime, but he shall have died before the instrument could be prepared and executed, such instructions shall be considered to constitute his will, although they may not have been reduced into writing in his presence, nor read over to him.

Sixth.—Such soldier or mariner as aforesaid may make a will by word of mouth by declaring his intentions before two witnesses present at the same time.

Seventh.—A will made by word of mouth shall be null at the expiration of one month after the testator shall have ceased to be entitled to make a privileged will.

PART X.

Of the Attestation, Revocation, Alteration, and Revival of Wills.

Effect of gift to attesting witness.

54. A will shall not be considered as insufficiently attested by reason of any benefit thereby given, either by way of bequest or by way of appointment, to any person attesting it, or to his or her wife or husband:

but the bequest or appointment shall be void so far as concerns the person so attesting, or the wife or husband of such person, or any person claiming under either of them.

Explanation.—A legatee under a will does not lose his legacy by attesting a codicil which confirms the will.

Witness not disqualified by interest or by being executor.

55. No person, by reason of interest in, or of his being an executor of, a will, is disqualified as a witness to prove the execution of the will or to prove the validity or invalidity thereof.

Revocation of will by testator's marriage.

56. Every will shall be revoked by the marriage of the maker, except a will made in exercise of a power of appointment, when the property over which the power of appointment is exercised would not, in default of such appointment, pass to his or

her executor or administrator, or to the person entitled in case of intestacy.

Explanation.—Where a man is invested with power to determine the disposition of property of which he is not the owner, he is said to have power to appoint such property.

Power of appointment defined.

57. No unprivileged will or codicil, nor any part thereof, shall be revoked otherwise than by marriage, or by another will or codicil, or by some writing declaring an intention to revoke the same, and executed in the manner in which an unprivileged will is hereinbefore required to be executed, or by the burning, tearing, or otherwise destroying the same by the testator, or by some person in his presence and by his direction, with the intention of revoking the same.

Revocation of unprivileged will or codicil.

Illustrations.

(*a.*) A has made and unprivileged will. Afterwards A makes another unprivileged will which purports to revoke the first. This is a revocation.

(*b.*) A has made an unprivileged will. Afterwards A, being entitled to make a privileged will, makes a privileged will which purports to revoke his unprivileged will. This is a revocation.

58. No obliteration, interlineation, or other alteration made in any unprivileged will after the execution thereof shall have any effect, except so far as the words or meaning of the will shall have been thereby rendered illegible or undiscernible, unless such alteration shall be executed in like manner as hereinbefore is required for the execution of the will; save that the will, as so altered, shall be deemed to be duly executed if the signature of the testator and the subscription of the witnesses be made in the margin or on some other part of the will opposite or near to such alteration or at the foot or end of, or opposite to, a memorandum referring to such alteration, and written at the end or some other part of the will.

Effect of obliteration, interlineation, or alteration in unprivileged will.

59. A privilleged will or codicil may be revoked by the testator, by an unprivileged will or codicil, or by any act expressing an intention to revoke it, and accompanied with such formalities as would be sufficient to give validity to a privileged will, or by the burning, tearing, or otherwise destroying the same by the testator, or by some person in his presence and by his direction, with the intention of revoking the same.

Revocation of privileged will or codicil.

Explanation.—In order to the revocation of a privileged will or codicil by an act accompanied with such formalities as would be sufficient to give validity to a privileged will, it is not necessary that the testator should, at the time of doing that act, be in a situation which entitles him to make a privileged will.

Revival of unprivileged will.

60. No unprivileged will or codicil, nor any part thereof which shall be in any manner revoked, shall be revived otherwise than by the re-execution thereof, or by a codicil executed in manner hereinbefore required, and showing an intention to revive the same;

Extent of revival of will or codicil partly revoked, and afterwards wholly revoked.

and when any will or codicil which shall be partly revoked, and afterwards wholly revoked, shall be revived, such revival shall not extend to so much thereof as shall have been revoked before the revocation of the whole thereof, unless an intention to the contrary shall be shown by the will or codicil.

PART XI.

OF THE CONSTRUCTION OF WILLS.

Wording of will.

61. It is not necessary that any technical words or terms of art shall be used in a will, but only that the wording shall be such that the intentions of the testator can be known therefrom.

Enquiries to determine questions as to object or subject of will

62. For the purpose of determining questions as to what person or what property is denoted by any words used in a will, a Court must enquire into every material fact relating to the persons who claim to be interested under such will, the property which is claimed as the subject of deposition, the circumstances of the testator and of his family, and into every fact, a knowledge of which may conduce to the right application of the words which the testator has used.

Illustrations.

(*a*) A, by his will, bequeaths 1,000 rupees to his eldest son, or to his youngest grandchild, or to his cousin Mary. A Court may make inquiry in order to ascertion to what person the description in the will applies.

(*b.*) A, by his will, leaves to B "his estate called Black Acre." It may be necessary to take evidence in order to ascertain what is the subject-matter of the bequest; that is to say, what estate of the testator's is called Black Acre.

(*c.*) A, by his will, leaves to B "the estate which he purchased of C." It may be necessary to take evidence in order to ascertain what estate the testator purchased of C.

63. Where the words used in the will to designate or describe a legatee, or a class of legatees, sufficiently show what is meant, an error in the name of description shall not prevent the legacy from taking effect.

Misnomer or misdescription of object.

A mistake in the name of a legatee may be corrected by a description of him, and a mistake in the description of a legatee may be corrected by the name.

Illustrations.

(*a.*) A bequeaths a legacy "to Thomas, the second son of his brother John." The testator has an only brother, named John, who has no son named Thomas, but has a second son whose name is William. William shall have the legacy.

(*b.*) A bequeaths a legacy "to Thomas, the second son of his brother John." The testator has an only brother, named John, whose first son is named Thomas, and whose second son is named William. Thomas shall have the legacy.

(*c.*) The testator bequeaths his property "to A and B, the legitimate children of C." C has no legitimate child, but has two illegitimate children, A and B. The bequest to A and B takes effect, although they are illegitimate.

(*d.*) The testator gives his residuary estate to be divided among "his seven children," and, proceeding to enumerate them, mentions six names only. This omission shall not prevent the seventh child from taking a share with the others.

(*e.*) The testator, having six grandchildren, makes a bequest to "his six grandchildren," and, proceeding to mention them by their Christian names, mentions one twice over, omitting another altogether. The one whose name is not mentioned shall take a share with the others.

(*f.*) The testator bequeaths "1,000 rupees to each of the three children of A." At the date of the will, A has four children. Each of these four children shall, if he survives the testator, receive a legacy of 1,000 rupees.

64. Where any word material to the full expression of the meaning has been omitted, it may be supplied by the context.

When words may be supplied.

Illustration.

The testator gives a legacy of "five hundred" to his daughter A, and a legacy of "five hundred rupees" to his daughter B. A shall take a legacy of five hundred rupees.

65. If the thing which the testator intended to bequeath can be sufficiently identified from the description of it given in the will, but some parts of the description do not apply, such parts of the description shall be rejected as erroneous, and the bequest shall take effect.

Rejection of erroneous particulars in description of subject.

Illustrations.

(*a.*) A bequeaths to B, "his marsh-lands lying in L, and in the occupation of X." The testator had marsh-lands lying in L, but had no marsh-lands in the occupation of X. The words "in the occupation of X." shall be rejected as erroneous, and the marsh-lands of the testator lying in L shall pass by the bequest.

(*b.*) The testator bequeaths to A "his zamindari of Rampur." He had an estate at Rampur, but it was a taluq, and not a zamindari. The taluk passes by this bequest.

When part of description may not be rejected as erroneous.

66. If the will mentions several circumstances as descriptive of the thing which the testator intends to bequeath, and there is any property of his in respect of which all those circumstances exist, the bequest shall be considered as limited to such property, and it shall not be lawful to reject any part of the description as erroneous, because the testator had other property to which such part of the description does not apply.

Explanation.—In judging whether a case falls within the meaning of this section, any words which would be liable to rejection under section 65 are to be considered as struck out of the will.

Illustrations.

(*a.*) A bequeaths to B "his marsh-lands lying in L, and in the occupation of X." The testator had marsh-lands lying in L, some of which were in the occupation of X, and some not in the occupation of X. The bequest shall be considered as limited to such of the testator's marsh-lands lying in L as were in the occupation of X.

(*b*) A bequeaths to B "his marsh-lands lying in L, and in the occupation of X comprising 1,000 bighas of land." The testator had marsh-lands lying in L, some of which were in the occupation of X, and some not in the occupation of X. The measurement is wholly inapplicable to the marsh-lands of either class, or to the whole taken together. The measurement shall be considered as struck out of the will, and such of the testator's marsh-lands lying in L as were in the occupation of X shall alone pass by the bequest.

Extrinsic evidence admissible in case of patent ambiguity.

67. Where the words of the will are unambiguous, but it is found by extrinsic evidence that they admit of applications, one only of which can have been intended by the testator, extrinsic evidence may be taken to show which of these applications was intended.

Illustrations.

(*a*) A man, having two cousins of the name of Mary, bequeaths a sum of money to "his cousin Mary," It appears that there are two persons, each answering the description in the will. That description, therefore, admits of two applications, only one of which can have been intended by testator. Evidence is admissible is show which of the two applications was intended.

(*b*) A, by his will, leaves to B "his estate called Sultanpur Khurd." It turns out that he had two estates called Sultanpur Khurd. Evidence is admissible to show which estate was intended.

Extrinsic evidence inadmissible in cases of patent ambiguity or deficiency.

68. Where there is an ambiguity or deficiency on the face of the will, no extrinsic evidence as to the intentions of the testator shall be admitted.

Illustrations.

(*a*) A man has an aunt Caroline and a cousin Mary, and has no aunt of the name of Mary. By his will he bequeaths 1,000 rupees to "his aunt Caroline" and 1,000 rupees to "his cousin Mary," and afterwards bequeaths 2,000 rupees to his "before mentioned aunt Mary." There is no person to whom the description given in the will can apply, and evidence is not admissible to show who was meant by "his before-mentioned aunt Mary." The bequest is therefore void for uncertainty under section 76.

(c) A bequeaths 1,000 rupees to , leaving a blank for the name of the legatee. Evidence is not admissible to show what name the testator intended to insert.

(*c*) A bequeaths to B rupees, or "his estate of ." Evidence is not admissible to show what sum or what estate the testator intended to insert.

Meaning of clause to be collected from entire will.

69. The meaning of any clause in a will is to be collected from the entire instrument, and all its parts are to be construed with reference to each other; and for this purpose a codicil is to be considered as part of the will.

Illustrations.

(*a*) The testator gives to B a specific fund or property at the death of A, and by a subsequent clause gives the whole of his property to A. The effect of the several clauses taken together is to vest the specific fund or property in A for life, and after his decease in B; it appearing from the bequest to B that the testator meant to use, in a restricted sense the words in which he describes what he gives to A.

(*b*) Where a testator, having an estate, one part of which is called Black Acre, bequeaths the whole of his estate to A, and in another part of his will bequeaths Black Acre to B, the latter bequest is to be read as an exception out of the first, as if he had said, "I give Black Acre to B, and all the rest of my estate to A."

When words may be understood in restricted sense, and when in sense wider than usual.

70. General words may be understood in a restricted sense where it may be collected from the will that the testator meant to use them in a restricted sense; and words may be understood in a wider sense than that which they usually bear, where it may be collected from the other words of the will that the testator meant to use them in such wider sense.

Illustrations.

(*a*) A testator gives to A "his farm in the occupation of B," and to C "all his marsh-lands in L." Part of the farm in the occupation of B consists of marsh-lands in L, and the testator also has other marsh-lands in L. The general words, "all his marsh-lands in L" are restricted by the gift to A. A takes the whole of the farm in the occupation of B, including that portion of the farm which consists of marsh lands in L.

(*b*) The testator (a sailor on ship-board) bequeathed to his mother his gold ring, buttons, and chest of clothes, and to his friend A (a ship-mate) his red box, clasp-knife, and all things not before bequeathed. The testator's share in a house does not pass to A under this bequest.

(*c*) A, by his will, bequeathed to B all his household furniture, plate, linen, China, books, pictures, and all other goods of whatever kind; and afterwards bequeathed to B a specified part of his property. Under the first bequest, B is entitled only to such articles of the testator's as are of the same nature with the articles therein enumerated.

Which of two possible constructions preferred.

71. Where a clause is susceptible of two meanings, according to one of which it has some effect, and according to the other it can have none, the former is to be preferred.

No part rejected if it can be reasonably construed.

72. No part of a will is to be rejected as destitute of meaning if it is possible to put a reasonable construction upon it.

Interpretation of words repeated in different parts of will.

73. If the same words occur in different parts of the same will, they must be taken to have been used everywhere in the same sense, unless there appears an intention to the contrary.

Testator's intention to be effectuated as far as possible.

74. The intention of the testator is not to be set aside, because it cannot take effect to the full extent, but effect is to be given to it as far as possible.

Illustration.

The testator, by a will made on his death-bed, bequeathed all his property to C D for life, and after his decease to a certain hospital. The intention of the testator cannot take effect to its full extent, because the gift to the hospital is void under section 105, but it shall take effect so far as regards the gift to C D.

The last of two inconsistent clauses prevails.

75. Where two clauses or gifts in a will are irreconcilable, so that they cannot possibly stand together, the last shall prevail.

Illustration.

(*a*) The testator, by the first clause of his will, leaves his estate of Ramnagar "to A," and, by the last clause of his will, leaves it to B, and not "to A." B shall have it.

(*b*) If a man, at the commencement of his will, gives his house to A, and at the close of it directs that his house shall be sold, and the proceeds invested for the benefit of B, the latter disposition shall prevail.

Will or bequest void for uncertainty.

76. A will or bequest not expressive of any definite intention is void for uncertainty.

Illustration.

If a testator says, "I bequeath goods to A"; or "I bequeath to A;" or "I leave to A all the goods mentioned in a schedule," and no schedule is found; or, "I bequeath 'money,' 'wheat,' 'oil,'" or the like, without saying how much, this is void.

Words describing subject refer to property answering description at testator's death.

77. The description contained in a will of property, the subject of gift, shall, unless a contrary intention appear by the will, be deemed to refer to and comprise the property answering that description at the death of the testator.

Power of appointment executed by general bequest.

78. Unless a contrary intention shall appear by the will, a bequest of the estate of the testator shall be construed to include any property which he may have power to appoint by will to any object he may think proper, and shall operate as an execution of such power;

and a bequest of property described in a general manner shall be construed to include any property to which such description may extend, which he may have power to appoint by will to any object he may think proper, and shall operate as an execution of such power.

Implied gift to objects of power in default of appointment.

79. Where property is bequeathed to or for the benefit of such of certain objects as a specified person shall appoint, or for the benefit of certain objects in such proportions as a specified person shall appoint, and the will does not provide for the event of no appointment being made, if the power given by the will be not exercised, the property belongs to all the objects of the power in equal shares.

Illustration.

A, by his will, bequeathed a fund to his wife for her life, and directs that at her death it shall be divided among his children in such proportions as she shall appoint. The widow dies without having made any appointment. The fund shall be divided equally among the children.

Bequest to "heirs" &c., of particular persons without qualifying terms.

80. Where a bequest is made to the "heirs" or "right heirs," or "relations," or "nearest relations," or "family," or "kindred," or "nearest of kin," or "next of kin," of a particular person without any qualifying terms, and the class so designated forms the direct and independent object of the

bequest, the property bequeathed shall be distributed as if it had belonged to such person, and he had died intestate in respect of it, leaving assets for the payment of his debts independently of such property.

Illustrations.

(*a.*) A leaves his property "to his own nearest relations." The property goes to those who would be entitled to it if A had died intestate, leaving assets for the payment of his debts independently of such property.

(*b.*) A bequeaths 10,000 rupees "to B for his life, and after the death of B to his own right heirs." The legacy after B's death belongs to those who would be entitled to it if it had formed part of A's unbequeathed property.

(*c.*) A leaves his property to B; but if B dies before him, to B's next of kin. B dies before A. The property devolves as if it had belonged to B, and he had died intestate, leaving assets for the payment of his debts independently of such property.

(*d.*) A leaves 10,000 rupees "to B for his life, and after his decease, to the heirs of C." The legacy goes as if it had belonged to C. and he had died intestate, leaving assets for the payment of his debts independently of the legacy.

Bequest to "representatives," &c., of particular person.

81. Where a bequest is made to the "representatives," or "legal representatives," or "personal representatives," or "executors or administrators," of a particular person, and the class so designated forms the direct and independent object of the bequest, the property bequeathed shall be distributed as if it had belonged to such person, and he had died intestate in respect of it.

Illustration.

A bequest is made to the "legal representative" of A. A has died intestate and insolvent. B is his administrator. B is entitled to receive the legacy, and shall apply it in the first place to the discharge of such part of A's debts as may remain unpaid if there be any surplus. B shall pay it to those persons who at A's death would have been entitled to receive any property of A's which might remain after payment of his debts, or to the representatives of such persons.

Bequest without words of limitation.

82. Where property is bequeathed to any person, he is entitled to the whole interest of the testator therein, unless it appears from the will that only a restricted interest was intended for him.

Bequest in alternative.

83. Where property is bequeathed to a person, with a bequest in the alternative to another person or to a class of persons, if a contrary intention does not appear by the will, the legatee first named shall be entitled to the legacy, if he be alive at the time when it takes

effect; but, if he be then dead, the person or class of persons named in the second branch of the alternative shall take the legacy.

Illustrations.

(*a.*) A bequest is made to A or to B. A survives the testator. B takes nothing.

(*b.*) A bequest is made to A or to B. A dies after the date of the will, and before the testator. The legacy goes to B.

(*c.*) A bequest is made to A or to B. A is dead at the date of the will. The legacy goes to B.

(*d.*) Property is bequeathed to A or his heirs. A survives the testator. A takes the property absolutely.

(*e.*) Property is bequeathed to A or his nearest of kin. A dies in the lifetime of the testator. Upon the death of the testator, the bequest to A's nearest of kin takes effect.

(*f.*) Property is bequeathed to A for life, and after his death to B or his heirs. A and B survive the testator. B dies in A's lifetime. Upon A's death the bequest to the heirs of B takes effect.

(*g.*) Property is bequeathed to A for life, and after his death to B or his heirs. B dies in the testator's lifetime. A survives the testator. Upon A's death the bequest to the heirs of B takes effect.

Effect of words, describing a class added to bequest to a person.

84. Where property is bequeathed to a person, and words are added which describe a class of persons, but do not denote them as direct objects of a distinct and independent gift, such person is entitled to the whole interest of the testator therein, unless a contrary intention appears by the will.

Illustrations.

(*a.*) A bequest is made—

to A and his children,
to A and his children by his present wife,
to A and his heirs,
to A and the heirs of his body,
to A and the heirs male of his body,
to A and the heirs female of his body,
to A and his issue,
to A and his family,
to A and his descendants,
to A and his representatives,
to A and his personal representatives,
to A, his executors, and administrators:

In each of these cases, A takes the whole interest which the testator had in the property.

(*b.*) A bequest is made to A and his brothers. A and his brothers are jointly entitled to the legacy.

(*c.*) A bequest is made to A for life, and after his death to his issue. At the death of A the property belongs in equal shares to all persons who shall then answer the description of issue of A.

85. Where a bequest is made to a class of persons under a general description only, no one to whom the words of the description are not in their ordinary sense applicable shall take the legacy.

Bequest to class of persons under general description only.

Construction of terms.

86. The word "children" in a will applies only to lineal descendants in the first degree;

the word "grandchildren" applies only to lineal descendants in the second degree of the person whose "children" or "grand-children" are spoken of;

the words "nephews" and "nieces" apply only to children of brothers or sister;

the words "cousins," or "first cousins," or "cousins-german," apply only to children of brothers or of sisters of the father or mother of the person whose "cousins," or "first cousins," or "cousins-german," are spoken of;

the words "first cousins once removed" apply only to children of cousins-german, or to cousins-german of a parent of the person whose "first cousins once removed," are spoken of;

the words "second cousins" apply only to grandchildren of brothers or of sisters of the grandfather or grandmother of the person whose "second cousins" are spoken of;

the words "issue" and "descendants" apply to all lineal descendants whatever of the person whose "issue" or "descendants" are spoken of.

Words expressive of collateral relationship apply alike to relatives of full and of half-blood.

All words expressive of relationship apply to a child in the womb who is afterwards born alive.

Words expressing relationship denote only legitimate relatives, or, failing such, relatives reputed legitimate.

87. In the absence of any intimation to the contrary in the will, the term "child," "son," or "daughter," or any word which expresses relationship is to be understood as denoting only a legitimate relative, or, where there is no such legitimate relative, a person who has acquired, at the date of the will, the reputation of being such relative.

Illustrations.

(*a*) A, having three children, B, C. and D, of whom B and C are legitimate, and D is illegitimate, leaves his property to be equally divided among "his children." The property belongs to B and C in equal shares to the exclusion of D.

(*b*) A, having a niece of illegitimate birth, who has acquired the reputation of being his niece, and having no legitimate niece, bequeaths a sum of money to his niece. The illegitimate niece is entitled to the legacy.

(*c*) A, having in his will enumerated his children, and named as one of them B, who is illegitimate, leaves a legacy to "his said children." B will take a share in the legacy along with the legitimate children.

(*d*) A leaves a legacy to the "children of B." B is dead, and has left none but illegitimate children. All those who had, at the date of the will, acquired the reputation of being the children of B, are objects of the gift.

(*e*) A bequeathed a legacy to "the children of B." B never had any legitimate child. C and D had, at the date of the will, acquired the reputation of being children of B. After the date of the will, and before the death of the testator, E and F were born, and acquired the reputation of being children of B. Only C and D are objects of the bequest.

(*f*) A makes a bequest in favour of his child by a certain woman, not his wife. B had acquired, at the date of the will, the reputation of being the child of A by the woman designated. B takes the legacy.

(*g*) A makes a bequest in favour of his child to be born of a woman, who never becomes his wife. The bequest is void.

(*h*) A makes a bequest in favour of the child of which a certain woman, not married to him, is pregnant. The bequest is valid.

Rules of construction where will purports to make two bequests to same person.

88. Where a will purports to make two bequests to the same person, and a question arises whether the testator intended to make the second bequest instead of, or in addition to, the first, if there is nothing in the will to show what he intended, the following rules shall prevail in determining the construction to be put upon the will:—

First.—If the same specific thing is bequeathed twice to the same legatee in the same will, or in the will, and again in a codicil, he is entitled to receive that specific thing only.

Second.—Where one and the same will or one and the same codicil purports to make, in two places, a bequest to the same person of the same quantity or amount of anything, he shall be entitled to one such legacy only.

Third.—Where two legacies of unequal amount are given to the same person in the same will or in the same codicil, the legatee is entitled to both.

Fourth.—Where two legacies, whether equal or unequal in amount, are given to the same legatee, one by a will and the other by a codicil, or each by a different codicil, the legatee is entitled to both legacies.

Explanation.—In the four last rules, the word "will" does not include a codicil.

Illustrations.

(*a*) A, having ten shares, and no more, in the Bank of Bengal, made his will, which contains near its commencement the words, "I bequeath my ten shares in the Bank of Bengal to B." After other bequests, the will concludes with the words, "and I bequeath my ten shares in the Bank of Bengal to B." B is entitled simply to receive A's ten shares in the Bank of Bengal.

(*b*) A, having one diamond ring which was given him by B, bequeathed to C the diamond ring which was given by B. A afterwards made a codicil to his will, and thereby, after giving other legacies, he bequeathed to C the diamond ring which was given him by B. C can claim nothing except the diamond ring which was given to A by B.

(*c*) A, by his will, bequeaths to B the sum of 5,000 rupees, and afterwards, by the same will, repeats the bequest in the same words. B is entitled to one legacy of 5,000 rupees only.

(*d*) A, by his will, bequeaths to B the sum of 5,000 rupees, and afterwards, by the same will, bequeaths to B the same of 6,000 rupees. B is entitled to 11,000 rupees.

(*e*) A, by his will, bequeaths to B 5,000 rupees, and by a codicil to the will he bequeaths to him 5,000 rupees. B is entitled to receive 10,000 rupees.

(*f*) A, by one codicil to his will, bequeaths to B 5,000 rupees, and by another codicil bequeaths to him 6,000 rupees. B is entitled to receive 11,000 rupees.

(*g*) A, by his will, bequeaths "500 rupees to B, because she was his nurse," and in another part of the will bequeaths 500 rupees to B, "because she went to England with his children." B is entitled to receive 1,000 rupees.

(*h*) A, by his will, bequeaths to B the sum of 5,000 rupees, and also, in another part of the will, an annuity of 400 rupees. B is entitled to both legacies.

(*i*) A, by his will, bequeaths to B the sum of 5,000 rupees, and also bequeaths to him the sum of 5,000 rupees if he shall attain the age of 18. B is entitled absolutely to one sum of 5,000 rupees, and takes a contingent interest in another sum of 5,000 rupees.

Constitution of residuary legatee.

89. A residuary legatee may be constituted by any words that show an intention on the part of the testator that the person designated shall take the surplus or residue of his property.

Illustrations.

(*a*) A makes her will, consisting of several testamentary papers, in one of which are contained the following words: "I think there will be something left, after all funeral expenses, &c., to give to B, now at school, towards equipping him to any profession he may hereafter be appointed to." B is constituted residuary legatee.

(*b*) A makes his will with the following passage at the end of it: "I believe there will be found sufficient in my banker's hands to defray and discharge my debts, which I hereby desire B to do, and keep the residue for her own use and pleasure. B is constituted the residuary legatee.

(*c*) A bequeaths all his property to B, except certain stocks and funds which he bequeaths to C. B is the residuary legatee.

Property to which residuary legatee entitled.

90. Under a residuary bequest, the legatee is entitled to all property belonging to the testator at the time of his death of which he has not made any other testamentary disposition which is capable of taking effect.

Illustration.

A, by his will, bequeaths certain legacies, one of which is void under section 105, and another lapses by the death of the legatee. He bequeaths the residue of his property to B. After the date of his will, A purchases a zamindari, which belongs to him at the time of his death. B is entitled to the two legacies and the zamindari as part of the residue.

Time of vesting of legacy in general terms.

91. If a legacy be given in general terms, without specifying the time when it is to be paid, the legatee has a vested interest in it from the day of the death of the testator, and if he dies without having received it, it shall pass to his representatives.

In what case legacy lapses.

92. If the legatee does not survive the testator, the legacy cannot take effect, but shall lapse and form part of the residue of the testator's property, unless it appear by the will that the testator intended that it should go to some other person.

In order to entitle the representatives of the legatee to receive the legacy, it must be proved that he survived the testator.

Illustrations.

(*a*) The testator bequeaths to B "500 rupees which B owes him." B dies before the testator. The legacy lapses.

(*b.*) A bequest is made to A and his children. A dies before the testator, or happens to be dead when the will is made. The legacy to A and his children lapses.

(*c.*) A legacy is given to A, and, in case of his dying before the testator, to B. A dies before the testator. The legacy goes to B.

(*d.*) A sum of money is bequeathed to A for life, and after his death to B. A dies in the lifetime of the testator; B survives the testator. The bequest to B takes effect.

(*e.*) A sum of money is bequeathed to A on his completing his eighteenth year, and, in case he should die before he completes his eighteenth year, to B. A completes his eighteenth year, and dies in the lifetime of the testator. The legacy to A lapses, and the bequest to B does not take effect.

(*f.*) The testator and the legatee perished in the same shipwreck. There is no evidence to show which died first. The legacy will lapse.

Legacy does not lapse if one of two joint legatees die before testator.

93. If a legacy be given to two persons jointly, and one of them die before the testator, the other legatee takes the whole.

Illustrations.

The legacy is simply to A and B. A dies before the testator. B takes the legacy.

Effect of words showing testator's intention to give distinct shares.

94. But where a legacy is given to legatees in words which show that the testator intended to give them distinct shares of it, then, if any legatee die before the testator, so much of the legacy as

was intented for him shall fall into the residue of the testator's property.

Illustration.

A sum of money is bequeathed to A, B, and C, to be equally divided among them. A dies before the testator. B and C shall only take so much as they would have had if A had survived the testator.

When lapsed share goes as undisposed of.

95. Where the share that lapses is a part of the general residue bequeathed by the will, that share shall go as undisposed of.

Illustration.

The testator bequeaths the residue of his estate to A, B, and C, to be equally divided between them. A dies before the testator. His one-third of the residue goes as undisposed of.

When bequest to testator's child or lineal descendant does not lapse on his death in testator's lifetime.

96. Where a bequest shall have been made to any child or other lineal descendant of the testator, and the legatee shall die in the lifetime of the testator, but any lineal descendant of his survive the testator, the bequest shall not lapse, but shall take effect as if the death of the legatee had happened immediately after the death of the testator, unless a contrary intention shall appear by the will.

Illustration.

A makes his will, by which he bequeaths a sum of money to his son B, for his own absolute use and benefit. B dies before A, leaving a son C who survives A, and having made his will, whereby he bequeaths all his property to his widow D. The money goes to D.

Bequest to A for benefit of D does not lapse by A's death.

97. Where a bequest is made to one person for the benefit of another, the legacy does not lapse by the death, in the testator's lifetime, of the person to whom the bequest is made.

Survivorship in case of bequest to described class.

98. Where a bequest is made simply to a described class of persons, the thing bequeathed shall go only to such as shall be alive at the testator's death.

Exception.—If property is bequeathed to a class of persons described as standing in a particular degree of kindred to a specified individual, but their possession of it is deferred until a time later than the death of the testator by reason of a prior bequest or otherwise, the property shall at that time go to such of them as shall be then alive, and to the representatives of any of them who have died since the death of the testator.

Illustrations.

(*a*) A bequeaths 1,000 rupees to "the children" of B without saying when it is to be distributed among them. B had died previous to the date of the will, leaving three children, C, D, and E. E died after the date of the will, but before the death of A. C and D survive A. The legacy shall belong to C and D to the exclusion of the representatives of E.

(*b*) A bequeaths a legacy to the children of B. At the time of the testator's death, B has no children. The bequest is void.

(*c*) A lease for years of a house was bequeathed to A for his life, and after his decease to the children of B. At the death of the testator, B had two children living C and D; and he never had any other child. Afterwards, during the lifetime of A, C died leaving E his executor. D had survived A. D and E are jointly entitled to so much of the leasehold term as remains unexpired.

(*d*) A sum of money was bequeathed to A for her life, and after her decease to the children of B. At the death of the testator, B had two children living, C and D, and after that event, two children, E and F, were born to B. C and E died in the lifetime of A, C having made a will, E having made no will. A has died, leaving D and F surviving her. The legacy is to be divided into four equal parts, one of which is to be paid to the executor of C, one to D, one to the administrator of E, and one to F.

(*e*) A bequeaths one-third of his lands to B for his life, and after his decease to the sisters of B. At the death of the testator, B had two sisters living, C and D, and after that event another sister E was born. C died during the life of B; D and E have survived B. One-third of A's lands belongs to D, E, and the representatives of C in equal shares.

(*f*) A bequeaths 1,000 rupees to B for life, and after his death equally among the children of C. Up to the death of B, C had not had any child. The bequest after the death of B is void.

(*g*) A bequeaths 1,000 rupees to "all the children, born or to be born." of B, to be divided among them at the death of C. At the death of the testator, B has two children living, D and E. After the death of the testator, but in the lifetime of C, two other children, F and G, are born to B. After the death of C, another child is born to B. The legacy belongs to D, E, F, and G, to the exclusion of the after-born child of B.

(*h*) A bequeaths a fund to the children of B, to be divided among them when the elder shall attain majority. At the testator's death, B had one child living, named C. He afterwards had two other children, named D and E. E died, but C and D were living when C attained majority. The fund belongs to C, D, and the representatives of E to the exclusion of any child who may be born to B after C's attaining majority.

PART XII.

Of Void Bequests.

Bequest to person by particular description who is not in existence at testator's death.

99. Where a bequest is made to a person by a particular description, and there is no person in existence at the testator's death who answers the description, the bequest is void.

Exception.—If property is bequeathed to a person described as standing in a particular degree of kindred to a specified individual, but his possession of it is deferred until a time later than the death of the testator by reason of a prior bequest or otherwise, and if a person answering the description is alive at the death of the testator, or comes into existence between that event and such later time, the property shall, at such later time go to that person, or, if he be dead, to his representatives.

Illustrations.

(*a*) A bequeaths 1,000 rupees to the eldest son of B. At the death of the testator, B has no son. The bequest is void.

(*b*) A bequeaths 1,000 rupees to B for life, and after his death to the eldest son of C. At the death of the testator, C had no son. Afterwards, during the life of B, a son is born to C. Upon B's death the legacy goes to C's son.

(*c*) A bequeaths 1,000 rupees to B for life, and after his death to the eldest son of C. At the death of the testator, C had no son; afterwards, during the life of B, a son named D is born to C. D dies; then B dies. The legacy goes to the representative of D.

(*d*) A bequeaths his estate of Green Acre to B for life, and at his decease to the eldest son of C. Up to the death of B, C has had no son. The bequest to C's eldest son is void.

(*e*) A bequeaths 1,000 rupees to the eldest son of C, to be paid to him after the death of B. At the death of the testator, C has no son, but a son is afterwards born to him during the life of B, and is alive at B's death. C's son is entitled to the 1,000 rupees.

Bequest to person not in existence at testator's death, subject to prior bequest.

100. Where a bequest is made to a person not in existence at the time of the testator's death, subject to a prior bequest contained in the will, the later bequest shall be void unless it comprises the whole of the remaining interest of the testator in the thing bequeathed.

Illustrations.

(*a*) Property is bequeathed to A for his life, and after his death to his eldest son for life, and after the death of the latter to his eldest son. At the time of the testator's death, A has no son. Here the bequest to A's eldest son is a bequest to a person not in existence at the testator's death. It is not a bequest of the whole interest that remains to the testator. The bequest to A's eldest son for his life is void.

(b) A fund is bequeathed to A for his life, and after his death to his daughters. A survives the testator. A has daughters, some of whom were not in existence at the testator's death. The bequest to A's daughters comprises the whole interest that remains to the testator in the thing bequeathed. The bequest to A's daughters is valid.

(c) A fund is bequeathed to A for his life, and after his death to his daughters, with a direction that, if any of them marries under the age of eighteen, her portion shall be settled, so that it may belong to herself for life, and may be divisible among her children after her death. A has no daughters living at the time of the testator's death, but has daughters born afterwards who survive him. Here the direction for a settlement has the effect, in the case of each daughter who marries under eighteen, of substituting, for the absolute bequest to her, a bequest to her merely for her life; that is to say, a bequest to a person not in existence at the time of the testator's death of something which is less than the whole interest that remains to the testator in the thing bequeathed. The direction to settle the fund is void.

(d) A bequeaths a sum of money to B for life, and directs that, upon the death of B, the fund shall be settled upon his daughters, so that the portion of each daughter may belong to herself for life, and may be divided among her children after her death. B has no daughter living at the time of the testator's death. In this case the only bequest to the daughters of B is contained in the direction to settle the fund, and this direction amounts to a bequest, to persons not yet born, of a life-interest in the fund, that is to say, of something which is less than the whole interest that remains in the testator in the thing bequeathed. The direction to settle the fund upon the daughters of B is void.

Rule against perpetuity.

101. No bequest is valid whereby the vesting of the thing bequeathed may be delayed beyond the lifetime of one or more persons living at the testator's decease, and the minority of some person who shall be in existence at the expiration of that period, and to whom, if he attains full age, the thing bequeathed is to belong.

Illustrations.

(a) A fund is bequeathed to A for his life; and after his death to B for his life; and after B's death to such of the sons of B as shall first attain the age of 25. A and B survive the testator. Here the son of B, who shall first attain the age of 25, may be a son born after the death of the testator; such son may not attain 25 until more than 18 years have elapsed from the death of the longer liver of A and B; and the vesting of the fund may thus be delayed beyond the lifetime of A and B and the minority of the sons of B. The bequest after B's death is void.

(b) A fund is bequeathed to A for his life; and after his death to B for his life; and after B's death to such of B's sons as shall first attain the age of 25. B dies in the lifetime of the testator, leaving one or more sons. In this case the sons of B are persons living at the time of the testator's decease and the time when either of them will attain 25, necessarily falls within his own lifetime. The bequest is valid.

(c.) A fund is bequeated to A for his life, and after his death to B for his life, with a direction that after B's death it shall be divided amongst such of B's children as shall attain the age of 18; but that, if no child of B shall attain that age, the fund shall go to C. Here the time for the division of the fund must arrive at the latest at the expiration of 18 years from the death of B, a person living at the testator's decease. All the bequests are valid.

(*d.*) A fund is bequeathed to trustees for the benefit of the testator's daughters, with a direction that if any of them marry under age, her share of the fund shall be settled, so as to devolve after her death upon such of her children as shall attain the age of 18. Any daughter of the testator to whom the direction applies must be in existence at his decease, and any portion of the fund which may eventually be settled as directed must vest not later than 18 years from the death of the daughter whose share it was. All these provisions are valid.

Bequest to a class, some of whom may come under rules in sections 100 and 101.

102. If a bequest is made to a class of persons with regard to some of whom it is inoperative by reason of the rules contained in the two last preceding sections, or either of them, such bequest shall be wholly void.

Illustrations.

(*a.*) A fund is bequeathed to A for life, and after his death to all his children who shall attain the age of 25. A survives the testator, and has some children living at the testator's death. Each child of A's living at the testator's death must attain the age of 25 (if at all) within the limits allowed for a bequest. But A may have children after the testator's decease, some of whom may not attain the age of 25 until more than 18 years have elapsed after the decease of A. The bequest to A's children, therefore, is inoperative as to any child born after the testator's death; and, as it is given to all his children as a class, it is not good as to any division of that class, but is wholly void.

(*b.*) A fund is bequeathed to A for his life, and after his death to B, C, D, and all other the children of A who shall attain the age of 25. B, C, D, are children of A living at the testator's decease In all other respects the case is the same as that supposed in illustration *a*. The mention of B, C, and D by name does not prevent the bequest from being regarded as a bequest to a class, and the bequest is wholly void.

Bequest to take effect on failure of bequest void under section 100, 101, or 102.

103. Where a bequest is void by reason of any of the rules contain in the three last preceding sections, any bequest contained in the same will, and intended to take effect after or upon failure of such prior bequest, is also void.

Illustrations.

(*a.*) A fund is bequeathed to A for his life, and after his death to such of his sons as shall first attain the age of 25, for his life, and after the decease of such son, to B. A and B survive the testator. The bequest to B is intended to take effect after the bequest to such of the sons of A as shall first attain the age of 25, which bequest is void under section 101. The bequest to B is void.

(*b.*) A fund is bequeathed to A for his life, and after his death to such of his sons as shall first attain the age of 25, and, if no son of A shall attain that age, to B. A and B survive the testator. The bequest to B is intended to take effect upon failure of the bequest to such of A's sons as shall first attain the age of 25, which bequest is void under section 101. Te bequest to B is void.

Effect of direction for accumulation.

104. A direction to accumulate the income arising from any property shall be void; and the property shall be disposed of as if no accumulation had been directed.

Exception.—Where the property is immovable, or where accumulation is directed to be made from the death of the testator, the direction shall be valid in respect only of the income arising from the property within one year next following the testator's death;

and at the end of the year such property and income shall be disposed of respectively as if the period during which the accumulation has been directed to be made had elapsed.

Illustrations.

(*a*) The will directs that the sum of 10,000 rupees shall be invested in Government securities, and the income accumulated for 20 years, and that the principal, together with the accumulation, shall then be divided between A, B, and C. A, B, and C, are entitled to receive the sum of 10,000 rupees at the end of the year from the testator's death.

(*b*) The will directs that 10,000 rupees shall be invested, and the income accumulated until A shall marry, and shall then be paid to him. A is entitled to receive 10,000 rupees at the end of a year from the testator's death.

(*c*) The will directs that the rents of the farm of Sultanpur shall be accumulated for ten years,and that the accumulation shall be then paid to the eldest son of A. At the death of the testator, A has an eldest son living, named B. B shall receive at the end of one year from the testator's death the rents which have accrued during the year, together with any interest which may have been made by investing them.

(*d*) The will directs that the rents of the farm of Sultanpur shall be accumulated for ten years and that the accumulation shall then be paid to the eldest son of A. At the death of the testator, A has no son. The bequest is void.

(*e*) A bequeaths a sum of money to B. to be paid to him when he shall attain the age of 18, and directs the interest to be accumulated till he shall arrive at the age. At A's death the legacy becomes vested in B; and so much of the interest as is not required for his maintenance and education is accumulated, not by reason of the direction contained in the will, but in consequence of B's minority.

Bequest to religious or charitable uses.

105. No man having a nephew or niece or any nearer relative shall have power to bequeath any property to religious or charitable uses, except by a will executed not less than twelve months before his death, and deposited within six months from its execution in some place provided by law for the safe custody of the wills of living persons.

Illustration.

A, having a nephew, makes a bequest by a will not executed nor deposited as required—

for the relief of poor people ;
for the maintenance of sick soldiers ;
for the erection or support of a hospital ;
for the education and preferment of orphans ;
for the support of scholars ;
for the erection or support of a school ;
for the building and repairs of a bridge ;
for the making of roads ;
for the erection or support of a church ;
for the repairs of a church ;
for the benefit of ministers of religion ;
for the formation or support of a public garden.

All these bequests are void.

PART XIII.

Of the Vesting of Legacies.

Date of vesting of legacy when payment or possession postponed.

106. Where, by the terms of a bequest, the legatee is not entitled to immediate possession of the thing bequeathed, a right to receive it at the proper time shall, unless a contrary intention appears by the will, become vested in the legatee on the testator's death, and shall pass to the legatee's representatives if he dies before that time, and without having received the legacy.

And in such cases the legacy is, from the testator's death, said to be vested in interest.

Explanation.—An intention that a legacy to any person shall not become vested in interest in him is not to be inferred merely from a provision whereby the payment or possession of the thing bequeathed is postponed, or whereby a prior interest therein is bequeathed to some other person, or whereby the income arising from the fund bequeathed is directed to be accumulated until the time of payment arrives, or from a provision that, if a particular event shall happen, the legacy shall go over to another person.

Illustrations.

(*a*.) A bequeaths to B 100 rupees to be paid to him at the death of C. On A's death the legacy becomes vested in interest in B, and if he dies before C, his representatives are entitled to the legacy.

(*b.*) A bequeaths to B. 100 rupees to be paid to him upon his attaining the age of 18. On A's death, the legacy becomes vested in interest in B.

(*c.*) A fund is bequeathed to A for life, and after his death to B. On the testator's death the legacy to B. becomes vested in interest in B.

(*d.*) A fund is bequeathed to A until B attains the age of 18, and then to B. The legacy to B is vested in interest from the testator's death.

(*e.*) A bequeaths the whole of his property to B upon trust to pay certain debts out of the income, and then to make over the fund to C. At A's death the gift to C becomes vested in interest in him.

(*f.*) A fund is bequeathed to A, B, and C in equal shares to be paid to them on their attaining the age of 18 respectively, with a proviso that, if all of them die under the age of 18, the legacy shall devolve upon D. On the death of the testator, the shares vest in interest in A, B, and C, subject to be divested in case A, B, and C shall all die under 18, and upon the death of any of them (except the last survivor) under the age of 18, his vested interest passes, so subject, to his representatives.

Date of vesting when legacy contingent upon specified uncertain event.

107. A legacy bequeathed in case a specified uncertain event shall happen does not vest until that event happens.

A legacy bequeathed in case a specified uncertain event shall not happen does not vest until the happening of that event becomes impossible.

In either case, until the condition has been fulfilled, the interest of the legatee is called contingent.

Exception.—Where a fund is bequeathed to any person upon his attaining a particular age, and the will also gives to him absolutely the income to arise from the fund before he reaches that age, or directs the income, or so much of it as may be necessary, to be applied for his benefit, the bequest of the fund is not contingent.

Illustrations.

(*a.*) A legacy is bequeated to D in case A, B, and C, shall all die under the age of 18. D has a contingent interest in the legacy until A, B, and C all die under 18, or one of them attains that age.

(*b.*) A sum of money is bequeathed to A "in case he shall attain the age of 18," or "when he shall attain the age of 18." A's interest in the legacy is contingent until the condition shall be fulfilled by his attaining that age.

(*c.*) An estate is bequeathed to A for life, and after his death to B, if B shall then be living, but, if B shall not be then living, to C. A, B, and C, survive the testator. B and C each take a contingent interest in the estate until the event which is to vest it in one or in the other shall have happened.

(*d.*) An estate is bequeathed as in the case last supposed. B dies in the lifetime of A and C. Upon the death of B, C acquires a vested right to obtain possession of the estate upon A's death.

(e.) A legacy is bequeathed to A when she shall attain the age of 18 or shall marry under that age with the consent of B, with a proviso that, if she shall not attain 18, or marry under that age without B's consent, the legacy shall go to C. A and C each take a contingent interest in the legacy. A attains the age of 18. A becomes absolutely entitled to the legacy, although she may have married under 18 without the consent of B.

(f.) An estate is bequeathed to A until he shall marry, and after that event to B. B's interest in the bequest is contingent until the condition shall be fulfilled by A's marrying.

(g.) An estate is bequeathed to A until he shall take advantage of the Act for the Relief of Insolvent Debtors, and after that event to B. B's interest in the bequest is contingent until A takes advantage of the Act.

(h.) An estate is bequeathed to A if he shall pay 500 rupees to B. A's interest in the bequest is contingent until he has paid 500 rupees to B.

(i.) A leaves his farm of Sultanpur Khurd to B, if B shall convey his own farm of Sultanpur Buzurg to C. B's interest in the bequest is contingent until he has conveyed the latter farm to C.

(j) A fund is bequeathed to A if B shall not marry C within five years after the testator's death. A's interest in the legacy is contingent, until the condition shall be fulfilled by the expiration of the five years without B's having married C, or by the occurrence, within that period, of an event which makes the fulfilment of the condition impossible.

(k) A fund is bequeathed to A if B shall not make any provision for him by will. The legacy is contingent until B's death.

(l) A bequeaths to B 500 rupees a year upon his attaining the age of 18, and directs that the interest, or a competent part thereof, shall be applied for his benefit until he reaches that age. The legacy is vested.

(m) A bequeaths to B 500 rupees when he shall attain the age of 18, and directs that a certain sum, out of another fund, shall be applied for his maintenance until he arrives at that age. The legacy is contingent.

Vesting of interest in bequest to such members of a class as shall have attained particular age.

108. Where a bequest is made only to such members of a class as shall have attained a particular age, a person who has not attained that age cannot have a vested interest in the legacy.

Illustration.

A fund is bequeathed to such of the children of A as shall attain the age of 18, with a direction that, while any child of A shall be under the age of 18, the income of the share to which it may be presumed he will be eventually entitled, shall be applied for his maintenance and education. No child of A, who is under the age of 18, has a vested interest in the bequest.

PART XIV.

OF ONEROUS BEQUESTS.

109. Where a bequest imposes an obligation on the legatee, he can take nothing by it unless he accepts it fully.

Onerous bequest.

Illustration.

A, having share in (X), a prosperous joint-stock company, and also shares in (Y), a joint-stock company in difficulties, in respect of which shares heavy calls are expected to be made, bequeaths to B all his shares in joint-stock companies. B refuses to accept the shares in (Y). He forfeits the shares in (X.)

110. Where a will contains two separate and independent bequest to the same person the legatee is at liberty to accept one of them, and refuses the other, although the former may be beneficial, and the latter onerous.

One of two separate and independent bequests to same person may be accepted, and the other refused.

Illustrations.

A, having a lease for a term of years of a house at a rent which he and his representatives are bound to pay during the term, and which is higher than the house can be left for, bequeaths to B the lease and a sum of money. B refuses to accept the lease. He shall not, by his refusal, forfeit the money.

PART XV.

OF CONTINGENT BEQUESTS.

111. Where a legacy is given if a specified uncertain event shall happen, and no time is mentioned in the will for the occurrence of that event, the legacy cannot take effect unless such event happens before the period when the fund bequeathed is payable or distributable.

Bequest contingent upon specified uncertain event, no time being mentioned for its occurrence.

Illustrations.

(*a*) A legacy is bequeathed to A, and, in case of his death, to B. If A survives the testator the legacy to B does not take effect.

(*b*.) A legacy is bequeathed to A, and, in case of his death without children, to B. If A survives the testator, or dies in his lifetime leaving a child, the legacy to B does not take effect.

(*c*.) A legacy is bequeathed to A when and if he attains the age of 18, and, in case of his death, to B. A attains the age of 18. The legacy to B does not take effect.

(*d*.) A legacy is bequeathed to A for life, and after his death to B, and, "in case of B's death without children," to C. The words "in case of B's death without children" are to be understood as meaning "in case B shall die without children during the lifetime of A."

(e.) A legacy is bequeathed to A for life, and after his death to B, and, "in case of B's death," to C. The words "in case of B's death" are to be considered as meaning "in case B shall die in the lifetime of A."

Bequest to such of certain persons as shall be surviving at some period not specified.

112. Where a bequest is made to such of certain persons as shall be surviving at some period, but the exact period is not specified, the legacy shall go to such of them as shall be alive at the time of payment or distribution, unless a contrary intention appear by the will.

Illustrations.

(a.) Property is bequeathed to A and B, to be equally divided between them, or to the survivor of them. If both A and B survive the testator, the legacy is equally divided between them. If A dies before the testator, and B survives the testator, it goes to B.

(b.) Property is bequeathed to A for life, and after his death to B and C, to be equally divided between them, or to the survivor of them. B dies during the life of A; C survives A. At A's death the legacy goes to C.

(c.) Property is bequeathed to A for life, and after his death to B and C, or the survivor, with a direction that, if B should not survive the testator, his children are to stand in his place. C dies during the life of the testator; B survives the testator, but dies in the lifetime of A. The legacy goes to the representative of B.

(d.) Property is bequeathed to A for life and after his death to B and C, with a direction that, in case either of them dies in the lifetime of A, the whole shall go to the survivor. B dies in the lifetime of A. Afterwards C dies in the lifetime of A. The legacy goes to the representative of C.

PART XVI.

OF CONDITIONAL BEQUESTS.

Bequest upon impossible condition.

113. A bequest upon an impossible condition is void.

Illustrations.

(a.) An estate is bequeathed to A on condition that he shall walk one hundred miles in an hour. The bequest is void.

(b.) A bequeaths 500 rupees to B on condition that he shall marry A's daughter. A's daughter was dead at the date of the will. The bequest is void.

Request upon illegal or immoral condition.

114. A bequest upon a condition, the fulfilment of which would be contrary to law or to morality, is void.

Illustrations.

(a.) A bequeaths 500 rupees to B on condition that he shall murder C. The bequest is void.

(b.) A bequeaths 5,000 rupees to his niece if she will desert her husband. The bequest is void.

115. Where a will imposes a condition to be fulfilled before the legatee can take a vested interest in the thing bequeathed, the condition shall be considered to have been fulfilled if it has been substantially complied with.

Fulfilment of condition precedent to vesting of legacy.

Illustrations.

(*a.*) A legacy is bequeathed to A on condition that he shall marry with the consent of B, C, D, and E. A marries with the written consent of B. C is present at the marriage. D sends a present to A previous to the marriage. E has been personally informed by A of his intentions, and has made no objection. A has fulfilled the condition.

(*b*) A legacy is bequeathed to A on condition that he shall marry with the consent B, C, and D. D dies. A marries with the consent of B and C. A has fulfilled the condition.

(*c*) A legacy is bequeathed to A on condition that he shall marry with the consent of B, C, and D. A marries in the lifetime of B, C, and D. with the consent of B and C only. A has not fulfilled the condition.

(*d*) A legacy is bequeathed to A on condition that he shall marry with the consent of B, C, and D. A obtains the unconditional assent of B, C, and D, to his marriage with E. Afterwards B, C, and D capriciously retract their consent. A marries E. A has fulfilled the condition.

(*e*) A legacy is bequeathed to A on condition that he shall marry with the consent of B, C, and D. A marries without the consent of B, C, and D, but obtains their consent after the marriage. A has not fulfilled the condition.

(*f*) A makes his will, whereby he bequeaths a sum of money to B if B shall marry with the consent of A's executors. B marries during the lifetime of A, and A afterwards expresses his approbation of the marriage. A dies. The bequest to B takes effect.

(*g*) A legacy is bequeathed to A if he executes a certain document within a time specified in the will. The document is executed by A within a reasonable time, but not within the time specified in the will. A has not performed the condition, and is not entitled to receive the legacy.

116. Where there is a bequest to one person, and a bequest of the same thing to another, if the prior bequest shall fail, the second bequest shall take effect upon the failure of the prior bequest, although the failure may not have occurred in the manner contemplated by the testator.

Bequest to A, and, on failure of prior bequest, to B.

Illustrations.

(*a*) A bequeaths a sum of money to his own children surviving him, and, if they all die under 18, to B. A dies without having ever had a child. The bequest to B takes effect.

(*b*) A bequeaths a sum of money to B, on condition that he shall execute a certain document within three months after A's death, and, if he should neglect to do so, to C. B dies in the testator's lifetime. The bequest to C takes effect.

117. Where the will shows an intention that the second bequest shall take effect only in the event of the first bequest failing in a particular manner, the second bequest shall not take effect unless the prior bequest fails in that particular manner.

When second bequest not to take effect on failure of first.

Illustration.

A makes a bequest to his wife, but in case she should die in his lifetime, bequeaths to B that which he had bequeathed to her. A and his wife perish together under circumstances which make it impossible to prove that she died before him. The bequest to B does not take effect.

118. A bequest may be made to any person with the condition superadded that, in case a specified uncertain event shall happen, the thing bequeathed shall go to another person; or that, in case a specified uncertain event shall not happen, the thing bequeathed shall go over to another person.

Bequest over conditional upon happening or not happening of specified uncertain event.

In each case the ulterior bequest is subject to the rules contained in sections 107, 108, 109, 110, 111, 112, 113, 114, 116, and 117.

Illustrations.

(*a*) A sum of money is bequeathed to A, to be paid to him at the age of 18, and, if he shall die before he attains that age, to B. A takes a vested interest in the legacy, subject to be divested and to go to B in case A shall die under 18.

(*b*) An estate is bequeathed to A, with a proviso that, if A shall dispute the competency of the testator to make a will the estate shall go to B. A disputes the competency of the testator to make a will. The estate goes to B.

(*c*) A sum of money is bequeathed to A for life, and after his death to B, but if B shall then be dead, leaving a son, such son is to stand in the place of B. B takes a vested interest in the legacy, subject to be divested if he dies leaving a son in A's lifetime.

(*d*) A sum of money is bequeathed to A and B, and if either should die during the life of C, then to the survivor living at the death of C. A and B die before C. The gift over cannot take effect, but the representative of A takes one-half of the money, and the representative of B takes the other half.

(*e*.) A bequeaths to B the interest of a fund for life, and directs the fund to be divided at her death equally among her three children, or such of them as shall be living at her death. All the children of B die in B's lifetime. The bequest over cannot take effect, but the interest of the children pass to their representatives.

119. An ulterior bequest of the kind contemplated by the last preceding section cannot take effect, unless the condition is strictly fulfilled.

Condition must be strictly fulfilled.

Illustrations.

(*a.*) A legacy is bequeathed to A with a proviso that, if he marries without the consent of B, C, and D, the legacy shall go to E. D dies. Even if A marries without the consent of B and C, the gift to E does not take effect.

(*b.*) A legacy is bequeathed to A with a proviso that, if he marries without the consent of B, the legacy shall go to C. A marries with the consent of B. He afterwards becomes a widower, and marries again without the consent of B. The bequest to C does not take effect.

(*c.*) A legacy is bequeathed to A, to be paid at 18, or marriage, with a proviso that, if A dies under 18, or marries without the consent of B, the legacy shall go to C. A marries under 18 without the consent of B. The bequest to C takes effect.

Original bequest not affected by invalidity of secoud.

120. If the ulterior bequest be not valid, the original bequest is not affected by it.

Illustrations.

(*a.*) An estate is bequeathed to A for his life, with a condition superadded that, if he shall not, on a given day, walk 100 miles in an hour, the estate shall go to B. The condition being void, A retains his estate as if no condition had been inserted in the will.

(*b.*) An estate is bequeathed to A for her life, and if she do not desert her husband, to B. A is entitled to the estate during her life as if no condition had been inserted in the will.

(*c.*) An estate is bequeathed to A for life, and, if he marries, to the eldest son of B for life. B, at the date of the testator's death, had not had a son. The bequest over is void under section 92, and A is entitled to the estate during his life.

Bequest conditioned that it shall cease to have effect in case specified uncertain event shall happen or not happen.

121. A bequest may be made with the condition superadded that it shall cease to have effect in case a specified uncertain event shall happen, or in case a specified uncertain event shall not happen.

Illustrations.

(*a.*) An estate is bequeathed to A for his life, with a proviso that, in case he shall cut down a certain wood, the bequest shall cease to have any effect. A cuts down the wood; he loses his life-interest in the estate.

(*b.*) An estate is bequeathed to A, provided that, if the marries under the age of 25, without the consent of the executors named in the will, the estate shall cease to belong to him. A marries under 25 without the consent of the executors. The estate ceases to belong to him.

(*c.*) An estate is bequeathed to A provided that, if he shall not go to England within three years after the testator's death his interest in the estate shall cease. A does not go to England within the time prescribed. His interest in the estate ceases.

(*d.*) An estate is bequeathed to A, with a proviso that, if she becomes a nun, she shall cease to have any interest in the estate. A becomes a nun. She loses her interest under the will.

(*e.*) A fund is bequeathed to A for life, and after his death to B, if B shall be then living, with a proviso that, if B shall become a nun, the bequest to her shall cease to have any effect. B becomes a nun in the life-time of A. She thereby loses her contingent interest in the fund.

Such condition must not be invalid under section 107.

122. In order that a condition that a bequest shall cease to have effect may be valid, it is necessary that the event to which it relates be one which could legally constitute the condition of a bequest as contemplated by the 107th section.

Result of legatee rendering impossible or indefinitely postponing act for which no time specified, and on non-performance of which subject-matter to go over.

123. Where a bequest is made with a condition superadded that unless the legatee shall perform a certain act, the subject matter of the bequest shall go to another person, or the bequest shall cease to have effect, but no time is specified for the performance of the act, if the legatee takes any step which renders impossible or indefinitely postpones the performance of the act required, the legacy shall go as if the legatee had died without performing such act.

Illustrations.

(*a*) A bequest is made to A with a proviso that, unless he enters the army, the legacy shall go over to B. A takes holy orders, and thereby renders it impossible that he should fulfil the condition. B is entitled to receive the legacy.

(*b*) A bequest is made to A, with a proviso that it shall cease to have any effect if he does not marry B's daughter. A marries a stranger, and thereby indefinitely postpones the fulfilment of the condition. The bequest ceases to have effect.

Performance of condition, precedent or subsequent, within specified time.

124. Where the will requires an act to be performed by the legatee within a specified time, either as a condition to be fulfilled before the legacy is enjoyed, or as a condition upon the non-fulfilment of which the subject-matter of the bequest is to go over to another person, or the bequest is to cease to have effect, the act must be performed within the time specified unless the performance of it be prevented by fraud, in which case such further time shall be allowed as shall be requisite to make up for the delay caused by such fraud.

Further time in case of fraud.

PART XVII.

OF BEQUESTS WITH DIRECTIONS AS TO APPLICATION OR ENJOYMENT.

Direction that funds be employed in particular manner following absolute bequest of same to or for benefit of any person.

125. Where a fund is bequeathed absolutely to or for the benefit of any person, but the will contains a direction that it shall be applied or enjoyed in a particular manner, the legatee shall be entitled to receive the fund as if the will had contained no such direction.

Illustrations.

A sum of money is bequeathed towards purchasing a country-residence for A, or to purchase an annuity for A, or to purchase a commission in the army for A, or to place A in any business. A chooses to receive the legacy in money. He is entitled to do so.

Direction that mode of enjoyment of absolute bequest is to be restricted, to secure specified benefit for legatee.

126. Where a testator absolutely bequeaths a fund, so as to sever it from his own estate, but directs that the mode of enjoyment of it by the legatee shall be restricted so as to secure a specified benefit for the legatee, if that benefit cannot be obtained for the legatee, the fund belongs to him as if the will had contained no such direction.

Illustrations.

(*a*) A bequeaths the residue of his property to be divided equally among his daughters, and directs that the shares of the daughters shall be settled upon themselves respectively for life, and be paid to their children after their death. All the daughters die unmarried. The representatives of each daughter are entitled to her share of the residue.

(*b*) A directs his trustees to raise a sum of money for his daughter, and he then directs that they shall invest the fund, and pay the income arising from it to her during her life, and divide the principal among her children after her death. The daughter dies without having ever had a child. Her representatives are entitled to the fund.

Bequest of fund for certain purposes, some of which cannot be fulfilled.

127. Where a testator does not absolutely bequeath a fund, so as to sever it from his own estate, but gives it for certain purposes, and part of those purposes cannot be fulfilled, the fund, or so much of it as has not been exhausted upon the objects contemplated by the will, remains a part of the estate of the testator.

Illustrations.

(*a*) A directs that his trustees shall invest a sum of money in a particular way, and shall pay the interest to his son for life, and, at his death, shall divide the principal among the children: the son dies without having ever had a child. The fund, after the son's death, belongs to the estate of the testator.

(b) A bequeaths the residue of his estate to be divided equally among his daughters, with a direction that they are to have the interest only during their lives, [and that at their decease the fund shall go to their children. The daughters have no children. The fund belongs to the estate of the testator.

PART XVIII.

Of Bequest to an Executor.

Legatee named as executor cannot take unless he shows intention to act as executor.

128. If a legacy is bequeathed to a person who is named an executor of the will, he shall not take the legacy unless he proves the will, or otherwise manifests an intention to act as executor.

Illustration.

A legacy is given to A, who is named an executor. A orders the funeral according to the directions contained in the will, and dies a few days after the testator, without having proved the will, A has manifested an attention to act as executor.

PART XIX.

Of Specific Legacies.

Specific legacy defined.

129. Where a testator bequeaths to any person a specified part of his property which is distinguished from all other parts of his property, the legacy is said to be specific.

Illustrations.

(a) A bequeaths to B—

"the diamond-ring presented to him by C:"
"his gold chain:"
"a certain bale of wood:"
"a certain piece of cloth:"
"all his household-goods, which shall be in or about his dwelling-house, in M Street, in Calcutta, at the time of his death:"
"the sum of 1,000 rupees in a certain chest:"
"the debt which B owes him."
"all his bills, bonds, and securities belonging to him, lying in his lodgings in Calcutta:"
"all his furniture in his house in Calcutta:"
"all his goods on board a certain ship then lying in the river Hugli:"
"2,000 rupees which he has in the hands of C:"
"the money due to him on the bond of D:"
"his mortgage on the Rampur factory:"
"one-half of the money owing to him on his mortgage of Rampur factory:"

"1,000 rupees, being part of a debt due to him from C:"
"his capital stock of 1,000*l.* in East India stock:"
"his promissory notes of the Government of India, for 10,000 rupees, in their four per cent loan:"
"all such sums of money as his executors may, after his death, receive in respect of the debt due to him from the insolvent firm of D and company:"
"all the wine which he may have in his cellar at the time of his death:"
"such of his horses as B may select:"
"all his shares in the Bank of Bengal:"
"all the shares in the Bank of Bengal which he may possess at the time of his death:"
"all the money which he has in the 5½ per cent. loan of the Government of India:"
"all the Government securities he shall be entitled to at the time of his decease."

Each of these legacies is specific.

(*b.*) A, having Government promissory notes for 10,000 rupees, bequeaths to his executors "Government promissory notes for 10,000 rupees in trust to sell" for the benefit of B.

The legacy is specific.

(*c.*) A having property at Benares, and also in other places, bequeaths to B all his property at Benares.

The legacy is specific.

(*d.*) A bequeaths to B—
his house in Calcutta:
his zamindari of Rampur:
his taluq of Ramnagar:
his lease of the indigo-factory of Salkya:
an annuity of 500 rupees out of the rents of his zamindari of W.

A directs his zamindari of X. to be sold, and the proceeds to be invested for the benefit of B.

Each of these bequests is specific.

(*e.*) A, by his will, charges his zamindari of Y with an annuity of 1,000 rupees to C during his life, and subject to this charge he bequeaths the zamindari to D.

Each of these bequests is specific.

(*f.*) A bequeaths a sum of money—
to buy a house in Calcutta for B:
to buy an estate in zilla Faridpur for B:
to buy a diamond-ring for B:
to buy a horse for B:
to be invested in shares in the Bank of Bengal for B:
to be invested in Government securities for B:

A bequeaths to B—
"a diamond-ring:"
"a horse:"
"10,000 rupees worth of Government securities:"

"an annuity of 500 rupees :"
"2,000 rupees to be paid in cash :"
"so much money as will produce 5,000 rupees four per cent. Government securities :"

These bequests are not specific.

(*g*.) A having property in England and property in India, bequeaths a legacy to B, and directs that it shall be paid out of the property which he may leave in India. He also bequeaths a legacy to C, and directs that it shall be paid out of the property which he may leave in England.

No one of these legacies is specific.

Bequest of sum certain where stocks, &c., in which invested are described.

130. Where a sum certain is bequeathed, the legacy is not specific merely because the stocks, funds or securities in which it is invested, are described in the will.

Illustration.

A bequeaths to B—
"10,000 rupees of his funded property :"
"10,000 rupees of his property now invested in shares of the East Indian Railway Company :"
"10,000 rupees, at present secured by mortgage of Rampur factory."

No one of these legacies is specific.

Bequest of stock where testator had, at date of will, equal or greater amount of stock of same kind.

131. Where a bequest is made, in general terms, of a certain amount of any kind of stock, the legacy is not specific merely because the testator was, at the date of his will, possessed of stock of the specified kind, to an equal or greater amount than the amount bequeathed.

Illustration.

A bequeaths to B 5,000 rupees five per cent. Government securities. A had, at the date of the will, five per cent. Government securities for 5,000 rupees.

The legacy is not specific.

Bequest of money where not payable until part of testator's property disposed of in certain way.

132. A money-legacy is not specific merely because the will directs its payment to be postponed until some part of the property of the testator shall have been reduced to a certain form, or remitted to a certain place.

Illustration.

A bequeaths to B 10,000 rupees, and directs that this legacy shall be paid as soon as A's property in India shall be realized in England.

The legacy is not specific.

When enumerated articles not deemed specifically bequeathed.

133. Where a will contains a bequest of the residue of the testator's property along with an enumeration of some items of property not previously bequeathed, the articles enumerated shall not be deemed to be specifically bequeathed.

134. Where property is specifically bequeathed to two or more persons in succession, it shall be retained in the form in which the testator left it, although it may be of such a nature that its value is continually decreasing.

Retention, in form, of specific bequest to several persons in succession.

Illustrations.

(*a*) A, having a lease of a house for a term of years, 15 of which were unexpired at the time of his death, has bequeathed the lease to B for his life, and, after B's death, to C. B is to enjoy the property as A left it, although, if B lives for 15 years, C can take nothing under the bequest.

(*b*) A having an annuity during the life of B, bequeaths it to C for his life, and after C's death to D. C is to enjoy the annuity as A left it, although, if B dies before D, D can take nothing under the bequest.

135. Where property comprised in a bequest to two or more persons in succession is not specifically bequeathed, it shall, in the absence of any direction to the contrary, be sold, and the proceeds of the sale shall be invested in such securities as the High Court may, by any general rule to be made from time to time, authorize or direct, and the fund thus constituted shall be enjoyed by the successive legatees according to the terms of the will.

Sale and investment of proceeds of property bequeathed to two or more persons in succession.

Illustration.

A, having a lease for a term of years, bequeaths "all his property" to B for life, and after B's death to C. The lease must be sold, and the proceeds invested as stated in the text, and the annual income arising from the fund is to be paid to B for life. At B's death the capital of the fund is to be paid to C.

Where deficiency of assets to pay legacies, specific legacy not to abate with general legacies.

136. If there be a deficiency of assets to pay legacies, a specific legacy is not liable to abate with the general legacies.

PART XX.

OF DEMONSTRATIVE LEGACIES.

137. Where a testator bequeaths a certain sum of money or a certain quantity of any other commodity, and refers to a particular fund or stock so as to constitute the same the primary fund or stock out of which payment is to be made, the legacy is said to be demonstrative.

Demonstrative legacy defined.

Explanation.—The distinction between a specific legacy and a demonstrative legacy consists in this, that, where specified property is given to the legatee, the legacy is specific:

where the legacy is directed to be paid out of a specified property, it is demonstrative.

Illustrations.

(*a*) A bequeaths to B 1,000 rupees, being part of a debt due to him from W. He also bequeaths to C 1,000 rupees, to be paid out of the debt due to him from W. The legacy to B is specific; the legacy to C is demonstrative.

(*b*) A bequeaths to B—

"ten bushels of the corn which shall grow in his field of Greenacre:"

"80 chests of the indigo which shall be made at his factory of Rampur:"

"10,000 rupees out of his five per cent. promissory notes of the Government of India:"

an annuity of 500 rupees "from his funded property:"

"1,000 rupees out of the sum of 2,000 rupees due to him by C:"

A bequeaths to B an annuity, and directs it to be paid out of the rents arising from his taluq of Ramnagar.

A bequeaths to B—

"10,000 rupees out of his estate at Ramnagar, or charges it on his estate at Ramnagar:"

"10,000 rupees, being his share of the capital embarked in a certain business."

Each of these bequests is demonstrative.

Order of payment when legacy directed to be paid out of fund the subject of specific legacy.

138. Where a portion of a fund is specifically bequeathed, and a legacy is directed to be paid out of the same fund, the portion specifically bequeathed shall first be paid to the legatee, and the demonstrative legacy shall be paid out of the residue of the fund, and, so far as the residue shall be deficient, out of the general assets of the testator.

Illustration.

A bequeaths to B 1,000 rupees, being part of a debt due to him from W. He also bequeaths to C 1,000 rupees to be paid out of the debt due to him from W. The debt due to A from W is only 1,500 rupees; of these 1,500 rupees, 1,000 rupees belong to B, and 500 rupees are to be paid to C. C is also to receive 500 rupees out of the general assets of the testator.

PART XXI.

Of Ademption of Legacies.

Ademption explained.

139. If anything which has been specifically bequeathed does not belong to the testator at the time of his death, or has been converted into property of a different kind, the legacy is adeemed; that is, it cannot take effect by reason of the subject-matter having been withdrawn from the operation of the will.

Illustrations.

(*a.*) A bequeaths to B—

"the diamond-ring presented to him by C:"
"his gold-chain:"
"a certain bale of wool:"
"a certain piece of cloth:"
"all his household-goods which shall be in or about his dwelling house in M. Street in Calcutta, at the time of his death,"

A, in his lifetime—

sells or gives away the ring:
converts the chain into a cup:
converts the wool into cloth:
makes the cloth into a garment:
takes another house into which he removes all his goods.

Each of these legacies is adeemed.

(*b.*) A bequeaths to B—

"the sum of 1,000 rupees in a certain chest:"
"all the horses in his stable."

At the death of A, no money is found in the chest, and no horses in the stable. The lagacies are adeemed.

(*c.*) A bequeaths to B certain bales of goods. A takes the goods with him on a voyage. The ship and goods are lost at sea, and A is drowned. The legacy is adeemed.

Non-ademption of demonstrative legacy.

140. A demonstrative legacy is not adeemed by reason that the property on which it is charged by the will does not exist at the time of the death of the testator, or has been converted into property of a different kind; but it shall, in such case, be paid out of the general assets of the testator.

Ademption of specific bequest of right to receive something from third party.

141. Where the thing specifically bequeathed is the right to receive something of value from a third party, and the testator himself receives it, the bequest is adeemed.

Illustrations.

(*a.*) A bequeaths to B—

"the debt which C owes him:"
"2,000 rupees which he has in the hands of D:"
"the money due to him on the bond of E:"
"his mortgage on the Rampur factory."

All these debts are extinguished in A's lifetime, some with and some without his consent. All the legacies are adeemed.

(*b.*) A bequeaths to B "his interest in certain policies of life assurance." A in his lifetime receives the amount of the policies. The legacy is adeemed.

Ademption *pro tanto* by testator's receipt of part of entire thing specifically bequeathed.

142. The receipt by the testator of a part of an entire thing specifically bequeathed, shall operate as an ademption of the legacy to the extent of the sum so received.

Illustration.

A bequeaths to B "the debt due to him by C." The debt amounts to 10,000 rupees. C pays to A 5,000 rupees, the one-half of the debt. The legacy is revoked by ademption so far as regards the 5,000 rupees received by A.

Ademption *pro tanto* by testator's receipt of portion of entire fund of which portion has been specifically bequeathed.

143. If a portion of an entire fund or stock be specifically bequeathed, the receipt by the testator of a portion of the fund or stock shall operate as an ademption only to the extent of the amount so received; and the residue of the fund or stock shall be applicable to the discharge of the specific legacy.

Illustration.

A bequeaths to B one-half of the sum of 10,000 rupees due to him from W. A in his lifetime receives 6,000 rupees, part of the 10,000 rupees. The 4,000 rupees which are due from W to A at the time of his death belong to B under the specific bequest.

Order of payment where portion of fund specifically bequeathed to one legatee, and legacy charged on same fund to another, and testator having received portion of that fund, remainder insufficient to pay both legacies.

144. Where a portion of a fund is specifically bequeathed to one legatee, and a legacy charged on the same fund is bequeathed to another legatee, if the testator receives a portion of that fund, and the remainder of the fund is insufficient to pay both the specific and the demonstrative legacy, the specific legacy shall be paid first, and the residue (if any) of the fund shall be applied, so far as it will extend, in payment of the demonstrative legacy, and the rest of the demonstrative legacy shall be paid out of the general assets of the testator.

Illustration.

A bequeaths to B 1,000 rupees, part of the debt of 2,000 rupees due to him from W. He also bequeaths to C 1,000 rupees to be paid out of the debt due to him from W. A afterwards receives 500 rupees part of that debt, and dies leaving only 1,500 rupees due to him from W. Of these 1,500 rupees; 1,000 rupees belong to B, and 500 rupees are to be paid to C. C is also to receive 500 rupees out of the general assets of the testator.

Ademption where stock specifically bequeathed does not exist at testator's death.

145. Where stock, which has been specifically bequeathed, does not exist at the testator's death, the legacy is adeemed.

Illustration.

A bequeaths to B—

"his capital stock of 1,000*l.* in East India Stock:"

"his promissory notes of the Government of India for 10,000 rupees in their four per cent. loan."

A sells the stock and the notes. The legacies are adeemed.

Ademption *pro tanto* where stock, specifically bequeathed, exists in part only at testator's death.

146. Where stock, which has been specifically bequeathed, does only in part exist at the testator's death, the legacy is adeemed, so far as regards that part of the stock which has ceased to exist.

Illustration.

A bequeaths to B "his 10,000 rupees in the 5½ per cent. loan of the Government of India." A sells one-half of his 10,000 rupees in the loan in question. One-half of the legacy is adeemed.

Non-ademption of specific bequest of goods described as connected with certain place, by reason of removal.

147. A specific bequest of goods under a description connecting them with a certain place is not adeemed by reason that they have been removed from such place from any temporary cause, or by fraud, or without the knowledge or sanction of the testator.

Illustrations.

A bequeaths to B "all his household goods which shall be in or about his dwelling-house in Calcutta at the time of his death." The goods are removed from the house to save them from fire. A dies before they are brought back.

A bequeaths to B "all his household goods which shall be in or about his dwelling-house in Calcutta at the time of his death." During A's absence upon a journey, the whole of the goods are removed from the house. A dies without having sanctioned their removal.

Neither of these legacies is adeemed.

When removal of things bequeathed does not constitute ademption.

148. The removal of the thing bequeathed from the place in which it is stated in the will to be situated does not constitute an ademption, where the place is only referred to in order to complete the description of what the testator meant to bequeath.

Illustrations.

A bequeaths to B all the bills, bonds, and other securities for money belonging to him, then lying in his lodgings in Calcutta. At the time of his death, these effects had been removed from his lodgings in Calcutta.

A bequeaths to B all his furniture than in his house in Calcutta. The testator has a house at Calcutta and another at Chinsurah, in which he lives alternately, being possessed of one set of furniture only, which he removes with himself to each house. At the time of his death, the furniture is in the house at Chinsurah.

A bequeaths to B all his goods on board a certain ship then lying in the river Hugli. The goods are removed by A's directions to a warehouse, in which they remain at the time of A's death.

No one of these legacies is revoked by ademption.

When thing bequeathed is a valuable to be received by testator from third person; and testator himself or his representative receives it.

149. Where the thing bequeathed is not the right to receive something of value from a third person, but the money or other commodity which shall be received from the third person by the testator himself or by his representatives, the receipt of such sum of money or other commodity by the testator shall not constitute an ademption;

but, if he mixes it up with a general mass of his property, the legacy is adeemed.

Illustration.

A bequeaths to B whatever sum may be received from his claim on C. A receives the whole of his claim on C, and sets it apart from the general mass of his property. The legacy is not adeemed.

Change by operation of law of subject of specific bequest between date of will and testator's death.

150. Where a thing specifically bequeathed undergoes a change between the date of the will and the testator's death, and the change takes place by operation of law, or in the course of execution of the provisions of any legal instrument under which the thing bequeathed was held, the legacy is not adeemed by reason of such change.

Illustration.

A bequeaths to B "all the money which he has in the $5\frac{1}{2}$ per cent. loan of the Government of India." The securities for the $5\frac{1}{2}$ per cent. loan are converted during A's lifetime into five per cent. stock.

A bequeaths to B the sum of 2,000*l.* invested in Consols in the names of trustees for A. The sum of 2,000*l.* is transferred by the trustees into A's own name.

A bequeaths to B the sum of 10,000 rupees in promissory notes of the Government of India, which he has power, under his marriage settlement, to dispose of by will. Afterwards, in A's lifetime, the fund is converted into Consols by virtue of an authority contained in the settlement.

No one of these legacies has been adeemed.

151. Where a thing specifically bequeathed undergoes a change between the date of the will and the testator's death, and the change takes place without the knowledge or sanction of the testator, the legacy is not adeemed.

Change of subject without testator's knowledge.

Illustration.

A bequaths to B "all his three per cent. Consols." The Consols are without A's knowledge, sold by his agent, and the proceeds converted into East India Stock. This legacy is not adeemed.

152. Where stock, which has been specifically bequeathed, is lent to a third party on condition that it shall be replaced and it is replaced accordingly, the legacy is not adeemed.

Stock specifically bequeathed, lent to third party on condition that it be replaced.

153. Where stock specifically bequeathed is sold, and an equal quantity of the same stock is afterwards purchased, and belongs to the testator at his death, the legacy is not adeemed.

Stock specifically bequeathed sold but replaced, and belonging to testator at his death.

PART XII.

OF THE PAYMENT OF LIABILITIES IN RESPECT OF THE SUBJECT OF A BEQUEST.

154. Where property specifically bequeathed is subject, at the death of the testator, to any pledge, lien, or incumbrance, created by the testator himself, or by any person under whom he claims, then, unless a contrary intention appears by the will, the legatee, if he accepts the bequest, shall accept it subject to such pledge or incumbrance, and shall (as between himself and the testator's estate) be liable to make good the amount of such pledge or incumbrance.

Non-liability of executor to exonerate specific legatees.

A contrary intention shall not be inferred from any direction which the will may contain for the payment of the testator's debts generally.

Explanation.—A periodical payment in the nature of land-revenue or in the nature of rent is not such an incumbrance as is contemplated by this section.

Illustrations.

(*a.*) A bequeaths to B the diamond-ring given him by C. At A's death the ring is held in pawn by D, to whom it has been pledged by A. It is the duty of A's executors, if the state of the testator's assets will allow them, to allow B to redeem the ring.

(*b*) A bequeaths to B a zamindari, which at A's death, is subject to a mortgage for 10,000 rupees, and the whole of the principal sum, together with interest to the amount of 1,000 rupees, is due, at A's death. B, if he accepts the bequest, accepts it subject to this charge, and is liable, as between himself and A's estate, to pay the sum of 11,000 rupees thus due.

Completion of testator's title to things bequeathed to be at cost of his estate.

155. Where anything is to be done to complete the testator's title to the thing bequeathed it is to be done at the cost of the testator's estate.

Illustrations.

(*a*.) A, having contracted in general terms for the purchase of a piece of land at a certain price, bequeaths it to B, and dies before he has paid the purchase-money. The purchase-money must be made good out of A's assets.

(*b*.) A, having contracted for the purchase of a piece of land for a certain sum of money, one-half of which is to be paid down, and the other half secured by mortgage of the land, bequeaths it to B. and dies before he has paid or secured any part of the purchase-money. One-half of the purchase-money must be paid out of A's assets.

Exoneration of legatee's immoveable property for which land-revenue or rent payable periodically.

156. Where there is a bequest of any interest in immoveable property, in respect of which payment in the nature of land-revenue, or in the nature of rent, has to be made periodically, the estate of the testator shall (as between such estate and the legatee) make good such payments or a proportion of them up to the day of his death.

Illustration.

A bequeaths to B a house, in respect of which 365 rupees are payable annually by way of rent. A pays his rent at the usual time, and dies 25 days after. A's estate shall make good 25 rupees in respect of the rent.

Exoneration of specific legatee's stock in joint-stock company.

157. In the absence of any direction in the will where there is a specific bequest of stock in a joint-stock company, if any call or other payment is due from the testator at the time of his death in respect of such stock, such call or payment shall, as between the testator's estate and the legatee, be borne by such estate;

but, if any call or other payment shall, after the testator's death, become due in respect of such stock the same shall, as between the testator's estate and the legatee, be borne by the legatee if he accept the bequest.

Illustrations.

(*a*.) A bequeathed to B his shares in a certain railway. At A's death there was due from him the sum of 5*l*. in respect of each share, being the amount of a call which had been duly made, and the sum of 5*s*. in respect of each share, being the amount of interest which had accrued due in respect of the call. These payments must be borne by A's estate.

(*b.*) A has agreed to take 50 shares in an intended joint-stock company, and has contracted to pay up 5*l.* in respect of each share which sum must be paid before his title to the shares can be completed. A bequeaths these shares to B. The estate of A must make good the payments which were necessary to complete A's title.

(*c.*) A bequeaths to B his shares in a certain railway. B accepts the legacy. After A's death, a call is made in respect of the shares. B must pay the call.

(*d.*) A bequeaths to B his shares in a joint stock company. B accepts the bequest. Afterwards the affairs of the company are wound up, and each shareholder is called upon for contribution. The amount of the contribution must be borne by the legatee.

(*e.*) A is the owner of ten shares in a railway company. At a meeting held during his life-time a call is made of 3*l.* per share payable by three instalments A bequeaths his shares to B, and dies between the day fixed for the payment of the first and the day fixed for the payment of the second instalment, and without having paid the first instalment. A's estate must pay the first instalment, and B, if he accepts the legacy, must pay the remaining instalments.

PART XXIII.

OF BEQUESTS OF THINGS DESCRIBED IN GENERAL TERMS.

Bequest of thing described in general terms.

158. If there be a bequest of something described in general terms, the executor must purchase for the legatee what may reasonably be considered to answer the description.

Illustrations.

(*a*) A bequeaths to B *a* pair of carriage-horses, or *a* diamond-ring. The executor must provide the legatee with such articles if the state of the assets will allow it.

(*b*) A bequeaths to B "his pair of carriage-horses." A had no carriage-horses at the time of his death. The legacy fails.

PART XXIV.

OF BEQUESTS OF THE INTEREST OR PRODUCE OF A FUND.

Bequest of interest or produce of fund.

159. Where the interest or produce of a fund is bequeathed to any person, and the will affords no indication of an intention that the enjoyment of the bequest should be of limited duration, the principal as well as the interest shall belong to the legatee.

Illustrations.

(*a*) A bequeaths to B the interest of his five per cent. promissory notes of the Government of India. There is no other clause in the will affecting those securities. B is entitled to A's five per cent. promissory notes of the Government of India.

(*b*) A bequeaths the interest of his 5½ per cent. promissory notes of the Government of India to B for his life, and after his death to C. B is entitle to the interest of the notes during his life; and C is entitled to the notes upon B's death.

(*c*) A bequeaths to B the rents of his lands at X. B is entitled to the lands.

PART XXV.

OF BEQUESTS OF ANNUITIES.

Annuity created by will payable for life only unless contrary intention appears by will.

160. Where an annuity is created by will, the legatee is entitled to receive it for his life only, unless a contrary intention appears by the will. And this rule shall not be varied by the circumstance that the annuity is directed to be paid out of the property generally, or that a sum of money is bequeathed to be invested in the purchase of it.

Illustrations.

(*a*) A bequeaths to B 500 rupees a year. B is entitled, during his life, to receive the annual sum of 500 rupees.

(*b*) A bequeaths to B the sum of 500 rupees monthly. B is entitled during his life to receive the sum of 500 rupees every month.

(*c*) A bequeaths an annuity of 500 rupees to B for life, and on B's death to C. B is entitled to an annuity of 500 rupees during his life. C, if he survives B, is entitled to an annuity of 500 rupees from B's death until his own death.

Period of vesting where will directs that annuity be provided out of proceeds of property, or out of property generally, or where money bequeathed to be invested in purchase of annuity.

161. Where the will directs that an annuity shall be provided for any person out of the proceeds of property, or out of property generally, or where money is bequeathed to be invested in the purchase of any annuity for any person on the testator's death, the legacy vests in interest in the legatee, and he is entitled, at his option, to have an annuity purchased for him, or to receive the money appropriated for that purpose by the will.

Illustrations.

(*a.*) A by his will directs that his executors shall, out of his property, purchase an annuity of 1,000 rupees for B. B. is entitled, at his option, to have an annuity of 1,000 rupees for his life purchased for him, or to receive such a sum as will be sufficient for the purchase of such an annuity.

(b) A bequeaths a fund to B for his life, and directs that after B's death it shall be laid out in the purchase of an annuity for C. B and C survive the testator. C dies in B's lifetime. On B's death the fund belongs to the representative of C.

Abatement of annuity.

162. Where an annuity is bequeathed, but the assets of the testator are not sufficient to pay all the legacies given by the will, the annuity shall abate in the same proportion as the other pecuniary legacies given by the will.

Where gift of annuity and residuary gift, whole annuity to be first satisfied.

163. Where there is a gift of an annuity and a residuary gift, the whole of the annuity is to be satisfied before any part of the residue is paid to the residuary legatee, and, if necessary, the capital of the testator's estate shall be applied for that purpose.

PART XXVI.

Of Legacies to Creditors and Portioners.

Creditor *primâ facie* entitled to legacy as well as debt.

164. Where a debtor bequeaths a legacy to his creditor, and it does not appear from the will that the legacy is meant as a satisfaction of the debt, the creditor shall be entitled to the legacy as well as to the amount of the debt.

Child *primâ facie* entitled to legacy as well as portion.

165 Where a parent, who is under obligation by contract to provide a portion for a child, fails to do so, and afterwards bequeaths a legacy to the child, and does not intimate by his will that the legacy is meant as a satisfaction of the portion, the child shall be entitled to receive the legacy as well as the portion.

Illustration.

A, by articles entered into in contemplation of his marriage with B, covenanted that he would pay to each of the daughters of the intended marriage a portion of 20,000 rupees on her marriage. This covenant having been broken, A bequeaths 20,000 rupees to each of the married daughters of himself and B. The legatees are entitled to the benefit of this bequest in addition to their portions

No ademption by subsequent provision for legatee.

166. No bequest shall be wholly or partially adeemed by a subsequent provision made by settlement or otherwise for the legatee.

Illustrations.

(a) A bequeaths 20,000 rupees to his son B. He afterwards gives to B the sum of 20,000 rupees. The legacy is not thereby adeemed.

(b) A bequeaths 40,000 rupees to B, his orphan niece, whom he had brought up from her infancy. Afterwards, on the occasion of B's marriage, A settles upon her the sum of 30,000 rupees. The legacy is not thereby diminished.

PART XXVII.

OF ELECTION.

167. Where a man, by his will, professes to dispose of something which he has no right to dispose of, the person to whom the thing belongs shall elect either to confirm such disposition or to dissent from it, and, in the latter case, he shall give up any benefits which may have been provided for him by the will.

Circumstances in which election takes place.

168. The interest so relinquished shall devolve as if it had not been disposed of by the will in favour of the legatee, subject, nevertheless, to the charge of making good to the disappointed legatee the amount or value of the gift attempted to be given to him by will.

Devolution of interest relinquished by owner.

169. This rule will apply whether the testator does or does not believe that which he professes to dispose of by his will to be his own.

Testator's belief as to his ownership immaterial.

Illustrations.

(*a*) The farm of Sultanpur was the property of C. A bequeathed it to B, giving a legacy of 1,000 rupees to C. C has elected to retain his farm of Sultanpur, which is worth 800 rupees. C forfeits his legacy of 1,000 rupees of which 800 rupees goes to B, and the remaining 200 rupees falls into the residuary bequest, or devolves according to the rules of intestate succession, as the case may be.

(*b*) A bequeaths an estate to B in case B's elder brother (who is married and has children) shall leave no issue living at his death. A also bequeaths to C a jewel, which belongs to B. B must elect to give up the jewel or to lose the estate.

(*c*) A bequeaths to B 1,000 rupees, and to C an estate which will, under a settlement, belong to B if his elder brother (who is married and has children) shall leave no issue living at his death. B must elect to give up the estate, or to lose the legacy.

(*d*) A, a person of the age of 18, domiciled in British India, but owning real property in England, to which C is heir-at-law, bequeaths a legacy to C, and, subject thereto, devises and bequeaths to B "all his property whatsoever and wheresoever," and dies under 21. The real property in England does not pass by the will. C may claim his legacy without giving up the real property in England.

170. A bequest for a man's benefit is, for the purpose of election, the same thing as a bequest made to himself.

Bequest for man's benefit how regarded for purpose of election.

Illustration.

The farm of Sultanpur Khurd, being the property of B, A bequeathed it to C; and bequeathed another farm, called Sultanpur Buzurg, to his own executors, with a direction that it should be sold, and the proceeds applied in payment of B's debts. B must elect whether he will abide by the will, or keep his farm of Sultanpur Khurd in opposition to it.

171. A person taking no benefit directly under the will but deriving a benefit under it indirectly, is not put to his election.

Person deriving benefit indirectly not put to election.

Illustration.

The lands of Sultanpur are settled upon C for life, and after his death, upon D, his only child. A bequeaths the lands of Sultanpur to B, and 1,000 rupees to C. C dies intestate shortly after the testator, and without having made any election. D takes out administration to C, and as administrator elects on behalf of C's estate to take under the will. In that capacity he receives the legacy of 1,000 rupees, and accounts to B for the rents of the lands of Sultanpur which accrued after the death of the testator, and before the death of C. In his individual character he retains the lands of Sultanpur in opposition to the will.

172. A person who in his individual capacity takes a benefit under the will, may, in another character, elect to take in opposition to the will.

Person taking in individual capacity under will may, in other character, elect to take in opposition.

Illustration.

The estate of Sultanpur is settled upon A for life, and after his death upon B. A leaves the estate of Sultanpur to D, and 2,000 rupees to B, and 1,000 rupees to C, who is B's only child. B dies intestate, shortly after the testator, without having made any election. C takes out administration to B, and as administrator elects to keep the estate of Sultanpur in opposition to the will, and to relinquish the legacy of 2,000 rupees. C may do this, and yet claim his legacy of 1,000 rupees under the will.

Exception to the six last rules.—Where a particular gift is expressed in the will to be in lieu of something belonging to the legatee, which is also in terms disposed of by the will, if the legatee claims that thing, he must relinquish the particular gift, but he is not bound to relinquish any other benefit given to him by the will.

Illustration.

Under A's marriage-settlement his wife is entitled, if she survives him, to the enjoyment of the estate of Sultanpur during her life. A by his will bequeaths to his wife an annuity of 200*l.* during her life, in lieu of her interest in the estate of Sultanpur, which estate he bequeaths to his son. He also gives his wife a legacy of 1,000*l.* The widow elects to take what she is entitled to under the settlement. She is bound to relinquish the annuity, but not the legacy of 1,000*l.*

173. Acceptance of a benefit given by the will constitutes an election by the legatee to take under the will, if he has knowledge of his right to elect, and of those circumstances which would influence the judgment of a reasonable man in making an election, or if he waives inquiry into the circumstances.

When a acceptance of benefit given by will constitutes election to take under will.

Illustrations.

(*a.*) A is owner of an estate called Sultanpur Khurd, and has a life-interest in another estate called Sultanpur Buzurg, to which, upon his death, his son B will be absolutely entitled. The will of A gives the estate of Sultanpur Khurd to B, and the estate of Sultanpur Buzurg to C. B, in ignorance of his own right to the estate of Sultanpur Buzurg, allows C to take possession of it, and enters into possession of the estate of Sutanpur Khurd. B has not confirmed the bequest of Sultanpur Buzurg to C.

(*b.*) B, the eldest son of A, is the possessor of an estate called Sultanpur. A bequeaths Sultanpur to C, and to B the residue of A's property. B, having been informed by A's executors that the residue will amount to 5,000 rupees allows C to take possession of Sultanpur. He afterwards discovers that the residue does not amount to more than 500 rupees. B has not confirmed the bequest of the estate of Sultanpur to C.

Presumption arising from employment by legatee for two years.

174. Such knowledge or waiver of inquiry shall, in the absence of evidence to the contrary, be presumed if the legatee has enjoyed for two years the benefits provided for him by the will without doing any act to express dissent.

Confirmation of bequest by act of legatee.

175. Such knowledge or waiver of inquiry may be inferred from any act of the legatee which renders it impossible to place the persons interested in the subject matter of the bequest in the same condition as if such act had not been done.

Illustrations.

A bequeaths to B estate to which C is entitled, and to C a coal-mine. C takes possession of the mine, and exhausts it. He has thereby confirmed the bequest of the estate to B.

When testator's representatives may call upon legatee to elect.

176. If the legatee shall not, within one year after the death of the testator, signify to the testator's representatives his intention to confirm or to dissent from the will, the representatives shall, upon the expiration of that period, require him to make his election;

Effect of non-compliance.

and if he does not comply with such requisition within a reasonable time after he has received it, he shall be deemed to have elected to confirm the will.

Postponement of election in case of disability.

177. In case of disability, the election shall be postponed until the disability ceases, or until the election shall be made by some competent authority.

PART XXVIII.

OF GIFTS IN CONTEMPLATION OF DEATH.

178. A man may dispose, by gift made in contemplation of death, of any moveable property which he could dispose of by will.

Property transferable by gift made in contemplation of death.

A gift is said to be made in contemplation of death where a man, who is ill and expects to die shortly of his illness, delivers to another the possession of any moveable property to keep as a gift in case the donor shall die of that illness.

When gift said to be made in contemplation of death.

Such a gift may be resumed by the giver.

Such gift resumable.

It does not take effect if he recovers from the illness during which it was made; nor if he survives the person to whom it was made.

When it fails.

Illustrations.

(*a*.) A, being ill and in expectation of death, delivers to B to be retained by him in cases of A's death—

a watch:
a bond granted by C to A:
a bank-note:
a promissory note of the Government of India endorsed in blank:
a bill of exchange endorsed in blank:
certain mortgage-deeds.

A dies of the illness during which he delivered these articles.
B is entitled to

the watch:
the debt secured by C's bond:
the bank-note:
the promissory note of the Government of India:
the bill of exchange:
the money secured by the mortgage-deeds.

(*b*.) A, being ill, and in expectation of death, delivers to B the key of a trunk or the key of a warehouse in which goods of bulk belonging to A are deposited, with the intention of giving him the control over the contents of the trunk, or over the deposited goods, and desires him to keep them in case of A's death. A dies of the illness during which he delivered these articles. B is entitled to the trunk and its contents, or to A's goods of bulk in the warehouse.

(*c*.) A, being ill, and in expectation of death, puts aside certain articles in separate parcels, and marks upon the parcels respectively the names of B and C. The parcels are not delivered during the life of A. A dies of the illness during which he set aside the parcels. B and C are not entitled to the contents of the parcels.

PART XXIX.

Of Grant of Probate and Letters of Administration.

Character and property of executor or administrator as such.

179. The executor or administrator, as the case may be, of a deceased person, is his legal representative for all purposes, and all the property of the deceased person vests in him as such.

Administration with copy annexed of authenticated copy of will proved abroad.

180. When a will has been proved and deposited in a Court of competent jurisdiction, situated beyond the limits of the province, whether in the British dominions or in a foreign country, and a properly authenticated copy of the will is produced, letters of administration may be granted with a copy of such copy annexed.

Probate only to appointed executor.

181. Probate can be granted only to an executor appointed by the will.

Appointment express or implied.

182. The appointment may be express or by necessary implication.

Illustrations.

(*a*) A wills that C be his executor if B will not. B is appointed executor by implication.

(*b*) A gives a legacy to B and several legacies to other persons, among the rest to his daughter-in-law, C, and adds, "but should the within-named C be not living, I do constitute and appoint B my whole and sole executrix." C is appointed executrix by implication.

(*c*) A appoints several persons executors of his will and codicils, and his nephew residuary legatee, and in another codicil are these words: "I appoint my nephew my residuary legatee to discharge all lawful demands against my will and codicils, signed of different dates." The nephew is appointed an executor by implication.

Persons to whom probate cannot be granted.

183. Probate cannot be granted to any person who is a minor or is of unsound mind, nor to a married woman without the previous consent of her husband.

Grant of probate to several executors simultaneously or at different times.

184. When several executors are appointed, probate may be granted to them all simultaneously, or at different times.

Illustration.

A is an executor of B's will by express appointment, and C an executor of it by implication. Probate may be granted to A and C at the same time, or to A first and then to C, or to C first and then to A.

Separate probate of codicil discovered after grant of probate.

185. If a codicil be discovered after the grant of probate, a separate probate of that codicil may be granted to the executor, if it in no way repeals the appointment of executors made by the will.

If different executors are appointed by the codicil, the probate of the will must be revoked, and a new probate granted of the will and the codicil together.

Procedure when different executors appointed by codicil.

186. When probate has been granted to several executors, and one of them dies, the entire representation of the testator accrues to the surviving executor or executors.

Accrual of representation to surviving executor.

187. No right as executor or legatee can be established in any Court of Justice, unless a Court of competent jurisdiction within the province shall have granted probate of the will under which the right is claimed, or shall have granted letters of administration under section 180.

Right as executor or legatee when established.

188. Probate of a will when granted establishes the will from the death of the testator, and renders valid all intermediate acts of the executor, as such.

Effect of probate.

189. Letters of administration cannot be granted to any person who is a minor or is of unsound mind, nor to a married woman without the previous consent of her husband.

To whom administration may not be granted.

190. No right to any part of the property of a person who has died intestate can be established in any Court of Justice, unless letters of administration have first been granted by a Court of competent jurisdiction.

Right to intestate's property when established.

191. Letters of administration entitle the administrator to all rights belonging to the intestate as effectually as if the administration had been granted at the moment after his death.

Effect of letters of administration.

192. Letters of administration do not render valid any intermediate acts of the administrator tending to the diminution or damage of the intestat's estate.

Acts not validated by administration.

193 When a person appointed an executor has not renounced the executorship, letters of administration shall not be granted to any other person until a citation has been issued, calling upon the executor to accept or renounce his executorship;

Grant of administration where executor has not renounced.

except that, when one or more of several executors have proved a will, the Court may, on the death of the survivor of those who have proved, grant letters of administration without citing those who have not proved.

Exception.

Form and effect of renunciation of the executorship.

194 The renunciation may be made orally in the presence of the Judge or by a writing signed by the person renouncing, and when made, shall preclude him from ever thereafter applying for probate of the will appointing him executor.

Procedure where executor renounces or fails to accept within time limited.

195. If the executor renounce, or fail to accept, the executorship within the time limited for the acceptance or refusal thereof, the will may be proved, and letters of administration with a copy of the will annexed may be granted to the person who would be entitled to administration in case of intestacy.

Grant of administration to universal or residuary legatee.

196. When the deceased has made a will, but has not appointed an executor; or

when he has appointed an executor who is legally incapable, or refuses to act, or has died before the testator, or before he has proved the will; or

when the executor dies after having proved the will, but before he has administered all the estate of the deceased;

an universal or a residuary legatee may be admitted to prove the will, and letters of administration with the will annexed may be granted to him of the whole estate, or of so much thereof as may be unadministered.

Right to administration of representative of deceased residuary legatee.

197. When a residuary legatee who has a beneficial interest survives the testator, but dies before the estate has been fully administered, his representative has the same right to administration with the will annexed as such residuary legatee.

Grant of administration where no executor nor residuary legatee, nor representative of such legatee.

198. When there is no executor, and no residuary legatee or representative of a residuary legatee, or he declines or is incapable to act, or cannot be found, the person or persons who would be entitled to the administration of the estate of the deceased if he had died intestate, or any other legatee having a beneficial interest, or a creditor, may be admitted to prove the will, and letters of administration may be granted to him or them accordingly.

199. Letters of administration with the will annexed shall not be granted to any legatee other than an universal or a residuary legatee, until a citation has been issued and published in the manner hereinafter mentioned, calling on the next-of-kin to accept or refuse letters of administration.

Citation before grant of administration to legatee other than universal or residuary.

200. When the deceased has died intestate, those who are connected with him either by marriage or by consanguinity are entitled to obtain letters of administration of his estate and effects in the order, and according to the rules, hereinafter stated.

Order in which connections entitled to administer.

201. If the deceased has left a widow, administration shall be granted to the widow unless the Court shall see cause to exclude her, either on the ground of some personal disqualification, or because she has no interest in the estate of the deceased.

Administration to widow unless Court see cause to exclude her.

Illustrations.

(*a*) The widow is a lunatic, or has committed adultery, or has been barred by her marriage-settlement of all interest in her husband's estate; there is cause for excluding her from the administration.

(*b*) The widow has married again since the decease of her husband; this is not good cause for her exclusion.

202. If the Judge think proper, he may associate any person or persons with the widow in the administration who would be entitled solely to the administration if there were no widow.

Association with widow in administration.

203. If there be no widow, or if the Court see cause to exclude the widow, it shall commit the administration to the person or persons who would be beneficially entitled to the estate according to the rules for the distribution of an intestate's estate:

Administration where no widow, or widow excluded.

Provided that, when the mother of the deceased shall be one of the class of persons so entitled, she shall be solely entitled to administration.

Proviso.

204. Those who stand in equal degree of kindred to the deceased are equally entitled to administration.

Title of kindred to administration.

205. The husband, surviving his wife, has the same right of administration of her estate as the widow has in respect of the estate of her husband.

Right of widower to administration of wife's estate.

206. When there is no person connected with the deceased by marriage or consanguinity who is entitled to letters of administration, and willing to act, they may be granted to a creditor.

Grant of administration to creditor.

207. Where the deceased has left property in British India, letters of administration must be granted according to the foregoing rules, although he may have been a domiciled inhabitant of a country in which the law relating to testate and intestate succession differs from the law of British India.

Administration where property left in British India.

PART XXX.

OF LIMITED GRANTS.

(*a*)—*Grants limited in Duration.*

208. When the will has been lost or mislaid since the testator's death, or has been destroyed by wrong or accident, and not by any act of the testator and a copy or the draft of the will has been preserved, probate may be granted of such copy or draft, limited until the original or a properly authenticated copy of it be produced.

Probate of copy or draft of lost will.

209. When the will has been lost or destroyed, and no copy has been made, nor the draft preserved, probate may be granted of its contents, if they can be established by evidence.

Probate of contents of lost or destroyed will.

210. When the will is in the possession of a person residing out of the province in which application for probate is made, who has refused or neglected to deliver it up, but a copy has been transmitted to the executor, and it is necessary for the interests of the estate that probate should be granted without waiting for the arrival of the original, probate may be granted of the copy so transmitted limited until the will or an authenticated copy of it be produced.

Probate of copy where original exists.

211. Where no will of the deceased is forthcoming, but there is reason to believe that there is a will in existence, letters of administration may be granted, limited until the will or an authenticated copy of it be produced.

Administration until will produced.

(b) *Grants for the Use and Benefit of others having Right.*

Administration, with will annexed, to attorney of absent executor.

212. When any executor is absent from the province in which application is made, and there is no executor within the province willing to act letters of administration with the will annexed, may be granted to the attorney of the absent executor, for the use and benefit of his principal, limited until he shall obtain probate or letters of administration granted to himself.

Administration with will annexed, to attorney of absent person, who, if present, would be entitled to administer.

213. When any person to whom, if present, letters of administration with the will annexed, might be granted, is absent from the province, letters of administration with the will annexed, may be granted to his attorney, limited as above mentioned.

Administration to attorney of absent person entitled to administer in case of intestacy.

214. When a person entitled to administration in case of intestacy is absent from the province, and no person equally entitled is willing to act letters of administration may be granted to the attorney of the absent person, limited as before mentioned.

Administration during minority of sole executor or residuary legatee.

215. When a minor is sole executor or sole residuary legatee letters of administration with the will annexed, may be granted to the legal guardian of such minor, or to such other person as the Court shall think fit, until the minor shall have completed the age of eighteen years, at which period, and not before, probate of the will shall be granted to him.

Administration during minority of several executors or residuary legatees.

216. When there are two or more minor executors, and no executor who has attained majority, or two or more residuary legatees, and no residuary legatee who has attained majority, the grant shall be limited until one of them shall have completed the age of eighteen years.

Administration for use and benfit of lunatic *jus habens*.

217. If a sole executor or a sole universal or residuary legatee or a person who would be solely entitled to the estate of the intestate according to the rule for the distribution of intestates' estates, be a lunatic, letters of administration, with or without the will annexed, as the case may be, shall be granted to the person to whom the care of his estate has been committed by competent authority, or, if there be no such person, to such other person as the Court may think

fit to appoint, for the use and benefit of the lunatic until he shall become of sound mind.

Administration *pendente lite.*

218. Pending any suit touching the validity of the will of a deceased person, or for obtaining or revoking any probate or any grant of letters of administration, the Court may appoint an administrator of the estate of such deceased person, who shall have all the rights and powers of a general administrator, other than the right of distributing such estate, and every such administrator shall be subject to the immediate control of the Court, and shall act under its direction.

(*c.*)—*For Special Purposes.*

Probate limited to purpose specified in will.

219. If an executor be appointed for any limited purpose specified in the will, the probate shall be limited to that purpose, and, if he should appoint an attorney to take administration on his behalf, the letters of administration, with the will annexed, shall accordingly be limited.

Administration, with will annexed, limited to particular purpose.

220. If an executor appointed generally give an authority to an attorney to prove a will on his behalf, and the authority is limited to a particular purpose, the letters of administration, with the will annexed, shall be limited accordingly.

Administration limited to property in which person has beneficial interest.

221. Where a person dies, leaving property of which he was the sole or surviving trustee, or in which he had no beneficial interest on his own account, and leaves no general representatives, or one who is unable or unwilling to act as such, letters of administration, limited to such property, may be granted to the person beneficially interested in the property, or to some other person on his behalf.

Administration limited to suit.

222. When it is necessary that the representative of a person deceased be made a party to a pending suit, and the executor or person entitled to administration is unable or unwilling to act, letters of administration may be granted to the nominee of a party in such suit, limited for the purpose of representing the deceased in the said suit, or in any other cause or suit which may be commenced in the same or in any other Court betweeen the parties, or any other parties, touching the matters at issue in the said cause or suit, and until a final decree shall be made therein, and carried into complete execution.

223. If, at the expiration of twelve months from the date of any probate or letters of administration, the executor or administrator to whom the same has been granted is absent from the province within which the Court that has granted the probate or letters of administration is situate, it shall be lawful for such Court to grant, to any person whom it may think fit, letters of administration, limited to the purpose of becoming and being made a party to a suit to be brought against the executor or administrator, and carrying the decree which may be made therein into effect.

Administration limited to purpose of becoming party to suit to be brought against administrator.

224. In any case in which it may appear necessary for preserving the property of a deceased person, the Court within whose district any of the property is situate, may grant to any person whom such Court may think fit, letters of administration limited to the collection and preservation of the property of the deceased, and giving discharge for debts due to his estate, subject to the directions of the Court.

Administration limited to collection and preservation of deceased's property.

225. When a person has died intestate, or leaving a will of which there is no executor willing and competent to act, or where the executor shall at the time of the death of such person, be resident out of the province, and it shall appear to the Court to be necessary or convenient to appoint some person to administer the estate or any part thereof, other than the person who, under ordinary circumstances, would be entitled to a grant of administration, it shall be lawful for the Judge, in his discretion, having regard to consanguinity, amount of interest, the safety of the estate, and the probability that it will be properly administered, to appoint such person as he shall think fit to be administrator and in every such case letters of administration may be limited or not as the Judge shall think fit.

Appointment, as administrator, of person other than one who, under ordinary circumstances, would be entitled to administration.

(d.)—*Grants with Exception.*

226. Whenever the nature of the case requires that an exception be made, probate of a will, or letters of administration with the will annexed, shall be granted subject to such exception.

Probate or administration, with will annexed subject to exception,

227. Whenever the nature of the case requires that an exception be made, letters of administration shall be granted subject to such exception.

Administration with exception.

(e.)—Grants of the Rest.

228. Whenever a grant, with exception, of probate, or letters of administration, with or without the will annexed, has been made, the person entitled to probate or administration of the remainder or the deceased's estate may take a grant of probate or letters of administration, as the case may be, of the rest of the deceased's estate.

Probate or administration of rest.

(f.)—Grants of Effects unadministered.

229. If the executor to whom probate has been granted have died, leaving a part of the testator's estate unadministered, a new representative may be appointed for the purpose of administering such part of the estate.

Grant of effects unadministered.

230. In granting letters of administration of an estate not fully administered, the Court shall be guided by the same rules as apply to original grants, and shall grant letters of administration to those persons only to whom original grants might have been made.

Rules as to grants of effects unadministered.

231. When a limited grant has expired by efflux ion of time, or the happening of the event or contingency on which it was limited, and there is still some part of the deceased's estate unadministered, letters of administration shall be granted to those persons to whom original grants might have been made.

Administration when limited grant expired, and still some part of estate unadministered.

(g.)—Alteration in Grants.

232. Errors in names and descriptions, or in setting forth the time and place of the deceased's death, or the purpose in a limited grant, may be rectified by the Court, and the grant of probate or letters of administration may be altered and amended accordingly.

When errors may be rectified by Court.

233. If, after the grant of letters of administration with the will annexed, a codicil be discovered, it may be added to the grant on due proof and identification, and the grant altered and amended accordingly.

Procedure where codicil discovered after grant of administration with will annexed.

(h.)—Revocation of Grants.

234. The grant of probate or letters of administration may be revoked or annulled for just cause.

Revocation or annulment for just cause.

"Just cause."

Explanation.—Just cause is—

1*st*, that the proceedings to obtain the grant were defective in substance;

2*nd*, that the grant was obtained fraudulently by making a false suggestion, or by concealing from the Court something material to the case;

3*rd*, that the grant was obtained by means of an untrue allegation of a fact essential in point of law to justify the grant, though such allegation was made in ignorance or inadvertently;

4*th*, that the grant has become useless and inoperative through circumstances;

5*th*, that the person to whom the grant was made has wilfully and without reasonable cause omitted to exhibit an inventory or account in accordance with the provisions of Part XXXIV. of the Act, or has exhibited under that Part an inventory or account which is untrue in a material respect.

Illustrations.

(*a*) The Court by which the grant was made had no jurisdiction.

(*b*) The grant was made without citing parties who ought to have been cited.

(*c*) The will of which probate was obtained was forged or revoked.

(*d*) A obtained letters of administration to the estate of B, as his widow, but it has since transpired that she was never married to him.

(*e*) A has taken administration to the estate of B as if he had died intestate, but a will has since been discovered.

(*f*) Since probate was granted, a later will has been discovered.

(*g*) Since probate was granted, a codicil has been discovered, which revokes or adds to the appointment of executors under the will.

(*h*) The person to whom probate was, or letters of administration were, granted has subsequently become of unsound mind.

PART XXXI.

OF THE PRACTICE IN GRANTING AND REVOKING PROBATES AND LETTERS OF ADMINISTRATION.

Jurisdiction of District Judge in granting and revoking probates, &c.

235. The District Judge shall have jurisdiction in granting and revoking probates and letters of administration in all cases within his district.

Power to appoint Delegate of District Judge to deal with non-contentious cases.

235A. The High Court may, from time to time, appoint such judicial officers within any district as it thinks fit, to act for the District Judge as Delegates to grant probate and letters of administration in non-contentious cases, within such local limits as it may from time to time prescribe:

Persons so appointed shall be called "District Delegates."

District Judge's powers as to grant of probate and administration.

236. The District Judge shall have the like powers and authority in relation to the granting of probate and letters of administration, and all matters connected therewith, as are by law vested in him in relation to any civil suit or proceeding depending in his Court.

District Judge may order person to produce testamentary papers.

237. The District Judge may order any person to produce and bring into Court any paper or writing, being or purporting to be testamentary, which may be shown to be in the possession or under the control of such person;

and if it be not shown that any such paper or writing is in the possession or under the control of such person, but there is reason to believe that he has the knowledge of any such paper or writing, the Court may direct such person to attend for the purpose of being examined respecting the same;

and such person shall be bound to answer such questions as may be put to him by the Court, and, if so ordered, to produce and bring in such paper or writing, and shall be subject to the like punishment under the Indian Penal Code, in case of default in not attending, or in not answering such questions, or not bringing in such paper or writing, as he would have been subject to in case he had been a party to a suit, and had made such default,

and the costs of the proceeding shall be in the discretion of the Judge.

Proceedings of District Judge's Court in relation to probate and administration.

238. The proceedings of the Court of the District Judge in relation to the granting of probate and letters of administration shall, except as hereinafter otherwise provided, be regulated, so far as the circumstances of the case will admit, by the Code of Civil Procedure.

When and how District Judge to interfere for protection of property.

239. Until probate be granted of the will of a deceased person, or an administrator of his estate be constituted, the District Judge, within whose jurisdiction any part of the property of the deceased person is situate, is authorized and required to interfere for the protection of such property at the

instance of any person claiming to be interested therein, and in all other cases where the Judge considers that the property incurs any risk of loss or damage ; and for that purpose, if he shall see fit, to appoint an officer to take and keep possession of the property.

When probate or administration may be granted by District Judge.

240. Probate of the will or letters of administration to the estate of a deceased person may be granted by the District Judge under the seal of his Court, if it shall appear by a petition, verified as hereinafter mentioned, of the person applying for the same, that the testator or intestate, as the case may be, at the time of his decease, had a fixed place of abode, or any property, moveable or immoveable, within the jurisdiction of the Judge.

Disposal of application made to Judge of District in which deceased had no fixed abode.

241. When the application is made to the Judge of a District in which the deceased had no fixed abode at the time of his death, it shall be in the discretion of the Judge to refuse the application, if, in his judgment, it could be disposed of more justly or conveniently in another district, or, where the application is for letters of administration, to grant them absolutely or limited to the property within his own jurisdiction.

Probate and letters of administration may be granted by Delegate.

241A. Probate and letters of administration may, upon application for that purpose to any District Delegate, be granted by him in any case in which there is no contention, if it appears by petition (verified as hereinafter mentioned) that the testator or intestate, as the case may be, at the time of his death, resided within the jurisdiction of such Delegate.

Conclusiveness of probate or letters of administration.

242. Probate or letters of administration shall have effect over all the property and estate, moveable or immoveable, of the deceased, throughout the province in which the same is "or are" granted,

and shall be conclusive as to the representative title against all debtors of the deceased, and all persons holding property which belongs to him, and shall afford full indemnity to all debtors paying their debts, and all persons delivering up such property to the person to whom such probate or letters of administration shall have been granted :

Provided that probates and letters of administration granted by a High Court after the first day of April 1875 shall unless otherwise directed by the grant, have like effect throughout the whole of British India.

Effect of unlimited probates, &c., granted by High Court.

242A. Whenever a grant of probate or letters of administration is made by a High Court with such effect as last aforesaid, the Register, or such other officer as the High Court, making the grant appoints in this behalf, shall send to each of the other High Courts a certificate to the following effect:—

Transmission to other Courts of certificate by High Court granting probate, &c.

"I, *A. B.*, Registrar [*or as the case may be*] of the High Court of Judicature at [*or as the case may be*], hereby certify that, on the day of 187 , the High Court of Judicature at [*or as the case may be*], granted probate of the will [*or* letters of administration of the estate] or *C. D.* late of deceased, to *E. F.*, of , and *G. H.* of , and that such probate [*or* letters] has [*or* have] effect over all the property of the deceased throughout the whole of British India:"

and such certificate shall be filed by the High Court receiving the same.

243. The application for the probate or letters of administration, if made and verified in the manner hereinafter mentioned, shall be conclusive for the purpose of authorizing the grant of probate or administration;

Conclusiveness of application for probate or administration, if properly made and verified.

and no such grant shall be impeached by reason that the testator or intestate had no fixed place of abode, or no property within the district at the time of his death, unless by a proceeding to revoke the grant if obtained by a fraud upon the Court.

244. Application for probate shall be made by a petition distinctly written in English or in the language in ordinary use in proceedings before the Court in which the application is made, with the will annexed, and stating—

Petition for probate.

the time of the testator's death,

that the writing annexed is his last will and testament,

that it was duly executed,

the amount of assets which are likely to come to the petitioner's hands, and

that the petitioner is the executor named in the will;

and in addition to these particulars, when the application is to the District Judge, the petition shall further state that the deceased, at the time of his death, had his fixed place of abode, or had some property, moveable or immoveable, situate within the jurisdiction of the Judge;

and, when the application is to a District Delegate, the petition shall further state that the deceased, at the time of his death, resided within the jurisdiction of such Delegate.

In what cases translation of will to be annexed to petition.

245. In cases wherein the will is written in any language other than English, or than that in ordinary use in proceedings before the Court, there shall be a translation thereof annexed to the petition by a translator of the Court, if the language be one for which a translator is appointed; or, if the will be in any other language, then by any person competent to translate the same, in which case such translation shall be verified by that person in the following manner:—

Verification of translation by persons other than Court translator.

"I (*A. B.*) do declare that I read and perfectly understand the language and character of the original, and that the above is a true and accurate translation thereof."

Petition for letters of administrations.

246. Applications for letters of administration shall be made by petition distinctly written as aforesaid, and stating—

the time and place of the deceased's death,

the family or other relatives of the deceased, and their respective residences,

the right in which the petitioner claims,

that the deceased left some property within the jurisdiction of the District Judge or District Delegate, to whom the application is made, and

the amount of assets which are likely to come to the petitioner's hand's;

and, when the application is to a District Delegate, the petition shall further state that the deceased at the time of his death, resided within the jurisdiction of such Delegate.

Additional statements in petition for probate, &c.

246A. Every person applying to a High Court for probate of a will or letters of administration of an estate, intended to have effect throughout British India, shall state in his petition, in addition to the matters respectively required by section 244 and section 246 of this Act, that, to the best of his belief, no application has been made to any other High Court for a probate of the same will, or for letters of administration of the same estate, intended to have such effect as last aforesaid;

or, where any such application has been made, the High Court to which it was made, the person or persons by whom it was made, and the proceedings (if any) had thereon.

And the High Court, to which any application is made under the proviso to section 242 of this Act, may, if it think fit, reject the same.

Petition for probate or administration to be signed and verified.

247. The petition for probate or letters of administration shall, in all cases, be subscribed by the petitioner and his pleader (if any), and shall be verified by the petitioner in the following manner, or to the like effect:—

"I (*A. B.*), the petitioner in the above petition, declare that what is stated therein is true to the best of my information and belief."

Verification of petition for probate by one witness to will.

248. Where the application is for probate, the petition shall also be verified by at least one of the witness to the will (when procurable) in the manner or to the effect following:—

"I (*C. D.*), one of the witnesses to the last will and testament of the testator mentioned in the above petition, declare that I was present, and saw the said testator affix his signature (*or* mark) thereto (*as the case may be*) *or* that the said testator acknowledged the writing annexed to the above petition to be his last will and testament in my presence."

Punishment for false averment in petition or declaration.

249. If any petition or declaration which is hereby required to be verified shall contain any averment which the person marking the verification knows or believes to be false, such person shall be subject to punishment according to the provisions of the law for the time being in force for the punishment of giving or fabricating false evidence.

District Judge may examine petitioner in person.

250. In all cases it shall be lawful for the District Judge or District Delegate, if he shall think proper—

to examine the petitioner in person, upon oath or solemn affirmation, and also

require further evidence.

to require further evidence of the due execution of the will, or the right of the petitioner to the letters of administration, as the case may be, and to issue citations calling upon all persons claiming to have any interest in the estate of the deceased to come and see the proceedings before the grant of probate or letters of administration.

and issue citations to inspect proceedings.

The citation shall be fixed up in some conspicuous part of the Court-house, and also in the office of the Collector of the District, and otherwise published or made known in such manner as the Judge "or District Delegate" issuing the same may direct.

Publication of citation.

Caveats against grant of probate or administration.

251. Caveats against the grant of probate or administration may be lodged with the District Judge or a District Delegate;

and, immediately on any caveat being lodged with any District Delegate, he shall send a copy thereof to the District Judge;

and, immediately on a caveat being entered with the District Judge, a copy thereof shall be given to the District Delegate, if any, within whose jurisdiction it is alleged the deceased resided at the time of his death, and to any other Judge or District Delegate to whom it may appear to the District Judge expedient to transmit the same.

Form of caveat.

252. The caveat shall be to the following effect:—

"Let nothing be done in the matter of the estate of *A. B.*, late of , deceased, who died on the day of at , without notice to *C. D.*, of ."

253. No proceeding shall be taken on a petition for probate or letters of administration after a caveat against the grant thereof has been entered with the Judge "or officer" to whom the application has been made "or notice has been given of its entry with some other Delegate," until after such notice to the person by whom the same has been entered as the Court shall think reasonable.

After entry of caveat no proceeding taken on petition until after notice to caveator.

253A. A District Delegate shall not grant probate or letters of administration in any case in which there is contention as to the grant, or in which it otherwise appears to him that probate or letters of administration ought not to be granted in his Court.

District Delegate when not to grant probate or administrations.

Explanation.—By "contention" is understood the appearance of any one in person or by his recognized agent or by a pleader duly appointed to act on his behalf, to oppose the proceeding.

Power to transmit statement to District Judge in doubtful cases where no contention.

253B. In every case in which there is no contention, but it appears to the District Delegate doubtful whether the probate of letters of administration should or should not be granted, or when any question arises in relation to the grant, or application for the grant, of any probate or letters of administration, the District Delegate may, if he thinks proper, transmit a statement of the matter in question to the District Judge, who may direct the District Delegate to proceed in the matter of the application, according to such instructions as to the Judge may seem necessary, or may forbid any further proceeding by the District Delegate in relation to the matter of such application, leaving the party applying for the grant in question to make application to the Judge.

Procedure where there is contention, or District Delegate thinks probate or letters of administration should be refused in his Court.

253C. In every case in which there is contention, or the District Delegate is of opinion that the probate or letters of administration should be refused in his Court, the petition, with any documents that may have been filed therewith, shall be returned to the person by whom the application was made in order that the same may be presented to the District Judge; unless the District Delegate thinks it necessary, for the purposes of justice, to impound the same, which he is hereby authorized to do; and in that case the same shall be sent by him to the District Judge.

Grant of probate to be under seal of Court.

254. When it shall appear to the Judge "or District Delegate" that probate of a will should be granted, he will grant the same under the seal of his Court in manner following:—

Form of such grant.

"I, , Judge of the District of , [*or* Delegate appointed for granting probate or letters of administration in (*here insert the limits of the Delegate's jurisdiction*)], hereby make known that on the day of , in the year , the last will of , late of , a copy whereof is hereunto annexed, was proved and registered before me, and that administration of the property and credits of the said deceased, and in any way concerning his will, was granted to , the executor in the said will named he having undertaken to administer the same, and to make a full and true inventory of the said property and credits, and exhibit the same in this Court within six months from the date of this grant, or within such further time as the Court may from time to time appoint, and also to render to this Court a true account of the said property and credits within one year from the same date, or within such further time as the Court may from time to time appoint."

255. And, wherever it shall appear to the District Judge "or District Delegate" that letters of administration to the estate of a person deceased, with or without a copy of the will annexed, should be granted, he will grant the same under the seal of his Court in manner following :—

Grant of letters of administration to be under seal of Court.

"I, , Judge of the District of , [*or* Delegate appointed for granting probate or letters of administration in (*here insert the limits of the Delegate's jurisdiction*)], hereby make known that on the day of , letters of administration (with *or* without the will annexed, *as the case may be*), of the property and credits of , late of , deceased, were granted to , the father (*or as the case may be*) of the deceased he having undertaken to administer the same, and to make a full and true inventory of the said property and credits, and exhibit the same in this Court within six months from the date of this grant, or within such further time as the Court may from time to time appoint, and also to render to this Court a true account of the said property and credits within one year from the same date, or within such further time as the Court may from time to time appoint."

Form of such grant.

256. "Every person to whom any grant of letters of administration is committed" shall give a bond to the Judge of the District Court to enure for the benefit of the Judge for the time being, with one or more surety or sureties, engaging for the due collection, getting in, and administering the estate of the deceased, which bond shall be in such form as the Judge shall, from time to time, by any general or special order, direct.

Administration-bond.

257. The Court may, on application made by petition, and on being satisfied that the engagement of any such bond has not been kept,

Assignment of administration-bond.

and upon such terms as to security, or providing that the money received be paid into Court, or otherwise as the Court may think fit, assign the same to some person, his executors, or administrators,

who shall thereupon be entitled to sue on the said bond in his own name as if the same had been originally given to him instead of to the Judge of the Court, and shall be entitled to recover thereon, as trustee for all persons interested, the full amount recoverable in respect of any breach thereof.

Time for grant of probate and administration.

258. No probate of a will shall be granted until after the expiration of seven clear days, and no letters of administration shall be granted until after the expiration of fourteen clear days from the day of the testator or intestate's death.

Filing of original wills of which probate or administration, with will annexed, granted.

259. Every District Judge "or District Delegate" shall file and preserve all original wills of which probate or letters of administration, with the will annexed, may be granted by him among the records of his Court, until some public registry for wills is established;

and the Local Government shall make regulations for the preservation and inspection of the wills so filed as aforesaid.

Grantee of probate or administration alone to sue, &c., until same revoked.

260. After any grant of probate or letters of administration, no other than the person to whom the same shall have been granted, shall have power to sue or prosecute any suit, or otherwise act as representative of the deceased, throughout the province in which the same may have been granted, until such probate or letters of administration shall have been recalled or revoked.

Procedure in contentious cases.

261. In any case before the District Judge in which there is contention, the proceedings shall take, as nearly as may be, the form of a regular suit according to the provisions of the Code of Civil Procedure, in which the petitioner for probate or letters of administration, as the case may be, shall be the plaintiff, and the person who may have appeared as aforesaid to oppose the grant shall be the defendant.

Payment to executor or administrator before probate or administration revoked.

262. Where any probate is or letters of administration are revoked, all payments *bonâ fide* made to any executor or administrator under such probate or administration before the revocation, thereof shall, notwithstanding such revocation, be a legal discharge to the person making the same;

And the executor or administrator who shall have acted under any such revoked probate or administration may retain and reimburse himself in respect of any payments made by him, which the person to whom probate or letters of administration shall be afterwards granted might have lawfully made.

Right of such executor or administrator to recoup himself.

263. Every order made by a District Judge by virtue of the powers hereby conferred upon him, shall be subject to appeal to the High Court under the rules contained in the Code of Civil Procedure applicable to appeals.

Appeals from orders of District Judge.

264. The High Court shall have concurrent jurisdiction with the District Judge in the exercise of all the powers hereby conferred upon the District Judge.

Concurrent jurisdiction of High Court.

PART XXXII.

OF EXECUTORS OF THEIR OWN WRONG.

265. A person who intermeddles with the estate of the deceased, or does any other act which belongs to the office of executor, while there is no rightful executor or administrator in existence, thereby makes himself an executor of his own wrong.

Executor of his own wrong.

Exceptions.—First.—Intermeddling with the goods of the deceased for the purpose of preserving them, or providing for his funeral, or for the immediate necessities of his family or property, does not make an executor of his own wrong.

Second.—Dealing in the ordinary course of business with goods of the deceased received from another does not make an executor of his own wrong.

Illustrations.

(*a.*) A uses or gives away or sells some of the goods of the deceased, or takes them to satisfy his own debt or legacy, or receives payment of the debts of the deceased. He is an executor of his own wrong.

(*b.*) A, having been appointed agent by the deceased in his lifetime to collect his debts and sell his goods, continues to do so after he has become aware of his death. He is an executor of his own wrong in respect of acts done after he has become aware of the death of the deceased.

(*c.*) A sues as executor of the deceased, not being such. He is an executor of his own wrong.

266. When a person has so acted as to become an executor of his own wrong, he is answerable to the rightful executor or administrator, or to any creditor or legatee of the deceased, to the extent of the assets which may have come to his hands, after deducting payments made to the rightful executor or administrator, and payments made in a due course of administration.

Liability of executor of his own wrong.

PART XXXIII.

Of the Powers of an Executor or Administrator.

267. An executor or administrator has the same power to sue in respect of all causes of action that survive the deceased, and to distrain for all rents due to him at the time of his death, as the deceased had when living.

In respect of causes of action surviving deceased, and rents due at death.

268. All demands whatsoever, and all rights to prosecute or defend any action or special proceeding, existing in favour of or against a person at the time of his decease, survive to and against his executors or administrators; except causes of action for defamation, assault as defined in the Indian Penal Code, or other personal injuries not causing the death of the party; and except also cases where, after the death of the party, the relief sought could not be enjoyed, or granting it would be nugatory.

Demands and rights of action of or against deceased survive to and against executor or administrator.

Illustrations.

(*a.*) A collision takes place on a railway in consequence of some neglect or default of the officials, and a passenger is severely hurt, but not so as to cause death. He afterwards dies without having brought any action. The cause of action does not survive.

(*b.*) A sues for divorce. A dies. The cause of action does not survive to his representative.

269. An executor or administrator has power to dispose of the property of the deceased, either wholly or in part, in such manner as he may think fit.

Power of executor or administrator to dispose of property.

Illustrations.

(*a.*) The deceased has made a specific bequest of part of his property. The executor, not having assented to the bequest, sells the subject of it. The sale is valid.

(*b.*) The executor, in the exercise of his discretion, mortgages a part of the immoveable estate of the deceased. The mortgage is valid.

Purchase by executor or administrator of deceased's property.

270. If an executor or administrator purchases, either directly or indirectly, any part of the property of the deceased, the sale is voidable at the instance of any other person interested in the property sold.

Powers of several executors or administrators exerciseable by one.

271. When there are several executors or administrators, the powers of all may, in the absence of any direction to the contrary, be exercised by any one of them who has proved the will or taken out administration.

Illustrations.

(*a.*) One of several executors has power to release a debt due to the deceased.

(*b*.) One has power to surrender a lease.

(*c*.) One has power to sell the property of the deceased, moveable or immoveable.

(*d*.) One has power to assent to a legacy.

(*e*.) One has power to endorse a promissory note payable to the deceased.

(*f*.) The will appoints A, B, C, and D to be executors, and directs that two of them shall be a quorum. No act can be done by a single executor.

Survival of powers on death of one of several executors or administrators.

272. Upon the death of one or more of several executors or administrators, all the powers of the office become vested in the survivors or survivor.

Powers of administrator of effect unadministered.

273. The administrator of effects unadministered has, with respect to such effects, the same powers as the original executor or administrator.

Powers of administrator during minority.

274. An administrator during minority has all the powers of an ordinary administrator.

Powers of married executrix or administratrix.

275. When probate or letters of administration have been granted to a married woman, she has all the powers of an ordinary executor or administrator.

PART XXXIV.

OF THE DUTIES OF AN EXECUTOR OR ADMINISTRATOR.

276. It is the duty of an executor to perform the funeral of the deceased in a manner suitable to his condition, if he has left property sufficient for the purpose.

As to deceased's funeral.

277. (1) An executor or administrator shall, within six months from the grant of probate or letters of adminstration, or within such further time as the Court which granted the probate or letters may from time to time appoint, exhibit in that Court an inventory containing a full and true estimate of all the property in possession, and all the credits, and also all the debts owing by any person to which the executor or administrator is entitled in that character,

Inventory and account.

and shall in like manner, within one year from the grant, or within such further time as the said Court may from time to time appoint, exhibit an account of the estate, showing the assets which have come to his hands, and the manner in which they have been applied or disposed of.

(2) The High Court may from time to time prescribe the form in which an inventory or account under this section, is to be exhibited.

(3) If an executor or administrator, on being required by the Court to exhibit an inventory or account under this section, intentionally omits to comply with the requisition, he shall be deemed to have committed an offence under section 176 of the Indian Penal Code.

(4) The exhibition of an intentionally false inventory or account under this section shall be deemed to be an offence under section 193 of that Code.

277A. In all cases where "a grant has been made" of probate or letters of administration intended to have effect throughout the whole of British India, the executor or administrator to the effects of any person dying in British India and leaving property in more than one province shall include in the inventory of the effects of the deceased his moveable or immoveable property situate in each of the provinces;

Inventory to include property in any part of British India.

and the value of such property situate in the said provinces, respectively, shall be separately stated in such inventory;

and the probate or letters of administration shall be chargeable with a fee corresponding to the entire amount or value of the property affected thereby, wheresoever situate within British India.

As to property of, and debts owing to, deceased.

278. The executor or administrator shall collect, with reasonable diligence, the property of the deceased, and the debts that were due to him at the time of his death.

Expenses to be paid before all debts.

279. Funeral expenses to a reasonable amount, according to the degree and quality of the deceased, and death-bed charges, including fees for medical attendance, and board and lodging for one month previous to his death, are to be paid before all debts.

Expenses to be paid next after such expenses.

280. The expenses of obtaining probate or letters of administration, including the costs incurred for or in respect of any judicial proceedings that may be necessary for administering the estate, are to be paid next after the funeral expenses and death-bed charges.

Wages for certain services to be next paid, and then other debts.

281. Wages due for services rendered to the deceased within three months next preceeding his death by any labourer, artisan, or domestic servant, are next to be paid, and then the other debts of the deceased.

Save as aforesaid, all debts to be paid equally and rateably.

282. Save as aforesaid, no creditor is to have a right of priority over another, by reason that his debt is secured by an instrument under seal, or on any other account.

But the executor or administrator shall pay all such debts as he knows of, including his own, equally and rateably as far as the assets of the deceased will extend.

Application of moveable property to payment of debts where domicile not in British India.

283. If the domicile of the deceased was not in British India, the application of his moveable property to the payment of his debts is to be regulated by the law of "British India."

Creditor paid in part under section 283 to bring payment into account before sharing in proceeds of immoveable property.

284. No creditor who has received payment of a part of his debt by virtue of the last preceding section shall be entitled to share in the proceeds of the immoveable estate of the deceased unless he brings such payment into account for the benefit of the other creditors.

Illustration.

A dies, having his domicile in a country where instruments under seal have priority over instruments not under seal, leaving moveable property to the value of 5,000 rupees and immoveable property to the value of 10,000 rupees, debts on instruments under seal to the amount of 10,000 rupees, and debts on instruments not under seal to the same amount. The creditors holding instruments under seal receive half of their debts out of the proceeds of the moveable estate. The proceeds of the immoveable estate are to be applied in payment of the debts on instruments not under seal until one-half of such debts has been discharged. This will leave 5,000 rupees, which are to be distributed rateably amongst all the creditors without distinction, in proportion to the amount which may remain due to them.

Debts to be paid before legacies.

285. Debts of every description must be paid before any legacy.

Executor or administrator not bound to pay legacies without indemnity.

286. If the estate of the deceased is subject to any contingent liabilities, and executor or administrator is not bound to pay any legacy without a sufficient indemnity to meet the liabilities whenever they may become due.

Abatement of general legacies.

287. If the assets, after payment of debts, necessary expenses, and specific legacies, are not sufficient to pay all the general legacies in full, the latter shall abate or be diminished in equal proportions,

Executor not to pay one legatee in preference to another.

and the executor has no right to pay one legatee in preference to another, nor to retain any money on account of a legacy to himself or to any person for whom he is a trustee.

Non-abatement of specific legacy when assets sufficient to pay debts.

288. Where there is a specific legacy, and the assets are sufficient for the payment of debts and necessary expenses, the thing specified must be delivered to the legatee without any abatement.

Right under demonstrative legacy when assets sufficient to pay debts and necessary expenses.

289. Where there is a demonstrative legacy, and the assets are sufficient for the payment of debts and necessary expenses, the legatee has a preferential claim for payment of his legacy out of the fund from which the legacy is directed to be paid until such fund is exhausted, and, if, after the fund is exhausted, part of the legacy still remains unpaid, he is entitled to rank for the remainder against the general assets as for a legacy of the amount of such unpaid remainder.

290. If the assets are not sufficient to answer the debts and the specific legacies, an abatement shall be made from the latter rateably in proportion to their respective amounts.

Rateable abatement of specific legacies.

Illustration.

A has bequeathed to B a diamond-ring, valued at 500 rupees, and to C a horse, valued at 1,000 rupees. It is found necessary to sell all the effects of the testator, and his assets, after payment of debts, are only 1,000 rupees. Of this sum rupees 333-5-4 are to be paid to B, and rupees 666-10-8 to C.

291. For the purpose of abatement, a legacy for life, a sum appropriated by the will to produce an annuity, and the value of an annuity when no sum has been appropriated to produce it, shall be treated as general legacies.

Legacies treated as general for purpose of abatement.

PART XXXV.

Of the Executor's Assent to a Legacy.

Assent necessary to complete legatee's title.

292. The assent of the executor is necessary to complete a legatee's title to his legacy.

Illustrations.

(*a.*) A by his will bequeaths to B his Government paper, which is in deposit with the Bank of Bengal. The Bank has no authority to deliver the securities, nor B a right to take possession of them, without the assent of the executor.

(*b.*) A by his will has bequeathed to C his house in Calcutta in the tenancy of B. C is not entitled to receive the rents without the assent of the executor.

293. The assent of the executor to a specific bequest shall be sufficient to divest his interest as executor therein, and to transfer the subject of the bequest to the legatee, unless the nature or the circumstances of the property require that it shall be transferred in a particular way.

Effect of executor's assent to specific legacy.

This assent may be verbal, and it may be either expressed or implied from the conduct of the executor.

Nature of assent.

Illustrations.

(*a.*) A horse is bequeathed. The executor requests the legatee to dispose of it, or a third party proposes to purchase the horse from the executor, and he directs him to apply to the legatee. Assent to the legacy is implied.

(b.) The interest of a fund is directed by the will to be applied for the maintenance of the legatee during his minority. The executor commences so to apply it. This is an assent to the whole of the bequest.

(c.) A bequest is made of a fund to A, and after him to B. The executor pays the interest of the fund to A. This is an implied assent to the bequest to B.

(d.) Executors die after paying all the debts of the testator, but before satisfaction of specific legacies. Assent to the legacies may be presumed.

(e.) A person to whom a specific article has been bequeathed takes possession of it, and retains it without any objection on the part of the executor. His assent may be presumed.

Conditional assent

294. The assent of an executor to a legacy may be conditional, and if the condition be one which he has a right to enforce, and it is not performed, there is no assent.

Illustrations.

(a) A bequeaths to B his lands of Sultanpur, which at the date of the will, and at the death of A, were subject to a mortgage for 10,000 rupees. The executor assents to the bequest, on condition that B shall, within a limited time, pay the amount due on the mortgage at the testator's death. The amount is not paid. There is no assent.

(b.) The executor assents to a bequest on condition that the legatee shall pay him a sum of money. The payment is not made. The assent is nevertheless valid.

Assent of executor to his own legacy.

295. When the executor is a legatee, his assent to his own legacy is necessary to complete his title to it, in the same way as it is required when the bequest is to another person, and his assent may in like manner be expressed or implied.

Implied assent.

Assent shall be implied, if, in his manner of administering the property, he does any act which is referable to his character of legatee, and is not referable to his character of executor.

Illustration.

An executor takes the rent of a house, or the interest of Government securities bequeathed to him, and applies it to his own use. This is assent.

Effect of executor's assent.

296. The assent of the executor to a legacy gives effect to it from the death of the testator.

Illustrations.

(a.) A legatee sells his legacy before it is assented to by the executor. The executor's subsequent assent operates for the benefit of the purchaser, and completes his title to the legacy.

(b.) A bequeaths 1,000 rupees to B with interest from his death. The executor does not assent to his legacy until the expiration of a year from A's death. B is entitled to interest from the death of A.

297. An executor is not bound to pay or deliver any legacy until the expiration of one year from the testator's death.

Executor when to deliver legacies.

Illustration.

A by his will directs his legacies to be paid within six months after his death. The executor is not bound to pay them before the expiration of a year.

PART XXXVI.

Of the Payment and Apportionment of Annuities.

298. Where an annuity is given by the will, and no time is fixed for its commencement, it shall commence from the testator's death, and the first payment shall be made at the expiration of a year next after that event.

Commencement of annuity when no time fixed by will.

299. Where there is a direction that the annuity shall be paid quarterly or monthly, the first payment shall be due at the end of the first quarter or first month, as the case may be, after the testator's death; and shall, if the executor thinks fit, be paid when due, but the executor shall not be bound to pay it till the end of the year.

When annuity, to be paid quarterly or monthly, first falls due.

300. Where there is a direction that the first payment of an annuity shall be made within one month or any other division of time from the death of the testator, or on a day certain, the successive payments are to be made on the anniversary of the earliest day on which the will authorizes the first payment to be made;

Dates of successive payments when first payment directed to be made within given time, or on day certain.

and, if the annuitant should die in the interval between the times of payment, an apportioned share of the annuity shall be paid to his representative.

Apportionment where annuitant dies between times of payment.

PART XXXVII.

Of the Investment of Funds to provide for Legacies.

Investment of sum bequeathed where legacy, not specific, given for life.

301. Where a legacy, not being a specific legacy, is given for life, the sum bequeathed shall at the end of the year be invested in such securities as the High Court may, by any general rule to be made from time to time, authorize or direct, and the proceeds thereof shall be paid to the legatee as the same shall accrue due.

Investment of general legacy to be paid at future time.

302. Where a general legacy is given to be paid at a future time, the executor shall invest a sum sufficient to meet it in securities of the kind mentioned in the last preceding section.

Intermediate interest.

The intermediate interest shall form part of the residue of the testator's estate.

Procedure when no fund charged with, or appropriated to, annuity.

303. Where an annuity is given, and no fund is charged with its payment, or appropriated by the will to answer it, a Government annuity of the specified amount shall be purchased; or

if no such annuity can be obtained, then a sum sufficient to produce the annuity shall be invested for that purpose in such securities as the High Court may, by any general rule to be made from time to time, authorize or direct.

Transfer to residuary legatee of contingent bequest.

304. Where a bequest is contingent, the executor is not bound to invest the amount of the legacy, but may transfer the whole residue of the estate to the residuary legatee on his giving sufficient security for the payment of the legacy if it shall become due.

Investment of residue bequeathed for life, without direction to invest in particular securities.

305. Where the testator has bequeathed the residue of his estate to a person for life without any direction to invest it in any particular securities, so much thereof as is not at the time of the testator's decease invested in such securities as the High Court may for the time being regard as good securities shall be converted into money, and invested in such securities.

Investment of residue bequeathed for life, with direction to invest in specified securities.

306. Where the testator has bequeathed the residue of his estate to a person for life, with a direction that it shall be invested in certain specified securities, so much of the estate as is not at the time of his death invested in securities

of the specified kind shall be converted into money and invested in such securities.

Time and manner of conversion and investment.

307. Such conversion and investment as are contemplated by the two last preceding sections shall be made at such times and in such manner as the executor shall in his discretion think fit;

Interest payable until investment.

and, until such conversion and investment shall be completed, the person who would be for the time being entitled to the income of the fund when so invested shall receive interest at the rate of four per cent. per annum upon the market-value (to be computed as of the date of the testator's death) of such part of the fund as shall not yet have been so invested.

Procedure where minor entitled to immediate payment or possession of bequest, and no direction to pay to person on his behalf.

308. Where, by the terms of a bequest, the legatee is entitled to the immediate payment or possession of the money or thing bequeathed, but is a minor, and there is no direction in the will to pay it to any person on his behalf, the executor or administrator shall pay or deliver the same into the Court of the District Judge, by whom "or by whose District Delegate" the probate was, or letters of administration with the will annexed were, granted, to the account of the legatee, unless the legatee be a ward of the Court of Wards:

and, if the legatee be a ward of the Court of Wards, the legacy shall be paid into that Court to his account:

and such payment into the Court of the District Judge, or into the Court of Wards, as the case may be, shall be a sufficient discharge for the money so paid:

and such money, when paid in, shall be invested in the purchase of Government securities, which, with the interest thereon, shall be transferred or paid to the person entitled thereto, or otherwise applied for his benefit, as the Judge or the Court of Wards, as the case may be, may direct.

PART XXXVIII.

OF THE PRODUCE AND INTEREST OF LEGACIES.

Legatee's title to produce of specific legacy.

309. The legatee of a specific legacy is entitled to the clear produce thereof, if any, from the testator's death.

Exception.—A specific bequest, contingent in its terms, does not comprise the produce of the legacy between the death of the testator and the vesting to the legacy. The clear produce of it forms part of the residue of the testator's estate.

Illustrations.

(*a.*) A bequeaths his flock of sheep to B. Between the death of A and delivery by his executor the sheep are shorn, or some of the ewes produce lambs. The wool and lambs are the property of B.

(*b.*) A bequeaths his Government securities to B, but postpones the delivery of them till the death of C. The interest which falls due between the death of A and the death of C belongs to B, and must, unless he is a minor, be paid to him as it is received.

(*c.*) The testator bequeaths all his four per cent. Government promissory notes to A when he shall complete the age of 18. A, if he complete that age, is entitled to receive the notes, but the interest which accrues in respect of them, between the testator's death and A's completing 18, forms part of the residue.

Residuary, legatee's title to produce of residuary fund.

310. The legatee under a general residuary bequest is entitled to the produce of the residuary fund from the testator's death.

Exception.—A general residuary bequest, contingent in its terms, does not comprise the income which may accrue upon the fund bequeathed between the death of the testator and the vesting of the legacy. Such income goes as undisposed of.

Illustrations.

(*a.*) The testator bequeaths the residue of his property to A, a minor, to be paid to him when he shall complete the age of 18. The income from the testator's death belongs to A.

(*b.*) The testator bequeaths the residue of his property to A, when he shall complete the age of 18. A, if he complete that age, is entitled to receive the residue. The income which has accrued in respect of it since the testator's death goes as undisposd of.

Interest when no time fixed for payment of general legacy.

311. Where no time has been fixed for the payment of a general legacy, interest begins to run from the expiration of one year from the testator's death.

Exception.—(1.) Where the legacy is bequeathed in satisfaction of a debt, interest runs from the death of the testator.

(2.) Where the testator was a parent or a more remote ancestor of the legatee, or has put himself in the place of a parent of the legatee, the legacy shall bear interest from the death of the testator.

(3.) Where a sum is bequeathed to a minor with a direction to pay for his maintenance out of it, interest is payable from the death of the testator.

Interest when time fixed.

312. Where a time has been fixed for the payment of a general legacy, interest begins to run from the time so fixed. The interest up to such time forms part of the residue of the testator's estate.

Exception.—Where the testator was a parent or a more remote ancestor of the legatee, or has put himself in the place of a parent of the legatee, and the legatee is a minor, the legacy shall bear interest from the death of the testator, unless a specific sum is given by the will for maintenance.

Rate of interest.

313. The rate of interest shall be four per cent. per annum.

No interest on arrears of annuity within first year after testator's death.

314. No interest is payable on the arrears of an annuity within the first year from the death of the testator, although a period earlier than the expiration of that year may have been fixed by the will for making the first payment of the annuity.

Interest on sum to be invested to produce annuity.

315. Where a sum of money is directed to be invested to produce an annuity, interest is payable on it from the death of the testator.

PART XXXIX.

Of the Refunding of Legacies.

Refund of legacy paid under Judge's orders.

316. When an executor has paid a legacy under the order of a Judge, he is entitled to call upon the legatee to refund, in the event of the assets proving insufficient to pay all the legacies.

No refund if paid voluntarily.

317. When an executor has voluntarily paid a legacy, he cannot call upon a legatee to refund, in the event of the assets proving insufficient to pay all the legacies.

318. When the time prescribed by the will for the performance of a condition has elapsed without the condition having been performed, and the executor has thereupon, without fraud, distributed the assets; in such case, if further time has been allowed under the 124th section for the performance of the condition, and the condition has been performed accordingly, the legacy cannot be claimed from the executor, but those to whom he has paid it are liable to refund the amount.

Refund when legacy has become due on performance of condition within further time allowed under section 124.

319. When the executor has paid away the assets in legacies, and he is afterwards obliged to discharge a debt of which he had no previous notice, he is entitled to call upon each legatee to refund in proportion.

When each legatee compellable to refund in proportion.

320. Where an executor or administrator has given such notices as would have been given by the High Court in an administration-suit for creditors and others to send in to him their claims against the estate of the deceased, he shall, at the expiration of the time therein named for sending in claims, be at liberty to distribute the assets, or any part thereof, in discharge of such lawful claims as he knows of, and shall not be liable for the assets so distributed to any person of whose claim he shall not have had notice at the time of such distribution;

Distribution of assets.

but nothing herein contained shall prejudice the right of any creditor or claimant to follow the assets, or any part thereof, in the hands of the persons who may have received the same respectively.

Creditor may follow assets.

321. A creditor who has not received payment of his debt may call upon a legatee who has received payment of his legacy to refund, whether the assets of the testator's estate were or were not sufficient at the time of his death to pay both debts and legacies; and whether the payment of the legacy by the executor was voluntary or not.

Creditor may call upon legatee to refund.

322. If the assets were sufficient to satisfy all the legacies at the time of the testator's death, a legatee who has not received payment of his legacy, or who has been compelled to refund under the last preceding section, cannot oblige one who has received payment in full to refund, whether the legacy were paid to him with or without

When legatee not satisfied, or compelled to refund under section 321, cannot oblige one paid in full to refund.

suit, although the assets have subsequently become deficient by the wasting of the executor.

When unsatisfied legatee must first proceed against executor, if solvent.

323. If the assets were not sufficient to satisfy all the legacies at the time of the testator's death, a legatee who has not received payment of his legacy must, before he can call on a satisfied legatee to refund, first proceed against the executor, if he is solvent; but if the executor is insolvent or not liable to pay, the unsatisfied legatee can oblige each satisfied legatee to refund in proportion.

Limit to refunding of one legatee to another.

324. The refunding of one legatee to another shall not exceed the sum by which the satisfied legacy ought to have been reduced if the estate had been properly administered.

Illustrations.

A has bequeathed 240 rupees to B, 480 rupees to C, and 720 rupees to D. The assets are only 1,200 rupees, and if properly administered, would give 200 rupees to B, 400 rupees to C, and 600 rupees to D. C and D have been paid their legacies in full, leaving nothing to B. B can oblige C to refund 80 rupees, and D to refund 120 rupees.

Refunding to be without interest.

325. The refunding shall, in all cases be without interest.

Residue after usual payments to be paid to residuary legatee.

326. The surplus or residue of the deceased's property, after payment of debts and legacies, shall be paid to the residuary legatee when any has been appointed by the will.

Transfer of assets from British India to executor or administrator in country of domicile for distribution.

326A. Where person not having his domicile in British India has died leaving assets both in British India and in the country in which he had his domicile at the time of his death,

and there have been a grant of probate or letters of administration in British Iudia with respect to the assets there, and a grant of administration in the country of domicile with respect to the assets in that country,

the executor or administrator, as the case may be, in British India, after having given such notices as are mentioned in section 320, and after having discharged, at the expiration of the time therein named, such lawful claims as he knows of,

may, instead of himself distributing any surplus or residue of the deceased's property to persons residing out of British India who are entitled thereto, transfer, with the consent of the executor or administrator, as the case may be, in the country of domicile, the surplus or residue to him for distribution to those persons.

PART XL.

Of the Liability of an Executor or Administrator for Devastation.

Liability of executor or administrator for devastation.

327. When an executor or administrator misapplies the estate of the deceased, or subjects it to loss or damage, he is liable to make good the loss or damage so occasioned.

Illustrations.

(*a*) The executor pays out of the estate an unfounded claim. He is liable to make good the loss.

(*b*) The deceased had a valuable lease renewable by notice, which the executor neglects to give at the proper time. The executor is liable to make good the loss.

(*c*) The deceased had a lease of less value than the rent payable for it but terminable on notice at a particular time. The executor neglects to give the notice. He is liable to make good the loss.

Liability of executor or administrator for neglect to get in any part of property.

328. When an executor or administrator occasions a loss to the estate by neglecting to get in any part of the property of the deceased, he is liable to make good the amount.

Illustrations.

(*a*) The executor absolutely releases a debt due to the deceased from a solvent person, or compounds with a debtor who is able to pay in full. The executor is liable to make good the amount.

(*b*) The executor neglects to sue for a debt till the debtor is able to plead the Act for the limitation of suits, and the debt is thereby lost to the estate. The executor is liable to make good the amount.

PART XLI.

Miscellaneous.

329. *Stamps and Fees.* [*Repealed by Act VII of* 1870.]

330. *Saving as to Administrator-General.* [*Repealed by Act XXIV of* 1867.]

Succession of property of Hindus, &c., and certain wills, intestacies, and marriages not affected.

331. The provisions of this Act shall not apply to intestate or testamentary succession to the property of any Hindu, Mahomedan, or Buddhist; nor shall they apply to any will made, or any intestacy occurring, before the first day of January 1866,

The 4th section shall not apply to any marriage contracted before the same day.

332. The Governor-General of India in Council shall from time to time have power, by an order either restrospectively from the passing of this Act, or prospectively, to exempt from the operation of the whole or any part of this Act, the members of any race, sect, or tribe in British India, or any part of such race, sect, or tribe, to whom he may consider it impossible or inexpedient to apply the provisions of this Act, or of the part of the Act mentioned in the order.

Power of Governor-General in Council to exempt any race, sect, or tribe in British India from operation of Act.

The Governor-General of India in Council shall also have power from time to time to revoke such order, but not so that the revocation shall have any retrospective effect.

All orders and revocations made under this section shall be published in the *Gazette of India.*

333. (1) When a grant of probate or letters of administration is revoked or annulled under this Act, the person to whom the grant was made shall forthwith deliver up the probate or letters to the Court which made the grant.

Surrender of revoked probate or letters of administration.

(2) If such person wilfully and without reasonable cause omits so to deliver up the probate or letters, he shall be punished with fine which may extend to one thousand rupees, or with imprisonment of either description for a term which may extend to three months, or with both.

APPENDIX C.

Rules and Regulations for the Parsee Chief Matrimonial Court in the Presidency of Bombay.

CHAPTER XXXIV.

(OF THE RULES AND FORMS OF THE BOMBAY HIGH COURT. 1901.)

Procedure.

756. All proceedings shall be regulated by the provisions of the Code of Civil Procedure, save so far as such provisions may be varied or modified by the following rules.

Plaint for nullity, or dissolution of marriage to state non-existence of collusion or connivance.

757. In cases when the plaintiff is seeking for a decree of nullity of marriage, the plaint shall state that no collusion or connivance exists between the plaintiff and the other party to the marriage or alleged marriage, and in cases of dissolution of marriage on the grounds of adultery, that no collusion or connivance exists between the plaintiff and the person alleged to have committed adultery.

(Forms of plaints are given, Nos. I and III, in the Schedule to this Chapter.)

Summons to require that written statement should be filed. In default of written statement suit to proceed *exparte*.

758. The summons to the defendant shall require him (or her) to put in a written statement of his (or her) case, and of his (or her) answer to the material allegations in the plaint and to file the same, ten days at the least before the day appointed for the hearing of the suit. (Forms of written statements are given, Nos. II and IV, in the Schedule to this Chapter.)

No statement shall be received after such period without special order of the Court; in default, the Court shall be empowered to proceed *exparte* on the day appointed for the hearing of the suit.

Verification and stamping of plaint, &c.

759. All plaints, written statements, petitions and all responsive allegations must be duly verified and must be duly stamped, pursuant to the provisions of Act VII of 1870, or they will not be received or filed.

760. In cases involving a decree of nullity of marriage or a decree of judicial separation, or of dissolution of marriage, the defendant shall, in the written statement, state that there is not any collusion or connivance between the defendant and the other party to the marriage.

In certain cases written statements to state non-existence of collusion or connivance.

761. When a written statement admitting the fact of a marriage between the parties has been filed, and the husband has appeared in the suit, the wife may proceed to file an application for alimony, in substance according to the form V. in the Schedule to this Chapter, and a day shall be fixed for hearing such application.

Application by wife for alimony.

762. After an application for alimony has been filed, a copy thereof shall be served forthwith upon the husband, and within fifteen days after such service he shall file his answer thereto, which shall be subscribed and verified in the manner provided for subscribing and verfying plaints, or in default the Court will proceed *exparte*.

Answer of husband to such application after service.

763. After the answer of the husband has been filed, the wife may apply to the Court to decree her alimony *pendente lite*, provided that the wife shall, four days before she so moves the Court, give notice to her husband or to his agent or pleader of her intention to do so.

Application for alimony *pendente lite*.

764. The wife, subject to any order as to costs, may, if not satisfied with the husband's answer, apply to have a day fixed for hearing such application when witnesses may be examined in support of and against such application for alimony.

When witnesses may be examined on such application.

765. A wife, who has obtained a decree of judicial separation in her favour and has previously filed her application for alimony, may, unless in cases when an appeal is interposed, move the Court to decree her permanent alimony; provided that she shall, eight days at least before making any such application, give notice to the husband, his agent, or to his pleader, of her intention so to do.

Application or notice for permanent alimony.

766. The Court may receive in evidence and act upon affidavits produced in support of, or in opposition to, any interlocutory application or motion.

Affidavits to be received and acted on, on motion.

767. Such affidavits may be made before any Commissioner for taking affidavits at the Original Side or before the Registrar or Deputy Registrar at the Appellate Side of the High Court.

Affidavits, before whom made.

FORMS TO CHAPTER XXXIV.

(PARSI CHIEF MATRIMONIAL COURT.)

SCHEDULE.

No. I.

FORM OF PLAINT FOR DISSOLUTION OF MARRIAGE.

To,

The Judge of the Parsi Chief Matrimonial Court at Bombay.

A.B.

vs.

C.B. (and R.S. as the case may be).

The day of 19 .

1. That the plaintiff was on the day of 19 . lawfully married to *C. B.* at .

2. That after his said marriage the plaintiff lived and cohabited with his said wife at and at and that the plaintiff and his said wife have had issue of their said marriage, three children, one son and two daughters (*as the case may be*).

3. That on the of and other days between that day and the and said *C.B.* defendant at in the committed adultery with *R.S.*

4. That in and during the months of January, February, and March the said *C.B.* defendant, frequently met the said *R. S.* at and on divers such occasions committed adultery with the said *R.S.*

5. That there is not any collusion or connivance whatever between the plaintiff and the said defendant *C.B.* and *R.S.* or either of them in respect of this suit.

The plaintiff, therefore, prays that your Lordship will proceed to decree (*here state the relief sought*) and that plaintiff have further and other relief in the premises as to your Lordship may seem meet.

No. II.

FORM OF ANSWER TO PLAINT FOR DISSOLUTION OF MARRIAGE.

The day of 19 .

A.B.

vs.

C.B.

1. The defendant *C.B.* by *P.A.* his pleader, agent, (*or in person*) saith that she denies that she committed adultery with *R.S.* as is set forth in the said plaint.

2. The defendant further saith that on the day of 19 and on other days between that day and the said *A.B.* the plaintiff, at committed adultery with *X.Y.*, being a married woman, &c.

(In like manner the defendant is to state connivance, condonation, or other matters which may be relied on as a ground for dismissing the petition).

3. The defendant further saith that she is not colluding or conniving with the plaintiff that he may obtain a decree in this suit: wherefore this defendant humbly prays—

That your Lordship will be pleased to reject the prayer of the said plaint and decree, &c.

No. III.

FORM OF PLAINT TOR DECREE OF NULLITY OF MARRIAGE.

To

The Judge of the Parsi Chief Matrimonial Court at Bombay.

A.B.

vs.

C.D.

The day of 19 .

1. That the plaintiff, then a spinster, was on the day of 19 , married in fact, though not in law, to the defendant, then a bachelor, at

2. That from the said day of 19 until the day of 19 , the plaintiff lived and cohabited with the defendant at diverse places, and particularly at aforesaid.

3. That the said defendant has never consummated the said pretended marriage by carnal copulation.

4. That at the time of the celebration of the plaintiff's said pretended marriage, the said defendant was, by reason of his impotency or malformation, legally incompetent to enter into the contract of marriage.

5. That there is no collusion or connivance between the plaintiff and the said defendant with respect to the subject of this suit.

The plaintiff therefore prays that your Lordship will proceed to declare that the said marriage is null and void.

No. IV.

FORM OF ANSWER TO PLAINT FOR DECREE OF NULLITY OF MARRIAGE.

The day of 19 .

A.B.

vs.

C.D.

1. That I, the defendant, did consummate the said marriage so solemnized, and that the defendant was at the time of the said marriage, and from thence hitherto hath been and still is apt for coition, as will appear on inspection.

Wherefore the defendant humbly prays that your Lordship will be pleased to reject the said petition and decree, &c.

No. V.

APPLICATION FOR ALIMONY.

To,

The Judge of the Parsi Chief Matrimonial Court at Bombay.

C. B.

vs.

A. B.

The day of 19 .

The application of *C. B.*, defendant. the lawful wife of *A. B.*, showeth :

1. That the said plaintiff *A. B.* has for many years carried on the business of at and from such business derives the net annual income of Rs.

2. That the said plaintiff *A. B.* holds shares of the Railway Company amounting in value to Rs. and yielding a clear annual dividend to him of Rs.

3. That the said plaintiff *A. B.* is possessd of made in his said business of to the value of Rs. (and so on for any other property movable or immovable the husband may possess).

The defendant therefore humbly prays that your Lordship will be pleased to allow her such sum or sums of money by way of alimony *pendente lite* (or permanent alimony) as to your Lordship shall seem meet.

TABLE OF FEES.

The following fees only shall be allowed in cases tried under Act XV of 1865 :—

	Rs.	a.	p.
For every Plaint	20	0	0
For every other document	0	8	0
For issuing every summons and subpoena ...	1	0	0
For drawing and engrossing every decree or order	5	0	0
For sealing every document	1	0	0
For administering oath	1	0	0
For serving process	0	8	0
For attendance of attorney or pleader (when an advocate is not instructed) on the day of presenting plaint or written statement. ...	45	0	0
For attendance at settlement of issues (if not settled at the hearing of the suit) or hearing of any contested motion :			
For advocate	60	0	0
For attorney or pleader without advocate ...	45	0	0
For attorney or pleader with advocate	30	0	0
For attendance at hearing of suit on first-day :			
For advocate	75	0	0
For pleader or attorney	60	0	0
For pleader or attorney without advocate ...	45	0	0
For attendance for each succeeding day :			
For advocate	60	0	0
For attorney or pleader	45	0	0
For attorney or pleader with advocate	30	0	0
For taxing bill of costs	4	0	0
Costs of execution	45	0	0
For allowing search with proceedings	1	0	0
Charges for professional witnesses :			
Brigade Surgeon	100	0	0
Surgeon-Major	75	0	0
Surgeon	50	0	0
Assistant Surgeon over 20 years' standing ...	50	0	0
Assistant Surgeon under 20 years' standing ...	25	0	0

Costs of necessary translations will also be allowed.

Costs between party and party will be taxed by the Clerk of the Court.

Dated this 10th day of September 1902.

(Bombay High Court Rules, 1901, at p. 494.)

INDEX.

ABATEMENT
of legacies, 33, 34
of annuities, 34

ACCUMULATION,
direction for, 28, 29

ACT,
IX of 1837 (Parsi Chattels Real), 1, 2, 3 and *in extenso* in Appendix A.
X of 1865 (Indian Succession), 2, 4, 7, 14—42 and *in extenso* in Appendix B.
XV of 1865 (Parsi Marriage and Divorce), 2, 44, 45—67
XXI of 1865 (Parsi Intestate Succession), 2, 3, 4, 5—13
IV of 1869 (Indian Divorce), 57
III of 1874 (Married Woman's Property), 17,18
XIV of 1874 (Scheduled Districts), 5, 45
XV of 1874 (Laws Local Extent), 5, 45
IX of 1875 (Indian Majority), 19, 49
VI of 1890 (Charitable Endowments), 29

ADEMPTION,
of legacies, 32, 33

ADMINISTRATION,
letters of, 35
who cannot take, 36
letters of, do not validate intermediate acts if injurious to estate, 37

ADMINISTRATION,—*continued.*
limited grants of, 40, 41
in duration, 40
for use and benefit of others having right, 40
pendente lite, 41
for special purpose, 41
with exception, 41
of the rest, 41
of effects unadministered, 41
revocation of, 42
alteration in, 42

ADMINISTRATOR,
definition of, 35
on intestacy, 38
powers of, 38, 39
duties of, 39
liabilities of, 40

ADOPTION,
nothing like strict, amongst Parsis, 6

ADULTERY,
of wife, 57
of husband, 57

ALIMONY,
pendente lite, 59
permament, 59
payment of, to wife or to her trustee, 60

ANNUITIES, 27

APPEAL,
from decision of any Court established under Act XV of 1865, to High Court, 64

ASIRVAD, 46

BEQUESTS,
void, 28—30

BEQUESTS,—*continued.*
in perpetuity, 28
with direction for accumulation, 28
to charitable uses, 29, 30
upon impossible, or illegal or immoral conditions, 30
contingent, 31
onerous, 31
conditional, 31
with directions as to application or enjoyment, 32

Baj rozgar ceremonies, performance of, void, 29

BIGAMY,
punishment of, 51

BROTHER,
of intestate, right of, 10, 11
full-blood, right of, 10
full and half-blood, right of, 11
by same mother, right of, 12
widow of, right of, 12

CERTIFICATE,
of Parsi marriages, 51

Cessate GRANTS, 41

CHARITABLE bequests, 29, 30

CHILD,
division of share of predeceased, 8

CHILDREN,
share of, when widow of intestate alive, 5
share of, when widower of intestate alive, 7
share of, when no widow, 7
share of, when no widower, 7
posthumous, share of, 7

CHILDREN,—*continued.*
of predeceased brothers, rights of, 10
of predeceased sisters, rights of, 10
custody of, *pendente lite*, 65
orders as to custody of, after final decree, 65
settlement of wife's property for benefit of, 65

CODICIL,
definition of, 20

Cæterorum grants, 41

COMMON LAW,
wife's right under, as to her property, 14, 15

CONSENT,
of parents to Parsi marriage, when children under twenty-one, 46

CONSTRUCTION of wills, 23—25

COURT,
chief matrimonial, 53
district matrimonial, 54
in which suits to be brought under Parsi M. & D. Act, 55
appeal to High, from decision of any Court established under Parsi M. & D. Act, 64

CUSTODY,
of children *pendente lite*, 65
orders as to, of children, after final decree, 65

DAUGHTER,
share of, when widow and son of intestate alive, 5
step, share of, 6

DAUGHTER,—*continued.*
share of, when widower and son of intestate alive, 7
share of, when son alive, but no widow, 7
share of, when son alive, but no widower, 7
of grandfather, share of, 10
of great-grandfather, share of, 10
De bonis non grants, 41
DECREE,
of nullity of marriage, 56
of dissolution in case of absence, 56
for divorce, 58
for judicial separation, 58
for restitution of conjugal rights, 60
orders as to children's custody after final, 65
DELEGATES,
appointment of, 54
power to appoint new, 55
majority of, to determine questions of facts, 64
DEMONSTRATIVE LEGACY, 26
DHURM-PUTR, 6
DISSOLUTION,
of marriage in case of absense, 56
DIVORCE,
grounds of, 57
suits for, 58
decree for, 58
DOMICILE, 18—20
Donatio Mortis Causa, 35
Dosla ceremonies,
performance of, void, 29
ELECTION, 34, 35
EXECUTION OF unprivileged will, 20
EXECUTOR,
definition of, 35
renunciation by, 37
powers of, 38, 39
duties of 39, 40
liabilities of, 40
FATHER,
of intestate, right of, 8, 9, 10,
Gahambar ceremonies,
performance of, void, 29
GENERAL LEGACY, 25
GIFTS,
in contemplation of death, 35
GRANDFATHER,
right of, 10
sons and daughters of, rights of, 10
paternal, right of, 12
maternal, right of, 12
GRANDMOTHER,
right of, 10
paternal, right of, 12
maternal, right of, 12
GRANTS. (See limited grants).
GREAT-GRANDFATHER,
right of, 10
sons and daughters of, rights of, 10
GREAT-GRANDMOTHER,
right of, 10
GROUNDS,
of divorce, 57
of judicial separation, 58
HUSBAND,
right of, under Common Law over wife's property, 14, 15
this right of, removed by 4th Section of Indian Suc. Act, 14—16
definition of, 46

HUSBAND,—*continued.*
can obtain divorce, when, 57
IMMOVABLE PROPERTY,
definition of, 18
succession to, 18
INFANT MARRIAGES, 63
INTESTATE,
definition of, 5
succession among Parsis, 5—13
JUDICIAL SEPARATION,
grounds of, 58
suits for, 58
LAPSE OF LEGACIES, 27
LEGACY,
to attesting witness, 22
general, 25
specific, 25, 26
demonstrative, 26
lapse of, 27
vesting of, 30—32
ademption of, 32, 33
abatement of, 33, 34
refunding of, 34
LETTERS OF ADMINISTRATION, 35
with will annexed when and to whom given, 37, 38
LIMITED GRANTS, 40, 41
MAJORITY,
• age of, under Parsi M. and D. Act, 49, 50
MARRIAGE,
effect of, under 4th section of Succession Act, 14—16
effects of, before Succession Act, 14—16
Parsi, and Divorce Act, 45
definition of, 46
MARRIAGES,
between Parsi, 46—53
requisites to validity of Parsi, 46
in life-time of his or her wife or husband unlawful, 50
MARRIAGE-REGISTER,
to be open for public inspection, 52
MATRIMONIALS COURTS,
chief, 53
district, 54
practitioners in, 55
MATRIMONIAL SUITS, 56—65
MINOR,
definition of, 19
MINORITY,
definition of, 19
MORTMAIN GIFTS. (See charitable bequests.)
MOTHER,
of intestate, right of, 8, 9, 11
MOVABLE PROPERTY,
definition of, 18
succession to, 18
Nirangdin,
consecration of, void, 29
NULLITY OF MARRIAGE,
decree of, 56
ORDERS,
under Parsi M. & D. Act, 68, 69
order constituting Parsi Chief Matrimonial Court in Bombay and District Courts in Surat and Poona, 68
order constituting Parsi District Matrimonial Court for Sind, 68
Aden and its dependencies to be included within

ORDERS,—*continued.*
jurisdiction of Parsi Chief Matrimonial Court of Bombay, 69

ONEROUS BEQUEST, 31

PALUK, 6

PARSIS,
law of succession among, before 1865, 1, 2, 3
intestate succession among, regulated now by Parsi Intestate Succession Act, 4, 5
law as to marriages among, before 1865, 43
section 42 of Succession Act does not apply to, 10
Succession Act X of 1865 applies to testamentary succession of, 4, 14

PARSI MARRIAGE and Divorce Act, 44, 45—67
applies to whole of British India except Scheduled Districts, 45
Marriages between Parsis, 46—58
requisites to validity of, 46, 48
prohibited degrees of relationship, 47
re-marriage, save after divorce unlawful during life-time of first wife or husband, 50
Matrimonial Courts, 53—55
chief, 53
district, 54
appointment of delegates, 54

PARSI M. & D. Act,—*continued.*
appointment of new delegates, 55
practitioners in, 55
court in which suits to be brought, 55
when defendant has left British India, 55
Matrimonial Suits, 56, 65
(*a*) for decree of nullity, 56
(*b*) for decree of dissolution in case of absence, 56
(*c*) for divorce or judicial separation, 57—60
on ground of wife's adultery, 57
on ground of husband's adultery, &c., 57
grounds of judicial separation, 58
suits for divorce or judicial separation, 58
alimony, 59
(*d*) for restitution of conjugal rights, 60—65
suit for, 60
lawful grounds justifying refusal to cohabit, 62
no suit to enforce marriage or contract arising out of marriage when husband under 16 or wife under 14 years, 63
suits with closed doors, 64
civil procedure code applied, 64
all questions of law and procedure to be determined by presiding judge, 64

PARSI M. & D. Act,—*continued.*
decision on facts to be by majority of delegates, 64
appeal to High Court from decision of any Court established under this Act, 64
Children of Parties, 65
custody of, *pendente lite*, 65
orders as to custody of, after final decree, 65
settlement of wife's property for benefit of, 65
Mode of enforcing penalties, 65, 66
cognizance of offences under this Act, 65
levy of fines by distress, 66
imprisonment if no sufficient distress, 66
Miscellaneous, 66, 67
rules of procedure of matrimonial courts to be made by High Court, 66
Schedule to section 6 of this Act, 67

PARSI SUCCESSION ACT, 5—10
applies to whole of British India, except Scheduled Districts, 15
schedules to, 10—13
division among widow and children, 5
division among widower and children, 7
division amongst children, when there is no widow, 7

PARSI S. ACT,—*continued.*
division amongst children, when there is no widower, 7
division of predeceased child's share among widow or widower and issue of such child, 8
division where intestate leaves widow or widower, but no lineal descendants, 8, 9
division where intestate leaves neither widow nor widower nor lineal descendants, 9
exemption of Parsis from parts of Succession Act, 10

PENALTY (under Act XV of 1865),
for solemnizing marriage contrary to 4th section, 52
for priests' neglect of requirements of 6th section, 52
for omitting to subscribe and attest certificate, 52
for making or signing or attesting false certificate, 53
for not registering certificate, 53
for secreting destroying or altering register, 52

Pendente lite,
grants, 41
alimony, 59

PERPETUITY,
rule against, 28

POSTHNMOUS CHILD,
succession of, 7

PRACTITIONERS,
in matrimonial courts, 55

PRIEST,'
definition of, 46
PROBATE,
grant of, 35
definition of, 36
cannot be granted to, 36
effect of, when granted, 37
revocation of grant of, 42
QUESTIONS of facts, to be decided by majority of delegates, 64
QUESTIONS of law and procedure, to be determined by presiding judge, 64
REFUNDING OF LEGACIES, 34
REGISTRY,
of Parsi marriages, 51
REGULATION,
Bombay IV of 1827, 1—3, 50
RE-MARRIAGE,
lawful only after divorce, during lifetime of first wife or husband, 50
no restriction to, by a person in his or her lifetime, before Parsi M. and D. Act, 50
RE-MARRY,
liberty to parties to, after divorce, 64, 65
RENUNCIATION BY EXECUTOR, 37
RESIDUARY LEGATEE, 27
RESIDUE, 27
RESTITUTION OF CONJUGAL RIGHTS, 60—63
REVOCATION,
of grants, 42
of wills, 22, 23
SCHEDULE,
first, to Parsi Succession Act, 10
SCHEDULE,—*continued.*
second, to Parsi Succession Act, 11—13
to 6th section of Parsi M. and D. Act, 67
SETTLEMNNT,
of wife's property for children's benefit, 65
of Aden and its dependencies to be included within jurisdiction of Parsi Chief Matrimonial Court of Bombay, 69
SISTER,
of intestate, right of, 10, 11
full blood, right of, 10
full and half-blood, right of, 11
by same mother, 12
SON,
share of, when widow and daughter of intestate alive, 5
step, 6
adopted, 6
share of, when widower and daughter of intestate alive, 7
share of, when daughter alive but no widow, 7
share of, when daughter alive but no widower, 7
of grandfather, right of, 10
of great-grandfather, right of, 10
widow of, right of, 12
SPECIFIC LEGACY, 25, 26
STATUTE,
9 Geo. II C. 36 (Mortmain Act), 30

STATUTE,—*continued.*
4 Geo. IV C. 76 (English Marriage Act), 49
33 and 34 Vict. C. 93 (English Married Woman's Property Act), 17

STEP-CHILD, 5

SUCCESSION,
to property of intestate Parsis, 5—13
to immovable property in British India, 18
to movable property, 18
to movable property in British India, 20

SUCCESSION ACT,
extends to Parsis in regard to testamentary succession, 4, 14
4th section of, applies to Parsis, 14
by 4th section of, previous state of law completely altered, 14—17
summary of important portions of, 14—42
in extenso, appendix B.

SUITS,
matrimonial, 56—65
for decree of nullity of marriage, 56
for decree of dissolution in case of absence, 56
for divorce, 58
for judicial separation, 58
with closed doors, 64

TRUSTS,
for performance of *gahambár* and *doslá* ceremonies void, 29

VOID BEQUESTS, 28—30

WIDOW,

WIDOW,—*continued.*
share of, when there are children, 5
share of, when there are no lineal descendants, 9
of son, right of, 12
of brother, right of, 12

WIDOWER,
share of, when there are children, 7
meaning of, in section 7 of Parsi Succession Act, 8
share of, when there are no lineal descendants, 9
share of, of intestate's deceased daughter, 12

WIFE,
right of, over her property under Common law, 14, 15
right of, after 1st January 1866, 14—16
very limited right of, to will away property, if married before 1st January 1866, 16
definition of, 46
can obtain divorce, when, 57
can obtain judicial separation, when, 58

WILL,
definition of, 20
requisites of, 21, 22
revocation of, 22, 23
revival of, 23
construction of, 23—25

WITNESSES,
to will, 22
to Parsi marriage, 46

Yezashne,
recitation of, void, 29